# Transatlantic Stage Stars in Vaudeville and Variety

PALGRAVE STUDIES IN THEATRE AND PERFORMANCE HISTORY is a series devoted to the best of theatre/performance scholarship currently available, accessible, and free of jargon. It strives to include a wide range of topics, from the more traditional to those performance forms that in recent years have helped broaden the understanding of what theatre as a category might include (from variety forms as diverse as the circus and burlesque to street buskers, stage magic, and musical theatre, among many others). Although historical, critical, or analytical studies are of special interest, more theoretical projects, if not the dominant thrust of a study, but utilized as important underpinning or as a historiographical or analytical method of exploration, are also of interest. Textual studies of drama or other types of less traditional performance texts are also germane to the series if placed in their cultural, historical, social, or political and economic context. There is no geographical focus for this series and works of excellence of a diverse and international nature, including comparative studies, are sought.

The editor of the series is Don B. Wilmeth (EMERITUS, Brown University), Ph.D., University of Illinois, who brings to the series over a dozen years as editor of a book series on American theatre and drama, in addition to his own extensive experience as an editor of books and journals. He is the author of several award-winning books and has received numerous career achievement awards, including one for sustained excellence in editing from the Association for Theatre in Higher Education.

Also in the series:

# Transatlantic Stage Stars in Vaudeville and Variety

## Celebrity Turns

*Leigh Woods*

TRANSATLANTIC STAGE STARS IN VAUDEVILLE AND VARIETY
© Leigh Woods, 2006.

Cover Image    Cameo of Sarah Bernhardt set into a Palace Theatre program, 1913 (reprinted by permission of the Theatre Collection, Museum of the City of New York)

First published in 2006 by
PALGRAVE MACMILLAN™
175 Fifth Avenue, New York, N.Y. 10010 and
Houndmills, Basingstoke, Hampshire, England RG21 6XS
Companies and representatives throughout the world.

PALGRAVE MACMILLAN is the global academic imprint of the Palgrave Macmillan division of St. Martin's Press, LLC and of Palgrave Macmillan Ltd. Macmillan® is a registered trademark in the United States, United Kingdom and other countries. Palgrave is a registered trademark in the European Union and other countries.

ISBN-13: 978–1–4039–7536–2
ISBN-10: 1–4039–7536–1

Library of Congress Cataloging-in-Publication Data

Woods, Leigh.
    Transatlantic stage stars in vaudeville and variety : celebrity turns / Leigh Woods.
        p. cm.—(Palgrave studies in theatre and performance history)
    Includes bibliographical references.
        ISBN 1–4039–7536–1 (alk. paper)
            1. Vaudeville—United States—History—20th century.
    2. Vaudeville—United States—History—19th century. 3. Music-halls (Variety-theaters, cabarets, etc.)—United States—History—20th century. 4. Music-halls (Variety-theaters, cabarets, etc.)—United States—History—19th century. 5. Entertainers—Great Britain—Biography. I. Title. II. Series.

PN1968.USW66 2006
792.70973'0904—dc22                                              2006044752

A catalogue record for this book is available from the British Library.

Design by Newgen Imaging Systems (P) Ltd., Chennai, India.

First edition: November 2006

10 9 8 7 6 5 4 3 2 1

Printed in the United States of America.

Gift '|07

*To Ágústa*

# Contents ᔆ

# List of Illustrations ❧

# Acknowledgments ❧

This was a labor of love. It took a long time in the making, stretching out between two universities and several households, in the United States and abroad.

Early on, I spent time in New York City with assistance from Deans Morton Lowengrub and Albert Wertheim at the Office of Research and Graduate Development at Indiana University, and from Marianne, Helen, and Melvin Mencher, the last of Columbia University. My research was aided by Brooks McNamara and Marianne Chach at the Shubert Archive; Louis Rachow and Raymond Wemminger at the Hampden-Booth Theatre Library at the Players' Club; Faith Coleman at the Museum of the City of New York; Marianne Jenson and Michelle McEntire at the Firestone Library, Princeton University; Dorothy Swerdlove and her squads of librarians at the Billy Rose Theatre Collection in the Library of the Performing Arts at Lincoln Center; and staff at the Columbia University Library.

For research in London, a decade later, those to whom I'm grateful include J. S. Bratton, David Wiles, Fiona Kisby, Ellie Roper, and David Ward, from Royal Holloway, University of London; Graeme Cruickshank at the Palace Theatre Archive, London; Clare Colvin at the English National Opera Archive; Richard Mangan at the Mander and Mitchenson Theatre Collection; and the librarians and staff at the Theatre Museum Library, the British Library, the Westminster Reference Library, the Westminster City Archive, the British Library's newspaper archive at Colindale, the University of London Library at the Senate House, and David Cheshire.

My thanks go to the University of Michigan Library, and especially to its Rare Books and Special Collections' Kathryn Beam and Peggy Daub. I took advantage of the rich illustrations housed at the University of Michigan's Clements Library, courtesy of John Dann and Clayton Lewis. Andrew Coleman and Ben Chabot of the

University of Michigan's Economics Department helped me with currency conversions.

Others to whom I'm indebted include Noreen Barnes-McLain, Sarah Bay-Cheng, John Russell Brown, Anthony Cantrell, Marvin Carlson, Elisabeth Däumer, Judith Ebenstein, Erik Fredricksen, J. Ellen Gainor, Steven Gillis, Bill Grange, Barbara Grossman, John Hill, Ken Hurwitz, William Ingram, Ejner Jensen, Alison Kibler, Robert Knopf, Donald Lawniszak, Vanessa Luke, Holly Maples, Jeffrey Mason, Steve Morgan, Robyn Quick, Mary Resing, Cheyney Ryan, D. Ross, Laurence Senelick, Howard Singer, Daniel Watermeier, Livia Woods, and Phyllis Woods. My mother-in-law, Sigurlaug A. Stefánsdóttir, and my parents, Harry and Phyllis Woods, provided or found quiet places for me to write in Iceland and in San Diego, respectively.

My sabbaticals in 1991 and 1998 came with crucial assistance from Erik Fredricksen, Chair of Theatre & Drama at the University of Michigan, and from Dean Paul Boylan of the School of Music. My 1998 sabbatical was supplemented with travel grants from the Department of Theatre & Drama, the School of Music, and the International Institute at the University of Michigan. The School of Music also supported the second sabbatical through its Faculty Research Fund. Dean Boylan, in his capacity as Vice Provost for the Arts, joined Frederick C. Neidhardt, acting Vice President for Research at the University of Michigan, in extending the time I could spend in London, Iceland, and California in 1998. The Office of the Vice President for Research at the University of Michigan supplied the laptop I took overseas and on which I wrote drafts of the book.

The following journals, or presses that publish them, have graciously granted permission to use versions of the following articles under my name, and those are cited in full in the bibliography: " 'The Golden Calf': Noted English Actresses in American Vaudeville, 1904–1916," which appeared in *Journal of American Culture* in 1992, permission from Blackwell Publishing of Oxford, England; "Sarah Bernhardt and the Refining of American Vaudeville," which appeared in *Theatre Research International* in 1993, permission from the Cambridge University Press of London, England; "Ethel Barrymore and the Wages of Vaudeville," which appeared in *New England Theatre Journal*, in 1993; "Two-a-Day

Redemptions and Truncated Camilles: The Vaudeville Repertoire of Sarah Bernhardt," which appeared in *New Theatre Quarterly* in 1994; and " 'The Wooden Heads of the People': Arnold Daly and Bernard Shaw" that appeared in *New Theatre Quarterly* in February 2006.

Melissa Nosal at Palgrave Macmillan, joined later by Alessandra Bastagli and Emily Leithauser, made the book tighter. Don B. Wilmeth, series editor of the Palgrave Studies in Theatre and Performance History, was the first to read the entire book. He responded to it, whole, and assured me that some of what I was trying to do was coming through. He nursed me through revisions, and offered sage advice. I'm lucky to have been able to draw on Don, his knowledge, and his own distinguished scholarship in the field of popular entertainments.

My grandmother, Sadie Hill Ritter, was full of stories about the time she'd spent as a musician and chorus girl in New York City. She came alive for me, for a moment, as I sat in the Performing Arts Library at Lincoln Center beginning work toward this book. I came across her maiden name in a program for a musical revue called *Hokey Pokey*, produced in 1912. My grandmother was nineteen at the time, and she appeared onstage as a "Wandering Banderine," marching, probably dancing, and certainly playing the trombone her father had given her. She appeared with famous faces including Lillian Russell and *Hokey Pokey's* coproducers and chief comics, Joe Weber and Lew Fields, who were more famous as Weber and Fields. Within a few months, she was touring with the road company. Discoveries like this one may not add much weight to the scholarly enterprise, but, you know, so what.

Finally, my wife, Ágústa Gunnarsdóttir, planned, packed, repacked, and all of it while maintaining her alertness to detail, and, with maybe only a lapse or two, her good humor through two extended stays away from our home. She did this with our two daughters in tow, and by setting aside some of her own work. I haven't enough words or the right ones. Ágústa has made herself a worthy steward of the diamond my grandmother left me, in her flamboyant, vaudevillian way, and that my grandfather, Walter Ritter, had given to Sadie Hill. I hope this book makes Ágústa, and that it would have made my grandparents, proud.

# Introduction ᴥ

*I have always thought the actions of men the best interpreters of their thoughts.*

John Locke, *An Essay Concerning Human Understanding* (1690)[1]

Locke wasn't thinking of variety entertainment when he wrote these words. Nor is it likely that he would have included the theatre in his inventory of the most consequential places that men take action, and women, too, whom he excluded, casually and entirely, consistent with social and grammatical conventions of his day.

The theatre was a venerable institution when Locke lived, but it figured only in passing in his utopia. His "Second Treatise on Government," written at around the time of *An Essay Concerning Human Understanding*, remarks that any man facing the range of opinion and vested interest in the world, crammed onto a stage, would despair of comprehending the full scope and follow the noble Roman, Cato, in "coming into the theatre, only to go out again."[2] Even the theatre Locke invoked so fleetingly was worthy only in its classical lineage and most governable expressions. In this incarnation, at least, the theatre made a place for men to witness actions quickly and then depart, and with greater dispatch if they were systematic and conscionable. The theatre was a kind of sampler for rational men.

Fast-forward 200 years. Vaudeville in its glossier venues—with its nearest British cousin "variety" at the upper end of the beer-soaked music halls—were offering arenas for action, all right. The action they sponsored, though, was scarcely the admirable, utilitarian kind that Locke made key to his social contract. He wanted to reverse the sectarianism that had divided England for nearly two centuries. Given his high purpose, it may seem far-fetched to apply his words to performers who thrived two centuries after his passing. Vaudeville and variety moved in the spirit of mercantile contracts, not social ones.

Detractors of the day accused variety and vaudeville of stifling thought and nourishing self-absorption, or worse, a herd mentality that could turn ugly and violent. When variety and vaudeville were praised, it was for their ungainly egalitarianism. Locke might have applauded the egalitarianism. He would have disapproved of the escapism that made the bait.

Noted actors were hardly known for being social theorists, much less altruists. But given their almost heroic self-interest, why would they have chosen venues known for being more escapist than the theatre was? And when it came to giving turns, why would they have gravitated toward showing some of life's most heart-wrenching circumstances?

Part of the answer lay in the simple habit formed by the stars' success in the theatre. Another reason lay simply in the large amounts of money stars could earn by showing turns that bespoke noble purpose and high-toned culture. But whatever the reasons, the more fame stars brought with them, the more likely it was that their turn would show suffering, or, in the case of comic luminaries, toil. This went against the grain—except for the toil—but in ways that aggrandized the stars and challenged patrons to lift themselves up by their own bootstraps. The theatre had hosted displays of suffering for far longer and at greater length. But suffering was more arresting, it seems, with nothing but funmaking around it.

As in the theatre, the greater seamlessness that stars could suggest between themselves and their characterizations, the more compelling audiences found the exercise. And as surely as the theatre provided vehicles for stars to recapitulate their successes, vaudeville and variety offered more regular, indeed relentless sources of repetition that, in the stars' cases, required more frequent performance. Two daily shows were standard in big-time vaudeville and grew common in variety as well after a lag of a few years. The regimen called for repeating bills and each turn on them, including the song-and-dance and sharp-tongued comedy that were fixtures, and in America more than Britain, blackface. Actors profited from offering the least familiar and least frivolous turn on view.

Stars joined bills grudgingly oftentimes, and almost as often out of necessity. They risked losing face in the change, and this put its own strain on them. On the good side, the same professional and, when it could be known or visible, personal strain made another way of folding the actors and their characters into a single suffering entity. It was a familiar formula, but it offered a fresh way to put the pursuit of happiness on sale.

* * *

This book scrutinizes the actions that took the stars into halls of mirth and the actions they took while there. I press producers' actions, too, when they recruited stars. I try to proceed to audiences' actions, with caution, in finding reasons for their interest in the entertainment and their responses to it, where known or determinable. My premise is that popular taste influenced stars and producers who inflected popular taste, or tried to, to favor their own interests. To identify some of the linkages, I've named each chapter to suggest a mode of exchange.

The first chapter, "Patronizing," shows three actors hoping not to compromise themselves too grievously by leaving the theatre. On the other side of the curtain, simple acts of purchase show audiences fairly glorying in the added range of their consumption. Vaudeville producers profited from promising stellar attractions in compressed form at lower prices.

"Precious Brits" treats four stars in search of gain from an unfamiliar source. Americans' sense of cultural deficiency often demanded, in vaudeville as in theatre, actors who seemed superior to native ones. Reciprocity lay in the pay British stars took from producers as hungry for their presence as crowds were, and in the value crowds took from the occasion, or had come convinced that they should.

"Growing Pains" focuses on topline stars achieving mythic proportions. These actors endowed themselves in greater suffering than other actors could command. The foremost players appealed across lines of class and gender and showed how deeply sacrifice was inscribed in the two leading English-speaking, heavily Christian, evermore distinct imperial powers.

The fourth chapter, "Suffer the Women," shows fame applied to a political cause. A string of noted actresses showed turns to promote women's right to vote, or issues thereon contingent, such as divorce, separate property, equal protection under law, and greater discretion in sexual behavior. Activism will be seen coinciding, and at times colliding, with star turns right through the peak of the battle over women's suffrage. The British stars challenged their American sisters' relative reticence. Foreign stars took native ones' places, in effect, in broaching suffrage in vaudeville.

Chapter 5, "War and Peace," accounts for fully a dozen stars who gave turns during World War I. The paucity of American noteworthies owed more than a little to a national difficulty with engaging the same level of distress that left British subjects with little choice. A number of important actresses, emboldened by suffrage turns, trouped into ones on behalf of the war, or in fewer cases, the peace. In vaudeville, again, foreign stars stood in for native ones, in effect, in supporting the Allied war effort or, in fewer cases again, the cause of peace.

The final chapter, "Parting," captures the decline of vaudeville and variety as stars grappled with conditions that turned stardom over more quickly in the postwar era. Audiences took interest in seeing once-mighty actors struggle, and they found it easy to tax the formerly great for not living up to expectations. "Afterthoughts" considers celebrity's current state in light of figures from the book who pointed the way into politics, in the United States especially.

As "Celebrity Turns" suggests, celebrity is a shadow-player throughout. Partly this is because it was so ingratiating, and partly because it was still largely an unknown quantity. Celebrity will be seen winding its way through the lives of those who possessed it, who wanted it, and who were mesmerized by it. Celebrity will be seen taking on different contours depending on where and how it figured, and from the ways it was pursued, adapted, and applied.

Rare is the show nowadays, in any venue, that mixes registers of culture as promiscuously as "refined" vaudeville and its British counterpart did a century ago. The bills showed, besides staples of song-and-dance and comic patter, hoofing of every sort with ballet, ballroom dancing, and some of what came to be called modern dance well represented. There could be sentimental- or torch-singing, dreamy crooning, or classical music played, sung, or both. There were minstrels in blackface as often as not, and *émigrés* from the circus—slackwire artists, jugglers, acrobats, contortionists, animal acts, strongmen and strongwomen. Films, including some of the earliest ones shown for profit, seasoned bills first in the mid-1890s.

In this menagerie, dramatic stars were never the whole show or even the turn audiences relished most, necessarily. This book, for dwelling on star turns rather than the bills they headlined, grants the actors a prominence that, as you're about to see, didn't always match with responses they met.

Stars' doings, however, reveal decisions they made on their ways to the moment when all eyes would fall on them. In decisions the actors made, I look for ties that John Locke thought he saw between deed and thought. I hope to offer nearer if phantasmagorical glimpses into life from the 1890s into the 1930s. Stars' gift for searching out the heart of their audiences makes their actions, if not consequential in Locke's sense, indicative of the thoughts of many who sat in attendance, and of what had drawn them there in the first place.

Star turns were easy to list among life's simple pleasures. But the spectacle of pain set squarely into harmless diversions suggests that pleasure is never just simple. The patrons needed help to understand a world picking up speed at a rate that could be alarming. The patrons, with the stars and producers who catered to them, left their actions to speak, and in Locke's word, interpret thoughts that stood at some distance from customary notions of utility and reality.

# 1. Patronizing, 1890–1901 ᢙ

*The music-hall of our youth was a thing of tinsel and orange peel, reeking with smoke and obscenity. There are people who affect to deplore its disappearance. They exalt its freedom, its carelessness, its honest mirth. What they fail to recall is the fact of its filth. It was a noisome sewer, and one of the best signs of the times is that the sewer has been cleansed.*

A. G. Gardiner, "Pillars of Society" (1914)[1]

In 1890, the Empire house of varieties was not the most savory spot in London. It was, however, the choicest establishment of its kind. In the third year of its existence, with a prime location overlooking Leicester Square at the heart of the city's glittering West End, the Empire had gained a reputation not for being a sewer, exactly, but for needing cleansing nonetheless.

To remove some grime and raise the tone, variety hired a stage actress who was familiar though hardly famous. Amy Roselle (1854–1895) had chased fame long enough to know how stern a taskmaster it could be. She was ready to try a new approach. Variety wanted to woo a higher trade. Roselle's respectability, as much as anything, added to her luster.

Born the daughter of a stage-loving schoolmaster, Amy, if that had been her name, acted as a child opposite her brother, Percy, an "infant phenomenon" of the kind popular in nineteenth century. She soon established herself as a child-star in her own right in Wales. She passed Percy by on joining a stock company in England. An Anglo-American actor-manager named E. A. Sothern saw her and hired her to tour the provinces as his co-star. She traveled to America and through it with Sothern when she was still, by report, only sixteen. As an adolescent phenomenon, she made her debut in London the following year, in the early 1870s.

In the capital, as she would have been told to expect, her competition stiffened. As a mature actress she took work, as others did, when it came. She still aspired to stardom, though, and her ambitions were whetted by Arthur Dacre (*né* Culver James), the former physician turned striving actor whom Roselle married and made her agent and sometime co-star. The Dacres would take to the road to ply their trade, or play secondary roles in London. To tide themselves over, they gave readings for professional groups, religious fellowships, and literary societies. Roselle's voice was expressive and her delivery assured. She specialized in what were called "recitations" of inspirational, sentimental, or devotional verse.

She had the bad luck to reach her thirties with four times as many actresses looking for work as when she'd been born.[2] The large numbers of women trying the stage had created a glut of performers in London and left Roselle underemployed among those who had lost the bloom of youth. Music halls and variety were putting more women than ever on the stage, to be sure, but those were mostly younger ones, and flashier, who could sing, dance, and pose in skimpy outfits.

Squeezed between aging and the laws of supply-and-demand, Roselle saw prospects in variety. What she could earn there would pay her better than the music halls could, and it would shield her from at least some of the disdain that mere music halls were attracting. Her experience reciting had taught her how to keep audiences attentive and to improve them if they would have it. Dacre almost certainly blessed the Empire engagement by helping to arrange it.

Under the Empire's stage lights, between late January and early April 1890, she gave four different turns. They came, in order, in Alfred, Lord Tennyson's poem "Rizpah" for her first week and his better-known "Charge of the Light Brigade" for her next three. Then she changed into the American Frank Gassaway's "The Dandy Fifth, A Story of the American Civil War" for three more weeks, and finally into Henry Savile Clark's "The Siege of Lucknow" for her last five. She might have acted in a short play or in several. Her giving recitations owed at least partly to the Empire's having been prosecuted not long before for producing plays in defiance of the theatre's longstanding monopoly.

Roselle can't have missed hearing about the Empire's legal troubles. She knew that solo turns would cost her less than more fully cast and mounted pieces. "Rizpah," like each of the turns she used after it, had her onstage alone. Speaking lines from Tennyson made for a momentous occasion, though not for boisterousness of the kind variety was known for. Tennyson's Rizpah was the namesake of a Biblical character stricken with loss. The actress played the reincarnated Rizpah, "worn with sorrow and harrowed with grief " and looking ghoulish, actually, wearing "garments of a semi-mourning type" and a wig of "long grey, almost white hair hanging round her face."[3] Regulars at the Empire would have been struck by the difference between the Laureate's somber lines and the frolicsome turns on the bill. More in the ordinary line, for instance, was Geraldine, "as graceful as she is beautiful" hanging from a trapeze. Tending toward the excessive were production numbers called "Dream of Wealth" and "Paris Exhibition," both of them alive with leggy Italian dancers.[4]

It's possible that some of the Empire's better-heeled patrons had seen Roselle's Rizpah before at smaller, more genteel gatherings. Those who hadn't seen it would have been startled by the sight of Roselle's playing a "half demented mother . . . rescu[ing], bone by bone . . . the remains of her darling son [a thief], hanged in chains at the cross-roads."[5] Grimness and moralizing offered variety a way to purify itself. Moral laxity, for anyone who cared to look, lay in the number of easy women ranging the Empire's auditorium and the squads of continental chorines filling the stage with their colorful gear and shining bodies.

"Rizpah's" wallop had *Era* praising Roselle for silencing "the chatter of a music hall audience."[6] The reviewer felt, though, that she could do even better by showing some more "simple and sympathetic subject" to replace "Rizpah." *Stage*, another weekly trade paper, suggested that she try "a more stirring selection" such as "a transparency of a battlefield, or the saving of a crew from shipwreck." Although the Empire was paying Roselle to build its trade from the middle up, its management saw no reason to let its less moneyed patrons move on.

"Rizpah" and its preachifying commanded an upper-end traffic that drew more of the lower end with it. "Aristocratic men and women" were reported coming to see her, and they were "only too delighted to be supplied with those 'variety' features of entertainment" that the staid theatre couldn't provide.[7] Roselle had chosen a character lowly enough to flatter anyone, and who expressed mother love at its fiercest. Still, "Rizpah's" creepiness put off some of the diehards whose reactions the critics registered. Aiming to broaden her appeal, Roselle chose her next turn along more uplifting lines.

She stuck with Tennyson and spent the next three weeks reciting "The Charge of the Light Brigade." The poem would have been familiar to many as a bitter requiem for the doomed British cavalry who'd met their ends in the Crimea. For her third selection, after "The Light Brigade," she touched on battle again in "The Dandy Fifth," about the American Civil War. It let her strike a more triumphal note for calling up events at a more comfortable remove from her crowds' deepest sympathies.

Her last recitation, and the best received, came in "The Siege of Lucknow." Its author Clark was only a hack playwright, not in Tennyson's league. But he had written a tribute to empire tailored not only to Roselle's strengths but to the range of patrons at the Empire Varieties who had dreams of glory in India.

"Lucknow" has a woman speak to her fiancé in the British garrison's last stronghold. She can hear hordes of Indians howling for their blood. She has been reduced, in the words of one reviewer, to "praying to her lover to save one shot for her heart, so that if all fails, they can at least die together." "But in the midst of all" as the critic recalled it,

> a sound of [bag-] pipes is heard. Nearer and nearer they come. "It is the sound of the Pibroch [made by bagpipes]," deliverance is at hand, the marching of the Scots coming nearer still is a reality—their piping becomes louder and louder, the steels of the gallant fellows glitter—the waiting ones knew that "The peril was ended, that sorrow was past— they knew they were saved at last!"[8]

The Empire's management had laid on bagpipers to conjure up the Scottish saviors. The house orchestra joined the music that swelled with Roselle's voice to ring down the curtain, rescue and victory at hand.

Stirring stuff it was. *Stage* praised "the wisdom of the Empire management" in featuring such a noteworthy actress to show the one true Empire so stoutly defended. The turns around hers weren't inspirational in the same way, but they didn't need to be. For her first week in "Lucknow," Roselle was joined on the bill by Loie Fuller among others. An American pioneer of the modern dance, Fuller wore a white satin robe to sing and glide her way through "Rock-a-bye Baby" and the old Scottish air, "Coming Through the Rye."

The themes "Lucknow" sounded were as familiar as any Scottish air. The Empire was shown to prevail, and a gallant warrior's wife-to-be was saved from the fate worse than death. Roselle upheld Britain's imperial mission at a time when, as Martha Banta has written, "More often than not, the types that stood for national values were female."[9] Showing nations as women softened charges of exploitation and advanced more nurturing images. Any hostile colonized people could be shown to be aggressors, different in kind from the heroic British women joining the men to keep savagery in check. The women's steadfastness made them more worthy of defending, at home and abroad.

"Lucknow's" curtain-line, "The banner that never goes back," called up a Union Jack that flew over more parts of the world than ever. Clark's mention of the banner, with the sight of it onstage, rallied Britons of every stripe, poorer and richer, women with the men, and children, too. All British subjects had a stake in helping their small nation do its duty where the sun never set.

Those who had made the Empire on Leicester Square into variety's centerpiece were also using Roselle toward more parochial ends. The London County Council, then in the earliest months of its existence, was considering the proper role of variety around the metropolis. Killjoys on the council were intent on cutting variety back. The council's membership was dominated by urban reformers who wanted, at the least, to enforce a more wholesome tone. Concern for what measures the council might take had variety's chief entrepreneurs seeking attractions to protect their halls from moral censure and legal penalties.

Roselle did so well that she had *Era* credit the Empire Varieties for pointing audiences in the right direction. The correspondent ventured to hope that

> not only the Theatres Committee but many of the members of the Council itself will be paying patrons (at their own expense) of the London music halls during the ensuing year; and not only elevate the audience and the entertainment by their presence, but speak with unbiased minds of what they have actually seen and heard. This will be better for all parties than a system of perpetual passes which might easily lead to abuse.[10]

Variety, according to its dearest partisans, was ready to stake its standing on the culture it commanded rather than on the bribes it could bestow.

The Empire's management was hoping to draw leniency or even endorsement from London's civic officialdom. Such initiative would have satisfied many of "sensible people" who, as *Era* had written a while back, wanted only to

> divert their minds from politics and business alike [and not] to have the opinions of the daily papers reproduced in verse and flung at their heads by a music hall singer. . . . persons who go to a place of amusement to be amused, are too sensible to care to proclaim their private opinions by applauding senseless rubbish with a political meaning.[11]

Roselle's job was to help hold the fort by serving up bromides about the scourge of crime, the sanctity of love, the glory of God, and devotion to country, honor, and duty—always duty.

The reception she got showed, among other things, how essential consensus or its promise was to the conduct of empire. Whenever fresh ways of inspiring the faithful could be found, they were treasured and multiplied. And so it fell out at the Empire in the heart of London during the winter and early spring of 1890.

\*  \*  \*

For all the services Amy Roselle performed, she never returned to variety nor flourished anywhere else. She didn't give way easily. While she was still in mid-engagement at the Empire and considering how best to follow "The Charge of the Light Brigade," she had Dacre turn down an offer from a rival variety house. She'd made "previous arrangements," or so he said.[12] This may have been true, or he may have been driving up her price. The couple may have feared that her giving too many turns would compromise whatever future they saw for themselves in the theatre.

Whatever was driving the Dacres, they spent most of the rest of their careers together. They'd been known for requesting outlandish salaries before her engagement at the Empire, and it had cost them jobs. They found work not long after Roselle left variety when they gave a "recitation entertainment" entirely on their own—without benefit from any bill around them—at Prince's Hall near London's Piccadilly Circus. Even the bustling location didn't bring them much notice.

Toward the end of 1890 Dacre turned up in New York, suing an American star named Mrs. Leslie Carter for firing him. "My name was to be featured in the bill," he complained to the *New York Times*. He was bitter, he said, because "After selling out everything in England I came to this country, only to find that the part for which I was cast was a mean insignificant one."[13] Roselle joined Dacre in the 'States, but they couldn't pick up enough work for the two of them together. They returned to England, though not before flopping in what proved to be their last venture in the 'States, in a play called *Love and War*. They barely made it home after taking charity from a band of Yankee actors who threw a hasty benefit in their honor.[14]

Restored to London, they rented a theatre to star themselves in an American play called *Man and Woman* in which they can have done no better than to break even.[15] They lowered their fees, but not enough, according to *Stage*,

and even then strove to preserve the letter of them. That is to say, the old terms might figure in an agreement, but by private arrangement a portion of the joint salary might be returnable to the manager. This pathetic admiration and exaggeration of each other's abilities had much to do with the failure of the Dacres to obtain engagements.[16]

A trip to Australia proved conclusive. It was not to be the happy ending they were looking for.

Their tour of the antipodes faltered so badly that they felt as if they'd been cursed. Feeling stranded and alone, they gave way to despair. *Era*, whose readership included many of their friends and colleagues, saw that

> all the particulars of the Dacre-Roselle tragedy tend[ed] to show premeditation and the existence of a complete understanding between husband and wife. Both, in fact, had spoken to their friends from time to time of contemplating suicide.[17]

Roselle found her relatively picturesque end at the hotel she'd made her last stop in Sydney. There,

> Mr. and Mrs. Dacre remained in their bedroom throughout the morning of Sunday last [November 17, 1895]. In the afternoon their bell was rung violently, and the servant on entering the room found Mr. Dacre with his throat cut, but still alive. His wife lay on the bed in her nightdress, apparently asleep. Examination, however, showed that she was dead, with two bullet wounds in the breast. . . . The wounds showed medical knowledge.

Dacre, the one with medical knowledge, wasn't so lucky. When he was discovered,

> he gasped out, "Oh, my God, what agony!" and died. A doctor was at once sent for, and on arrival saw that Dacre had been struggling to throw himself on the bed beside the body of his wife. . . . At the inquest held on Monday the jury found that Amy Roselle had died by her husband's act, and that Dacre had committed suicide.[18]

This version of the Dacres' final hours joined other accounts in removing Roselle from any responsibility for her own death, even after the writer conceded that she appeared to have shown "complete understanding" in the manner of her demise. She'd taken a sleeping draught, the story went, before leaving her husband, the former physician, to shoot her in the most humane way before dispatching himself as best he could, which wasn't very well.

Eerily, this scenario resembled the one she'd played out in "The Siege of Lucknow." Sadly, this time, there was no expeditionary force to come to the lady's aid. Arthur was left to play the savior Amy needed. He made himself into something like the unseen soldier in "Lucknow," ready to kill his beloved rather than leave her to the fate worse than death. The fate worse than death for the Dacres in Australia was not rape, but their fear of humiliation and disgrace. Arthur was left, like Romeo, reaching out to his beloved with a last, dying, dutiful flourish.

Such images leaped straight from the stage, of course, and from what had grown into a teeming literature around suicide. The prevailing wisdom held that Roselle was heroic for the devotion and submissiveness she'd shown her husband. Dacre, on the other hand, was unmanly, unstable, and cowardly for taking his own life and hers. His dragging himself toward her body to redeem himself did make an arresting image. But it could never have matched the interest in Roselle's cleaner death, which put her more in the news than she'd been for some time. She had to die, and in quite the striking way, to reclaim the attention that had followed her through the provinces during her prodigal phase.

One account of the funeral mentioned the "small packet of English earth" she'd carried with her should she die far from home. She'd left instructions that the dirt be spread over her grave "so that she might be buried in English soil."[19] It would have mattered little, to all but the few who remembered, that she'd been raised and shown her quality first in Wales.

Her apparent innocence in folding Wales into England confirmed— to English eyes at least—that there was the *United* Kingdom that Henry Savile Clark had used the crack Scottish regiment in "Lucknow" to show. Roselle's last reading at the Empire evoked a nation united and worthy of the empire that had given London's leading variety establishment its name.

Amy Roselle entered variety in pursuit of fame and riches. She ended her life in an outpost of the Empire. In her last hours, locked to Arthur Dacre in their "previous arrangements," she saw no reason to look for anything other than the quick death that ended a career that had left her evermore haunted by the promise of her youth.

Her legacy wasn't one to celebrate. It showed how high the cost could be of seeking a public eye that tracked ambition to the grave.

*   *   *

Amy Roselle died a failure in her own eyes. For her, in the end, it had not been enough that she'd applied herself to upholding the Empire global at the Empire Varieties. Her variously inspiring turns helped draw crowds mixed enough by class to have pundits speaking of the gatherings in Shakespeare's time.

Variety's adherents believed that lowlier patrons stood to gain by soaking up what culture serious acting could supply. The common people's betters, said the party of tolerance, would do well to cultivate the broad-mindedness that came with communing with laborers.

Oscar Wilde was best known among the betters to frequent variety. He was drawn there, to the Empire especially, because he could see more polished acts than the music halls could offer, and racier ones than theatres would allow. He was only one of the men of means who could be seen slumming at the Empire, where it was easy, it seems, to take stimulation from sources other than the stage. The presence Wilde lent the proceedings showed a certain good humor on his part, snob that he was, and ever so mouthy.

Mixing the classes was one thing but degeneracy was another. Moralists decried the young men consorting with the well turned-out prostitutes that Leicester Square was known to attract. Reformers fulminated against the illicit contact that variety houses seemed to foster more than theatres did. The party of propriety pressed its case hardest against the Empire, known before and after Roselle played there for ladies of evening who strolled through what was called the "promenade" that took up the main lobby.

Less talked about were the men consorting with other men, or boys. Wilde himself, of course, may have been among those seeking dalliance in the upper galleries, or if that was too risky for his blood, winking at the goings-on there. Such a clientele and the concerns it raised helped keep serious actors, and all but a few respectable women, away from the Empire and variety at large for nearly a decade after Roselle came and went. Meanwhile, men of means, young and not so young, and the boys and the ladies for hire, kept the Empire and other varieties nearby flourishing as precincts of abandon.

During the summer and early fall of 1889, within months before Roselle turned up at the Empire, London authorities had closed the hall down, not for being a den of vice but for staging productions to rival the theatres'. The closing of the Empire had all the leading variety houses cozying up to customers with more savory connections than Oscar Wilde could claim, on the whole. Variety needed people other than inverts, pimps, and showpersons to stand up to some of London's most zealous Christians.

There were Christian zealots in New York City, too, and in other American cities. But mixing social classes didn't seem so subversive where egalitarianism might just as well have been embossed on the national seal. What had taken to calling itself "refined" vaudeville felt no need to bear up under the punishment its British counterpart was absorbing in the crossfires of class. The entertainment freshly named "vaudeville" had seen its audiences grow larger *and* more mixed by class, gender, and age after smoking and drinking were prohibited there in the 1880s. Any patron who entered its portals had to maintain a certain decorum to protect the sensibilities of the women and children in the house.

Vaudeville's trappings of respectability didn't persuade every pious American of its good intentions. Many guarantors of culture called it mindless. Vaudeville replied, in among other ways, by tapping the theatre as variety had done. The theatre fought back by warning actors that their reputations would suffer from giving turns. Foiled, partly, by such doom-saying, vaudeville went hunting for attractions from the grand opera, operetta, ballet, and classical music. It found them.

Across the water, Roselle had shown how stage actors could raise the level of the entertainment and the quality of the assembly. But respectable turns of the sort she'd shown demanded a restraint that sometimes provoked patrons to heckle, or what was worse, to take their patronage elsewhere. For popular entertainment to be of the people, truly, it had to build audiences, not narrow them as the theatre was doing to protect its fairly freshly hatched legitimacy.

Vaudeville recruited actors not only to enlarge its viewership, but to plunder what was still its major rival among entertainments. The word "vaudeville's" vaguely French derivation—the mere sound of it, really—offered a dash of pretension to spice up all the slapstick and the schmaltz.

In Maurice Barrymore (1849–1905), vaudeville found a man on whom to hang its refinement. He knew how to play the gentleman in life as onstage. Amy Roselle had drawn only a few thousand Londoners, at most, on her own account, and probably few tourists, if any, to see her at the Empire. Barrymore had star quality. He would stand as the cynosure of any bill he joined.

He'd been touring America for more than two decades. His eminence extended beyond the stage and those who'd seen him there. The impression he'd made on New York society, even before taking up his acting career in the 'States, had put him in line for celebrity as it emerged in the newer land. He hadn't become as celebrated as he'd hoped to do, given his talents. Vaudeville, he thought, might give him the boost he needed, or at least tide him through some tough times.

Barrymore was known to have pursued the bubble reputation more than anything else—unless, of course, it was the pretty ladies, including stars, whom he bedded before, during, and after his marriage to America's own Georgiana Drew, from one of the nation's leading theatrical families. Acting had come naturally to him, and he never showed it the devotion Amy Roselle did, or his own wife for that matter. Nor did he have a stage parent to drive him from the outset. Quite the contrary. He came from a family dismayed at the thought of one of theirs acting for hire.

Born in India as Herbert Blyth, the man who became Maurice Barrymore claimed ancestors of some means from England's County Essex. His father had gone out to India as a young surveyor before spending most of the rest of his life yearning for the gracious existence of an English country squire. In India, the senior Blyth had found other winters of discontent after his first wife, Herbert's mother, died bringing the boy into the world. The father had a hard time thereafter in giving his son the benefit of the doubt.

When Herbert was eight, his father remarried and shipped him back to England. The measure was taken at partly for the sake of the boy's education, and partly for his safekeeping around the time of the Sepoy Mutiny, in which the siege of Lucknow was only a single element. In England, the boy eked out an uneven education at Harrow, the Blackheath Proprietary School, and for a single undistinguished year, at Oxford. Still as Blyth, he fought his way to the all-England amateur middleweight boxing championship.[20] Boxing had been refined recently by the Marquess of Queensberry, who made it respectable for young swells such as Herbert. Championship in hand, Blyth carried some small recognition when he decided to try the stage. Out of respect to the family name—his father was mortified at his choice of profession—the young man who'd been christened Herbert Arthur Chamberlayne Hunter Blyth chose the moniker "Maurice Barrymore." His father disowned him anyway. Not long after, the father died, though not before being persuaded to restore his prodigal son's patrimony.[21]

Barrymore had advantages besides his legacy. He was highly companionable and very good-looking. He had a fine body, wore nice clothing well, and filled the stage with an animal grace (see figure 1). For the first two years of his career, he played a round of mostly upper-crust roles through the English provinces. He found that he was only one among a number of young actors of breeding to enter what had long been a rogue profession.

It's not clear how or whether he intended to resume acting on landing in America in 1874. He did try the stage there, and advanced to stardom fairly quickly. Still he craved something that would be more gratifying. Few on the stage or anywhere could rival him in ease, volubility, or wit. Once he'd settled into his new name—he was "Barry" to his friends and lovers—he spoke in ways that, even with a little slippage, sounded mellifluous to Yankee ears. He flourished in romantic roles of title, standing, and military rank. By the early 1880s, he'd put himself near the head of the most accomplished British expatriates and native Anglophiles in the American theatre of his day. He'd made himself a literary man, too, writing plays as vehicles for himself and the actresses he admired and adored, including Georgie Drew Barrymore, an important player in her own right and under her maiden name.

In 1897, the novelist and critic William Dean Howells saw fit to complain that America lacked "society in the rich, full, English

MAURICE BARRYMORE

949 BROADWAY N.Y.

**Figure 1** Maurice Barrymore, in one of his cup-and-saucer roles of the kind that vaudeville came to prize. (William L. Clements Library, University of Michigan.)

sense." More distressing to Howells was the feeling that "we have a number of people playing at society in that sense."[22] Barrymore didn't need to play at society in any sense at all. He was, he'd shown, the genuine article. He'd gained status simply by setting foot in a nation where some of the most refined of the citizenry believed that "British" meant "superior," and that the theatre used properly, with key assistance from British actors, could raise the resting state of the hoi polloi.

For all his advantages and accomplishments, Barrymore's career never blossomed in quite the way he hoped. As the years wound on, he found himself playing plum roles, though always second leads, to a string of European actresses on star-tours across the sprawling land. Through it all, he was known, not quite accurately, for being an English actor, for staying English, and for showing a touch of the eccentric—which carried its own savor of Englishness—away from the stage. It was his Englishness, in fact, which outranked the broader category of "Britishness" for being less generic and more class-bound. It qualified Barrymore as a proper leading man for some of the most famous actresses to be seen.

Fellow actors knew him as a "bad study." Even as a young man, he'd had a hard time committing lines to memory. To keep from embarrassing himself, he'd learned to improvise in ways that made it seem as if he was speaking his own golden words—as often, in truth, he was. His knack as a wordsmith served nicely when he had to make up dialogue as he went. It was no mean feat that he could do it under pressure. That, along with his other qualifications, put him in demand and kept him there.

Over time, the *ad libbing* came to seem more careless, less accountable to incidents in the plays in which he appeared. So did his wardrobe grow careless off-stage. His daughter Ethel remembered his becoming "perfectly appalling in his clothes . . . he seemed to have a mania to shock."[23] But the startling attire was taken as the latest sign of his flair. In 1897, the same year Howells was praising society "in the rich, full, English sense," Barrymore brought his own English sense to the New Union Square Theatre in New York City. Benjamin Franklin Keith had turned the former legitimate house into a showcase for vaudeville by mixing refined attractions with standard turns on bills like the ones on view at the Empire and other variety houses in London.

Barrymore gave his first turns at the New Union Square on March 29, 1897, afternoon and evening, in a one-act play called *A Man of the World*. Adapted by his friend Augustus Thomas from a story Thomas himself had written, *Man* had premiered in New York with Barrymore in it eight years before. The star had added it to his touring repertoire as a curtain-raiser before full-length plays. The play's brevity meant that for vaudeville, it needed no cutting. Better still for Barrymore, it gave him a vehicle that restored him to *Man's* hero, Captain Bradley, a former military officer who was, like Barry, a man of the world. Even better than that, for the sake of the crispness vaudeville demanded, he knew his lines cold.

The Captain sets out to save the marriage of his former ward, Jennie. She has a young husband who ignores her. Hurt by his indifference, she keeps ever fonder company with a young man who works for Bradley and who loves her. No sooner does the Captain learn about the threat of infidelity than he dispatches his employee to St. Louis and gives the young couple some advice. Years before, he tells them, he'd fallen in love with Jennie's mother, but she'd been married to another man and had died.

Bradley warns Jennie and her husband against the danger of their growing estrangement. The play sows suspicion that Jennie is his own daughter, and that the Captain wants to save her from what may have been her mother's fatal attraction. His sense of duty shades toward masochism as he cuts loose a capable employee, defends the sanctity of marriage though *he* has never married, and reconciles the young couple through the pain of his own lost love.

So heavy a dose of the bittersweet might have dragged down many a turn. With Barrymore in the lead, it didn't. Slender opportunities for the young supporting cast gave the star a *tour de force*. The piece lasted about twenty minutes, which made it ideal for vaudeville and efficient to rehearse and tour. The three youthful actors didn't require much experience, which meant that the star didn't need to pay them much, either. And again, *A Man of the World* let Barrymore speak dialogue he'd revisited for charity benefits during the years since he'd acted the play at its opening.

In vaudeville, Barrymore's stylishness brought "great delight to those who were amid strange surroundings, and amply satisfied regular patrons of the house."[24] Supporting him, playing young Jennie, was the star's second wife, Georgie having died four years since. Her successor was Marie (Mamie) Floyd, daughter of a vaudeville manager and young enough to be Barrymore's daughter. With Mamie in tow, he left as little as he could to chance by bringing along a claque to cheer him, made up of cronies from the Lambs Club. Its members included men from more dignified walks of life who enjoyed rubbing elbows with entertainers.

Barrymore's jolly crew joined the Union Square's regulars to make a warm occasion. Attendance through the week stayed high, "only limited by the capacity of the house."[25] The *New York Clipper* credited Barrymore, his play, and his friends for raising the tone of a bill including, together with live acts, bits of film showing young girls pillow-fighting, a Yale College football game, "Dancing Darkies," and President William McKinley's recent inauguration at the District of Columbia.[26]

It was hardly a surprise when Barrymore did well on the tour that followed. The $750 a week he made would be over $17,000 now, and three times what he'd been used to earning in the theatre.[27] The handsome salary was timely, coming four months after the failure of a play he'd written and helped produce called *Roaring Dick & Co.*, with himself in the title role. Only a month after *Roaring Dick* had closed, and adding insult to injury, he had another short run in Victorien Sardou's *Spiritisme*, produced by the powerful Theatrical Syndicate, which, he was convinced, closed the show to spite him. He was taking jobs from the Syndicate, but he loathed it. He blamed its members, increasingly in public, for the career he found wanting. Vaudeville offered him a haven and a hedge. Any money he made there stood to leave him more independent of the Syndicate, or of anyone else who meant only to throw him a bone.

And he still had big plans. Therefore, after finishing his first vaudeville tour, he accepted another offer from the Syndicate to play a leading role in *A Ward of France*. But even as he took the Syndicate's money, he kept up a withering commentary on its coarseness and its greed. His next theatrical outing didn't stand him in good stead with the Syndicate, either, coming in *Becky Sharp* as co-star to his fellow trust-buster, Minnie Maddern Fiske. The play was adapted from William Makepeace Thackeray's panoramic novel *Vanity Fair*, and it made one of the hits of New York's theatrical season of 1898–1899. But this success did not come until after Barrymore had toured vaudeville at least once more in *A Man of the World*. His dealings with the Syndicate had him depending on vaudeville, as one of his enemy's enemies, more than he can have wished.

He finally turned down the Syndicate when they offered him a cameo role as the Prince of Morocco in an all-star production of Shakespeare's *The Merchant of Venice*. At the time, the Prince of Morocco was played in blackface, which then was a sure way to raise laughter. The custom could easily have grated on an actor so recently removed from vaudeville, where burnt cork was standard application for face-darkening, and clown-white greasepaint, too, for enlarging the look of the lips on white and black minstrels alike. And the thought of putting on blackface *did* bother Barrymore, apparently, because his reply to the Syndicate was curt. "Existing conditions in theatrical management have driven me into vaudeville," he conceded before adding, at his lordliest, "I have not yet gone into negro minstrelsy."[28] He took the Syndicate's offer as another attempt to humiliate him. He may have been right. In the meantime, his resorts to vaudeville kept him in funds.

In the fall of 1900, he wasn't asked to tour *Becky Sharp* when Mrs. Fiske took it on the road. This hit Barrymore hard, because he knew how much he'd contributed to the play's success at its American premiere. Out of work in the theatre, he appeared at Frederick F. Proctor's Fifth Avenue vaudeville house, delivering recitations. His turn was lighter and less concentrated than any of Amy Roselle's had been, and it consisted of three poems he'd learned in his youth. They were "Etiquette" by W. S. Gilbert of Gilbert and Sullivan fame, "A Fable of Cloud-Land" by Alice Cary, and "Told to the Missionary" by George R. Sims. Barrymore may have thought he needed a change after touring *A Man of the World* as widely as he had. Speaking verse would have appealed to him, too, because for all his difficulty learning lines, he'd held on to some of the rhyming pieces he'd picked up as a boy and young man.[29]

He also wanted to sock some money away. Recitations didn't require a supporting cast and they let him perform on a bare stage—both ways of avoiding costs for a set, costumes, a small company, and the transport thereof. Nor is it likely that he had to pay royalties. Recitations were unregulated by international copyright laws, then not quite yet in full force.[30]

The pieces he chose were quintessentially English, and Proctor would have liked that. The producer had acquired the Fifth Avenue earlier that year. A former theatre as Keith's Union Square was, it stood only a short walk from the bustling shopping district known as "the Ladies' Mile" running up Broadway between 14th and 23d Streets. The choice location put Proctor in position to supplant Keith at the head of upper-end vaudeville in greater New York. With the Fifth Avenue for his jewel, Proctor needed to polish the fare to be shown there. Barrymore seemed again to be a man for the job, if no longer *the* man. Recitations were genteel stuff as far as vaudeville went, and in variety, too, with Amy Roselle to deliver them.

Barrymore's recitations were met with politeness more than enthusiasm, and the politeness was muted. The *New York Dramatic Mirror* handled him with kid gloves for what it called his

> debut as an elocutionist last week. His entertainment consisted of three selections in verse, which were attentively listened to and well received. If he should take the notion to abandon the footlights he would be sure of success on the Y.M.C.A. circuit, as his turn was on the order of those popular in church and lyceum circles.[31]

Gracious as this critic was, however, he couldn't help noticing Barrymore's bowing at the end of each selection.

The gesture made a way of prompting applause that ran against the steady builds and clean endings that vaudevillegoers favored. For lacking these, Barrymore had to troll for responses that had been within his easy reach before. On his first tour in *Man*, for instance, he and his fellow actors had been greeted by audiences like the one in Boston that kept applauding "until the curtain had lifted three times to enable the newcomers to bow their pleased acknowledgments."[32]

But at the Fifth Avenue in September of 1900, the *Dramatic Mirror* noticed that only Gilbert's "Etiquette" had been "delivered with good effect." The piety of the star's last two pieces hadn't struck home, it seems, for running against Barrymore's man-of-the-world image, spiffed up for the occasion by his evening dress or "monkey suit" in the slang of the day, and with real monkeys in similar attire not at all uncommon in vaudeville. Like Barrymore's recitations, his apparel was a departure, too, from the zany outfits he was sporting away from the stage.

Perhaps only Barrymore would have known that reciting in formal wear called up a deeper past. While studying at the Blackheath Proprietary School, he'd won the Moral Conduct Prize as "the boy who, in the opinion of the whole School and of the Masters, most commends himself, by his high moral and religious character, influence, and example."[33] The recitations returned him to the sober almost-English lad he'd been before becoming such a man of the world.

Whatever status, promise, solvency, or innocence he hoped to regain, events forced him to shed. In December of 1900, he had trouble learning lines for a theatrical tour of the Midwest. He chose, or was asked, to leave the company. He faltered during a benefit performance in Boston a few weeks later. He was industrious, still, but in bursts. He may not have known that something had gone wrong.

At loose ends back home in New Jersey, within commuting distance of Manhattan, he finished a play he called *The Lady and the Burglar*. He didn't notice that what he'd turned out was virtually identical to his friend Augustus Thomas's *The Burglar*.[34] He'd first acted Thomas's play at around the time he'd opened Thomas's *A Man of the World* in the late 1880s. Georgie had been alive then, and the three young children at home or nearby.

Thomas's plays may have called up the aura of this not-quite-so distant past for a star with dialogue from his glory days stuck in his head. More than a decade onward, whether in recollection, or forgetfulness, or both, Barrymore had written the same cockney lowlife for himself to play. As in Thomas's piece, the criminal meets and talks briefly with his young daughter, who doesn't recognize him as he rifles the elegant home of the couple who'd adopted her after he'd given himself over to a life of crime. "Writing" the play had Barrymore intent on performing it. He must have been seeking security in his own paraphrases of Thomas's original. He took comfort from playing a character fallen farther than he had.

Barrymore spent January 1901 alternating turns in *The Lady and the Burglar* and *A Man of the World*. This repertory would have helped make his Captain Bradley look as masterful as before, though as much by contrast, this time, as by skill. More worrisome for the star and his devotees was the fact that his engagement came at a vaudeville house in Worcester, Massachusetts, well away from the two-a-day's top-of-the-line, or even Boston's most refined vaudeville. The feeling of the backwater wasn't eased by his choice to include his younger son, John, then a rank novice of nineteen, among the trio that supported him onstage.[35]

The senior Barrymore's presence in Worcester showed him in exile from big-time vaudeville. He'd made it his latest crusade to take on Keith, Proctor, and their fellow producers for trying to monopolize vaudeville the way the Syndicate had monopolized the theatre. The thought of vaudeville going the way of the stage stung Barrymore into helping found a brotherhood of vaudevillians calling itself the Chivalrous Order of the White Rats of America, along the lines of the British music-hall union known, less ostentatiously, as the Grand Order of Water Rats. This latter group's name, its history, and its reversed spelling of "star" in "Rats," would have been known to Barrymore from his London connections. It would have been important to him that his fellow founding White Rats were white men.

The Rats, nesting in their exclusionary name, showed the same pugnacity Barrymore had flashed at the Syndicate's offer of minstrelsy. In late March, in front of a gathering of his fellow Rats, he appeared at a benefit in Harlem, then predominantly a white district, for the members who'd gone out on strike.[36] The content of his turn wasn't recorded, perhaps for being nondescript, or atypical, or buried among too many others, or delivered *extempore* to rally the strikers.

It was at his second appearance in front of the Rats, on the evening of March 28, 1901, that Barrymore lost his bearings. As his son John looked on, he "stopped in the middle of his performance and, advancing to the footlights, hurled bitter invective until those in the audience held their breath in astonishment."[37] His tirade was reported more widely than his acting had been for some time. He raged against the-atre producers, not the vaudeville magnates the Rats were fighting. His anti-Semitism would have been familiar to many who heard it, but not for being spoken with Jewish Rats in attendance. The explosion came one day short of Barrymore's fourth anniversary in vaudeville.

It's telling that an in-house performance for vaudevillians should have drawn so much venom from a man so well regarded for his good cheer. Barrymore had come to seeing vaudeville as desolate and him-self as a castaway in it. He believed that the Syndicate had pushed him out of the theatre, forced him into vaudeville, and kept him there. It was easier to blame the Jews who'd formed the Syndicate than it was to denounce the triumvirate of New England Christians—Keith, Albee, and Proctor—who were then heading refined vaudeville. Barrymore was convinced that the Syndicate had, out of avarice and envy, stifled the plays he'd written and taken away any chance they had of being produced to advantage. He took pride in his writing for being a more gentlemanly pursuit than acting was. He'd fixed on sta-tus much as his father had done when disowning him. But the former Herbert Blyth didn't have long to ponder his standing, or to consider which character, played where, would serve him best.

The White Rats' benefit was Barrymore's valedictory. When he remained agitated and abusive after the performance, he was deliv-ered to New York's Bellevue Hospital. A few days later, John Barrymore escorted his father to an asylum at Amityville on Long Island. The young man was said to have persuaded the older one to the journey by telling him, as one trouper to another, that Barry would be filling "an engagement in Philadelphia."[38] It was a town the star had known well. His in-laws, the Drews, had long made their home there and used the city as a base for their touring.

The cause of his breakdown was given out, fleetingly when at all, as paresis, a late stage of syphilis involving paralytic attacks and dementia. The *New York Dramatic Mirror* was kind if delicate in the euphemism it applied:

> "Barry's" extreme good-fellowship was the main cause of his pathetic
> fate. Always ready to entertain, he would sit with a crowd of boon

companions until the dawn broke. Perhaps for two or three days he would hardly sleep, and then when his exhausted vitality demanded rest, he would take too little.

If only Barrymore had taken better care of himself, it was implied, he might have avoided his unhappy fate. But as it was,

> he is of the temperament, the doctors say, that is most liable, if overtaxed, to mental derangement . . . It was inevitable that with his irregular life, his ceaseless working of a splendid brain, the human machine should some day break down, and his ardent sympathies become mania, and bring on the utter demoralization of an unusually talented man.[39]

The *Mirror's* account was one of a handful of what were eulogies, in effect, to check further criticism of a man beyond defending himself. "Demoralization" was a word that might have given his fans pause. At Amityville, he lived another four years, at the end in a vegetative state.

In 1900, the year before Barrymore broke down, the redoubtable critic William Winter accused him of "walking" Broadway instead of the more elegant Fifth Avenue. "His lover woos with a confident swagger rather than an elegant grace," Winter wrote derisively, adding that Barrymore "serenades his lady love with a banjo rather than a mandolin; his man about town is more at ease in a box coat than in evening dress—in short, Mr. Barrymore's acting lacks refinement."[40]

Winter may have been referring, obliquely, to Barrymore's junkets in vaudeville. But any rebuke from the dean of America's theatre critics would have been galling to an actor who'd based a career on refinement. Winter's opinion was more surprising for being written in a year when Barrymore actually had performed, in evening dress no less, at what until recently had been called the Fifth Avenue Theatre. On the down side, his appearances there, if Winter knew of them, came in a turn for Proctor. Such acting, by the critic's standard, was the nearest thing to fraud for someone of the star's caliber.

A few months after Barrymore broke down, he was entrusted to the care of "alienists," the psychiatrists of their day. They ministered to a patient who, to turn himself into Maurice Barrymore, had alienated himself from his birthplace, his birth family, and his given name. Then, years after having left England as his first adopted land, he left his former home in the theatre and turned his back on vaudeville, too, before it could turn its back on him. Even if he'd not suffered from a terrible disease, he had nowhere to look to find himself.

Excepting his anti-Semitism, the mean spirit he'd let fly with the White Rats and after, was out of character for him, as all who knew him assured all those who cared to listen. The delusions that took him over were fuelled not only by hatred but by grandiosity. Several hours after the debacle, he was still ranting on the ferry platform at Fort Lee, New Jersey, on his way home from the benefit. "I am Maurice Barrymore, the greatest actor this country ever saw," he screamed. "Why I'm greater than Lincoln."[41] His notions were in keeping with the standing he'd coveted, though scarcely with the modesty his friends knew or with the serial abjections he'd performed in vaudeville.

It wasn't only status that Barrymore had shed. He'd drifted away in stages from the masculinity rife in American politics, with Teddy Roosevelt's charge up San Juan Hill, the American Army's police actions in the Philippines and on the Chinese mainland, and a little later in the first President Roosevelt's bully-pulpit style and big-stick foreign policy. Barrymore had run squarely in the face of manly posturing, in a sequence of characters happy only in nostalgia, from the haunted Captain to the disgruntled drudges of Gilbert's "Etiquette" to the dematerialized cloud in Cary's "Cloud-Land" to the dying cockney of Sims's "Told to the Missionary" to the shiftless father in *The Lady and the Burglar* before coming back, full circle, to Captain Bradley, who was, after all, another sad case. In "Cloud-Land," the poem squarely in the middle of his turn at the Fifth Avenue, Barrymore identified so strongly with the bereft female cloud that when his friend, the former heavyweight boxing champion Jim Corbett asked him to recite Cary's poem after the first White Rats' benefit, Barry choked up on coming to the lesser cloud's lines of longing for simple companionship.[42]

In none of his turns, no matter how much he conceded, did Barrymore ever renounce his Englishness. Vaudeville used that

Englishness, and him, to cater to an Anglophilia nearly as rabid as it was in the theatre. But Anglophilia can call up its opposite, and so it may have done in Barrymore's case. The spectacle of a dimming star remained tolerable, or entertaining, even, to Americans disposed to read Britain's incipient decline as proof of their own worth.

Whoever saw Barry toward the end of his stint as a man of the world was left to redeem any resentment they felt toward Britain with their pity for its tottering angel. The kind of attention Barrymore got as he disintegrated supports Edward Said's contention that the lure of empire subordinates whatever divides the classes to the prospect of elevating them all.[43] Americans felt no differently than their counterparts in Britain did on this score, as the stellar career of Maurice Barrymore went toward proving.

*   *   *

The first Barrymore could, if he'd wanted, have used vaudeville for touting the Spanish-American War. In 1898, the two-a-day would have given him the perfect platform. But staunch Briton he remained, and only shared billing with the "War Graph" that included some of the earliest newsreels to show battle and to simulate it. The Spanish-American War, in fact, gave the American Biograph Company a trial run for capturing the Boer War on film when it broke out in South Africa the next year. As the century ran to its close, America was shaping the future of global communications and their extension into war coverage. Britain, meanwhile, was paying the price for its greatness.

Americans saw themselves forging a new kind of empire, conceived in commerce and dedicated to the proposition that all markets are created equal. Americans' trust in their benevolence had them believing that they deserved to pass the British by, whose dressy uniforms were looking as fussy as their military occupations had come to seem unending. People in the United States thought they could liberate the oppressed as they'd done, they liked to think, with remnants of the Spanish Empire in Cuba and the Philippines. Opinion settled in on both sides of the Atlantic that, as Bernard Porter has put it, "Britain's best hope in the future was to co-operate in her own snaffling." This might just work, the reasoning went, if the older nation could "persuade the United States to take her on as a kind of junior partner in whatever world scheme the latter might have in mind."[44] The path to the twenty-first century was being laid at the end of the nineteenth century.

With questions mounting as to how empires ought to be won, and run, British variety avoided images of decline such as the ones Maurice Barrymore gave out in vaudeville. Instead, toward the end of 1899, London took in turns from a star more imperial than Barrymore was, or Amy Roselle.

As she girded herself for her entrance into the new venue, Mrs. Herbert (Maud) Tree (1858–1937) could fall back on a sense of obligation that obscured whatever selfishness had brought her to the moment. Obligation came as naturally to her as masochism did to Roselle and Barrymore. Mrs. Tree's patrician presence offered something more elevated than variety had seen yet. This was no desperate woman, at least in the ordinary sense.

Maud Holt had grown up in London, well off and well educated. She'd studied at Queen's College there, taken honors in classics and trigonometry, and starred in amateur theatricals. She met Herbert Tree while she was still a beginner and he an up-and-coming young actor. Ambitious and able as he was, he won her only after he'd convinced her that he could support the sort of future she had in mind.[45] And that he did, for the most part.

On becoming Tree's bride, Maud made herself known as much for her philanthropy as her acting. She also fell into the mold of long-suffering Victorian wife in the face of her husband's epic womanizing. But she stayed with him, more or less, and became Lady Tree when he was knighted in 1909. After he died, she was awarded the Order of the British Empire for the public-spiritedness she'd shown throughout her life.

It was public-spiritedness, in part, that called her into variety. She wanted access to patrons she could never have reached otherwise, and who needed urging to meet a crisis in the Empire. She exercised a kind of control over her life on the stage, and in her household, that she would never find in her marriage.

The outbreak of the Boer War recommended her to the octogenarian Charles Morton at the London Palace. Aged as he was, Morton moved swiftly to have her give her first turn less than three weeks after mighty Britain had declared war on the South African Republic of Dutch-immigrant farmers. Nearly every British subject was expecting the Afrikaners to be routed. Optimism was rampant, and it bathed London in a rosy glow. Morton saw a windfall in the estimable Mrs. Tree.

She wasn't in it for the money. Her career was building still along with her husband's. She was known in exclusive circles for reciting at charity events in which she could combine "her gifts of being actress and social success," in the clear-sighted words of one of Beerbohm Tree's biographers.[46] The turn she settled on was Rudyard Kipling's newly written "The Absent-Minded Beggar." Her first recitation of it came on October 31, 1899, in the evening of the day when the piece appeared in print for the first time in the *Daily Mail*, London's leading tabloid.

Mrs. Tree joined Kipling on a mission to inspire subjects of the Crown—not least the *Daily Mail's* tens of thousands of working-class readers—to give to war-charities, or if they were young men, to enlist in the fighting forces. In air thick with hope and tobacco smoke, she applied herself to Kipling's frog-marching style. The poem had her repeat an appeal to compensate families of the dead and wounded. She spoke the first of "Beggar's" four stanzas as follows:

> When you've shouted "Rule Britannia," when you've sung "God Save the Queen,"
> When you've finished killing [Boer leader Paul] Kruger with your mouth,
> Will you kindly drop a shilling [~$5.50 now] in my little tambourine
>> For a gentleman in khaki ordered South?
> He's an absent-minded beggar, and his weaknesses are great—
>> But we and Paul [Kruger] must take him as we find him—
> He is out on active service, wiping something off a slate—
>> And he's left a lot of little things behind him!

Then the refrain:

> Duke's son—cook's son—son of a hundred kings—
>> (Fifty thousand horse and foot going to Table Bay!) [the harbor at Cape Town, South Africa]

> Each of 'em doing his country's work
>> (and who's to look after their things?)
> Pass the hat for your credit's sake,
>> and pay—pay—pay![47]

She spoke the "pay—pay—pay" at the end of each stanza in the tone of an officer barking orders. Mrs. Tree knew how to load her voice with authority. She did it something in the way Amy Roselle had done while recounting scenes of battle, and quite opposite to what Barrymore would do by exposing his softer side.

With tokens of male entitlement all around her, Mrs. Tree used "Beggar" to show that women could become more like men, or shame them if need be. As she, and Kipling, and producer Morton must have supposed the poem would do, it spoke more to women with her speaking it. It also appealed across class lines by calling on "Duke's son—cook's son—son of a hundred kings," with only slight variations before each of the "pay—pay—pay[s]!"

The nine-year-old Clarkson Rose, later a variety performer himself, would have been one of the younger sprites on hand, later in the run. Years onward, as he remembered it,

> This particular programme was a matinee, and started with overture prompt at two o'clock and it played for seven minutes. Promptly at two-seven, on came R. H. Douglass, whom I remember as one of the first comedians giving impressions. . . . [and later on the bill] the first-class character comedian George Bastow . . . [and] Paul Mill, a light comedian . . . Then there was that brilliant mimic, Marie Dainton, who announced that her impressions were given "by kind permission of A. W. Pinero, Esq. [playwright of note], John Hare, Esq. [actor-manager of note], and George Edwardes, Esq. [producer of musical entertainments, formerly at the Empire]."

Mrs. Tree was hardly the turn that Rose was most anticipating. Even as a grown man, he acknowledged the memory of her only in passing.

More impressive to him, in hindsight and in the moment, was the performer and his future friend Fred Russell following

Mrs. Tree, who

made his appearance at four thirty-three, billed as a ventriloquial come-
dian. Later, Fred was to be the guide, counsellor, and dearly loved "Uncle
Fred" of the Variety Artistes' Federation, and of the Grand Order of
Water Rats.[48]

Rose's account shows other turns catering to "Duke's son—cook's
son—son of a hundred kings" more playfully than "Beggar" did.

One other performer joined Mrs. Tree in bending gender. This
was none other than the so-said brilliant Marie Dainton, who
imitated some of the London theatre's most prominent men. Her
impressions, however, left out one of the greatest figures of the stage,
none other than Maud's husband, Herbert Beerbohm Tree. Even for
his turning up missing from Dainton's turn, and his wife's, Tree figured nevertheless, playing the title role in moving-pictures of
Shakespeare's war-ridden *King John*.[49] Tree's was only one of several
bits of footage put together by

"The American Biograph"—invented by Herman Casler of New York . . .
the list of pictures to be shown included, "Polo at Hurlingham," "A scene
from *King John*" (then playing at Her Majesty's Theatre), "The *Daily
Mail* War Express leaving Great Central Station, London," "Queen
Victoria Reviewing the Household Cavalry," "The Landing of General
Sir Redvers Buller at Capetown," "Afternoon Tea [with the royals] in the
Gardens of Clarence House," and "Train taking up water at full speed on
the London and North Eastern Railway."[50]

The Biograph offered an assortment to please the war-lovers, one
and all.

*King John*, available in brief on film at the Palace and running still
at full length onstage at Her Majesty's, stopped just short of being
pure propaganda. The war had been undeclared when Tree's stage
production had opened.[51] He had seen war in the offing, though,
and studded his show with patriotic moments to enlarge on
Shakespeare's vision. Most impressive among Tree's embellishments,
and the farthest beyond what the Bard had included, was a *tableau*
showing the signing of the Magna Carta.[52] *King John*, in Tree's

high-Victorian *homage*, made another way to call up the present war, along with "The Absent-Minded Beggar" and the troop- and shipboard-shots from the Biograph. The two Trees, in tandem across town, called on every British subject to fall into line behind the soldiers, beggarly lot though they were.

At Mrs. Tree's opening, the *Pall Mall Gazette* noted only a "few pessimists" in attendance in an auditorium that was

> literally packed. The best places had been sold out, and in the democratic first circle and amphitheatre [where the cheapest seats were] the "standing room only" notices were exhibited long before the curtain rose. Of course, we were in no doubt as to the meaning of the crush in this most ample house, or if any existed the conversation of our neighbours speedily set it at rest. "Not a bad programme this," observes a young fellow, smoking a stumpy briar pipe. "Oh, not *too* bad," drawls another youth coaxing a fat cigar, and, after a pause, "I came here for Kipling, you know." "Same here," rejoined the first; and with this common bond established they discussed the war news in exactly the same spirit that it was discussed all day all over London.

To dismiss the enemy would have belittled Britain's warriors. In that spirit, the *Gazette's* correspondent carried on his recording of the conversation he'd overheard:

> "They'll take some doing—these Boers," suggested the young artizan with a by no means ill-pleased expression. "Well," replied the other, "we could not expect to have a simple walk-over, could we?" "Of course not," was the response. "But it'll have to be got through"—a sentiment which was accepted with a significant little nod, which an American would translate into "You bet."[53]

As the evening wore on,

> the turns were of an average sort, but the house waited expectantly for what was to come, so long and so patiently that when Turn 13 [just before Mrs. Tree] was reached there was a round of applause which developed into a storm when Mrs. Tree, gowned in a deep tint of scarlet, came on. With the brief introduction, " 'The Absent-Minded Beggar,'

by Rudyard Kipling," she read the poem, simply and eloquently, with one solitary dramatic gesture at the last line of the last verse, leaving the words—and they could be heard distinctly in every part of the theatre— to make their own impression.

"The effect," as the *Gazette's* man relived the moment,

> was remarkable. It was not a Union Jack outburst, the prevailing note is not struck in that key—it was a warm but steady and somewhat restrained outburst, as if the sentiment of pride in the army was at the moment dominated by the determination that the nation would do its duty to the absent-minded beggar.

The evening closed fittingly with

> the orchestra play[ing] the National Anthem, and when the military pictures were shown [in the American Biograph], for the expression of national and military enthusiasm . . . for the time being the warlike sentiment was chastened by a deep touch of pathos . . . the loud patri- otic outburst in "God Save Our Queen" came as a relief to saddened feelings. The audience rose to the spirited expression of the national ideal, and broke into a single-hearted, triumphant expression of pride and loyalty.[54]

Celebrations such as this one may have eased some of the concern at what had become almost instant signs of trouble for the British side. In response, as the war heated up, American Biograph dropped the medievalized *King John* for more up-to-date footage showing the "Review of Gordon Highlanders by Lord Wolesley at Edinburgh" and the "Gordon Highlanders on Board the Transport." In the meantime, *King John* continued its run at Her Majesty's until nearly the new year that rang in the new century.

At the Palace, Mrs. Tree was facing something that not she, nor Kipling, nor Charles Morton could have foreseen. For all the respectability she and her husband were lending the proceedings, it may have helped arouse the mischief, overenthusiasm, or something like the "Union Jack outburst" the *Pall Mall Gazette* disclaimed. A fair number of the Palace patrons were taking Mrs. Tree's injunction to "pay—pay—pay" literally, showering coins on the stage where she stood.

The high spirits were partly a tribute to her expressive powers, and Kipling's. Some among the gatherings arrived already excited, flushed with the evening and with alcohol. The level of enthusiasm rose considerably once she hit the stage. When she rang out the "pay—pay—pay" at the end of each of stanza, she was hardly in a position to take it back, particularly on reaching the second or third repetition.

Her peremptory tone had friskier patrons following her orders in the most immediate way they could. She put them in position, without meaning to, to be good soldiers *and* rowdy in the same open-handed, full-bodied gesture. Some men may have resented her for taxing them so repeatedly, and she a woman. Her station and gender certainly didn't shield her once some of the assembly started measuring her where she stood, dressed all in crimson.

The sight of Palace patrons flinging coinage at his star alarmed the courtly Morton. He sprang to her aid by printing programs requesting patrons to refrain from tossing money. "Boxes are placed at the entrance for the reception of Donations," he pointed out.[55] All money collected, he assured the throngs, would be applied to "the Palace Theatre List for 'The Soldiers' Widows and Orphans Fund.' "

Gallant as it was, Morton's appeal couldn't stop the coins from raining down. No fool Mrs. Tree. She was reported speaking forcefully as ever more than six weeks into her run, but staying "well out of the line of fire" from "the officiousness of members of the audience, who would throw money over the footlights."[56] Nor was news that she was donating her salary of £100 a week (~$11,000) to the Widows' and Orphans' Fund enough to keep some among her audiences from taking a bead on her. For as long as she gave the turn, a few ticket holders delighted in making her into a highly polished version of a performing monkey. She might as well have been holding the tin cup, though that wouldn't have been a good idea, either, for giving the louts something shiny to aim at.

She stayed the good sport. The show went on, and she stood her ground in the cavalcade, or made it seem so. She continued raising money for dependents of the fallen, and more money for Morton and his shareholders at the Palace. Her presence on the bill, speaking in martial tones, showed how much the lines between men and women had blurred already, a decade before the campaign for women's suffrage hit full gear.[57] It's possible that this blurring of gender contributed to the fitful chivalry that greeted her.

Provocative as her "Beggar" was to the many, and profitable as it was to the few, Mrs. Tree didn't carry on in it for long beyond the new year. Just days before she'd given her first turn, British forces sustained the first in a series of stunning defeats that brought on the jitteriness among her opening-night audience. During her run came another round of military disasters capped by "Black Week" in mid-December 1899. Some of the people throwing money then may have felt a sense of helplessness, or guilt, that their vigor helped ease.

Attendance dwindled at shows across London.[58] The century turned without the festivity that might have marked it. Herbert Tree had weathered a dismal holiday season when, in the early January of 1900, he followed his brooding *King John* with a much lighter take on Shakespeare's *A Midsummer Night's Dream*, complete with live rabbits hopping about the stage. He drafted Mrs. Tree from the Palace to play the imperious Titania, queen of the fairies.

Her sponsorship of "Beggar" hadn't been for naught, apart from the money she'd raised. By the time she spoke the poem for the last time at the Palace, she'd inspired a round of imitators to carry on, including Harrison Brockbank delivering "Beggar" to Sir Arthur Sullivan's musical score at the Alhambra down the street, and Arthur Shirley with his own musical setting of "Beggar," tricked out as a revue showing a Boer villain lusting after an English soldier's wife.[59] The war, even going badly, couldn't drown out "The Absent-Minded Beggar."

Mrs. Tree may have left the Palace in retreat, but not before she'd touched on imperial issues with greater urgency than Amy Roselle or Maurice Barrymore had summoned. Even in the spirit of charity, though, Maud Tree's "Beggar" seemed presumptuous to those who determined to make her respond to *them*. Their patronizing her beyond the price of admission, especially the ones who least could afford it, was the reply to her patronizing them. If the Boer War was to be promoted for easing distinctions of class, Mrs. Tree in "The

Absent-Minded Beggar" reminded anyone who needed it that class and gender divide people in ways that not even the slickest jingoism can knit together.

* * *

Nearly sixty years later, John Osborne, angriest among the angry young British playwrights of the 1950s, quoted "The Absent-Minded Beggar." Osborne's play, *The Entertainer*, used the very few music halls that were left to mark Britain in decline. The subsequent film version, like the play, starred Laurence Olivier, who was far more celebrated by then than Mrs. Tree. In 1899 and 1900, she'd spoken "Beggar" to defend the Empire. By 1957, the Empire was all but gone when Osborne used the same verses to ring hollow after British diplomacy and the latest Queen's government had let the Union Jack down.

*The Entertainer* showed how far the source of renown had drifted from live entertainments. Hollywood had stood as the font of showbiz celebrity for more than forty years. The film capital had long since surpassed the London theatre in glitter and glamor, owing some part to its policy of recruiting stars from the mother stage. Even so, the London theatre, diminished in relative terms, was more vital than the tatty music halls where Olivier's character held forth. His corrosively cynical Archie Rice scarcely concealed his contempt for the few bored layabouts in attendance.

Osborne laid Victorian patriotism more deeply to rest by having a supporting actor speak snippets from "Beggar" instead of Sir Laurence himself, who alone among the cast could have matched Mrs. Tree in authority. Nor was it happenstance that had Olivier's celebrity crest in the same year he opened *The Entertainer* in London. His appearance opposite Marilyn Monroe in a lightweight Ruritanian costume drama called *The Prince and the Showgirl* had Hollywood using him to dignify her bosomy credulity, and her to refresh his renown as classical actor *par excellence*. Theirs wasn't a marriage like the Trees', nor any closer to being made in heaven. But it joined Olivier and Monroe, however uneasily, in grazing on the other's celebrity as a way of feeding their own.

Neither was it coincidence that had Olivier, at the height of his career, playing a burned out song-and-dance man as cheerless as any character Amy Roselle and Maurice Barrymore had dredged up. The sympathy Sir Larry gained in *The Entertainer*, with the nation joining his cankered showman in caterwauls of self-pity, helped gain him the title "Baron Olivier" a few years later. The pathetic spectacle he made as hollow-eyed music-hall veteran let audiences patronize his character in the act of lionizing him. As seeming opposites, the character, with Olivier in it, enlarged on the reputation the star had made by playing heroes as sterling, and as tortured, as any actor's of his era.

Even during his most extended interlude in Hollywood in the 1930s, Olivier stood more as the product of celebrity than its prophet as Mrs. Tree had been when she went off to meet Britain's last moment of truth in the nineteenth century that became its first one in the twentieth. For all their differences, Olivier, and Marilyn Monroe for that matter, were very like Mrs. Tree in showing how fame's larger version could inspire patrons who needed bucking up, as they always do, or will.

# 2. Precious Brits, 1904–1912 ❦

*Vaudeville . . . is coming to be something like the American tour of foreign actors, a respectable way of fattening a depleted bank account.*

Norman Hapgood, "The Life of a Vaudeville Artiste" (1901)[1]

*Americans for a long time had wanted to construct their own tradition, yet the European and English past was the only past that was available.*

Henry F. May, *The End of American Innocence* (1959)[2]

Whether the world was ready or not, the nineteenth century turned into the twentieth century. Britain hadn't yet set aside its foothold in the New World, nor been fought to a standstill by the undermanned, under-armed Boers. Easier travel, the common language, and a booming American economy were bringing more British actors to North American shores. Music-hall and variety performers were turning up in vaudeville, too, at the same time as vaudevillians filtered into variety and music halls on the other side.

Any major British actor might have shunned the venue that had drained Maurice Barrymore. On the other hand, audiences were no less eager to sample actors who spoke the King's English as Barrymore did. To fill his place, vaudeville courted stars from the mother lode. British stars knew that the rewards would be ample. They knew also that they would be settled into bills with run-of-the-mill performers showing heroic effort.

In 1904, vaudeville secured a pair of British stars who would have looked like laborers to no one. The actors were thoroughly English, more than Barrymore was, and harder working to boot. The woman of the two was Jessie Millward (1861–1932). She'd been a star in England and America for nearly twenty years when she came to give her first turn. She was also a true child of the stage, having grown up with a playwright for a father. It was his indisposition, in fact, that had brought her first to the stage to support the family. These events made the perfect setting for her debut, awash in sympathy.

Only in her early twenties on making her mark in London, she was fresh-faced, wholesome, and passionate in a maidenly sort of way. The great Henry Irving watched her and later hired her to play *ingénues* with a backbone. She joined his Lyceum Theatre company early in the 1880s. She toured the United States with Irving, and back home, acted for the first of many times opposite William Terriss at London's Adelphi Theatre.

Millward and Terriss flourished at what they helped rededicate as the citadel of British melodrama. In play after play, her spirited heroines stood by his sterling heroes. The bond between the stars was forged everlastingly in 1897, when, just outside the Adelphi's stage door, Terriss was stabbed by a crazed supernumerary. He died in Millward's arms, one of the first fatalities from the fanaticism the word "fan" chops short.[3]

Traumatized by the murder and some awkward publicity—it was whispered that she and Terriss, a married man, had been lovers—she took a sabbatical in Italy. There she agreed to Charles Frohman's terms for joining his Empire Stock Company in New York. In America, she tried a wider range of roles than the paragons she'd been known for. When her star didn't rise as she'd hoped it would, she signed on with Charles Dillingham, in league with the Theatrical Syndicate whose esthete-in-chief was Charles Frohman, with Frohman's brother Daniel to back him up.

It was Dillingham, though, who featured Millward in *A Clean Slate* in New York City in 1903. But the run wasn't strong enough to warrant taking the play on the road. When Millward found herself in debt in a country that was in the grips of recession, she looked to vaudeville to help her recover the clean slate she'd missed since

Terriss's death. She felt his absence onstage, and also in decisions about her career she was having to make on the fly.

She'd been no bigger a star than Barrymore, and a co-star like him at the top of her game. But her long sojourns in the 'States couldn't keep her from seeming more British than he'd been. The $1,000 a week F. F. Proctor paid her would be equivalent to about $21,000 now. It was the same sum that escape artist Harry Houdini had only hoped to get as one of vaudeville's premier acts the year before.[4]

With vaudeville beckoning, Millward hesitated. She buttonholed a high-powered American attorney who spoke of "the changing outlook in America on vaudeville." He told her that vaudeville's money men wanted "a change in the class of performance." Proctor's Fifth Avenue would be just the place to attract audiences to recognize her quality, she was told. It was this set of expectations that armed her against reservations she held as an artiste too apt, as she put it, "to look down on the music-halls as the abode of performing animals and red-nosed [i.e., alcoholic] singers."[5] She had a reputation to lose if things should go wrong.

She would have been reassured by the Fifth Avenue's rich history as a legitimate house, and by Proctor's offer, which was guaranteed. Vaudeville, if not growing by leaps and bounds at the moment, was doing well enough despite the recession. Walter Weyl, the social commentator and sage, wrote shortly after the American economy found its legs again, that the "salaries of actors, vaudeville artists, baseball players, etc., have enormously increased as a result of the flood of wealth pouring from the pockets of the people."[6] Millward's presence was sure to raise the price for stars, especially women. She decided to put herself in Proctor's pocket.

He saw fit to show her out twice as often as was usual. That meant that when she came to giving her first turn on the afternoon of May 23, 1904, it was not at Proctor's Fifth Avenue but at his 23d Street house before returning within the hour to the grander establishment a few city blocks away. Performing at more than one music hall or variety house in London was commonplace. There, lower salaries and fewer matinees encouraged mainstay performers to pick up as many turns of an evening as they could.

Whether Millward's dual appearances were her idea or Proctor's, she found them strenuous enough that,

> when the first week of it was over, I caught myself jumping out of bed in the middle of nights and rushing to the door mechanically as if I were going to take another [horse-]car to somewhere or other. It was an experience I certainly shall never go through again. Hereafter, I shall be content to appear in one theatre at a time, giving two performances, of course, each day, but not in places several miles [actually blocks] apart.[7]

Her skills were tested against turns like Clarice Vance's in blackface, doing "restrained and effective . . . coon songs" at the Fifth Avenue. At the 23d Street, meanwhile, she was billed with the "comedy foot dance cyclists" Wood and Berry, who helped fill a bill that included the latest in film tinting, the kalatechnoscope.[8] At least there were no red-nosed singers to block out the pastels. Millward gained from Proctor's paying what *Theatre Magazine* called "big salaries . . . for big names."[9] She made the kind of refined attraction to appeal to patrons whittling down their budgets with the economy on the slide.

Millward had always been a trouper, and all things considered, she held up well. She expected to stay in vaudeville quite a while, she said, to show "the serious side of my art."[10] She said later that she'd learned to stifle her serious side for fear of losing her grip after Terriss's death.[11]

Her turn in J. Hartley Manners's *A Queen's Messenger* was high seriousness by vaudeville's slap-happy standards. She played a Russian spy who seduces the young courier of the title. He carries

> very important papers . . . she is trying to obtain. . . . She lures him on with her wiles, and induces him to smoke a few drugged cigarettes, which bring on temporary insensibility. She opens the bag and secures the papers, and when the young man comes to he is much distressed.

In melodrama, the good couldn't die young even when they'd erred so dangerously. When the distraught messenger attempted

> to commit suicide with a pistol, mentioning the name of his English sweetheart [he] impresses the Russian woman, and moves her to tears.

She prevents the suicide, restores the precious papers and agrees to drive him to the station in time to catch his train.[12]

The diplomat's "English sweetheart" never showed up onstage. Instead, she made a shadow version of the pure but fiery young things Millward had played opposite William Terriss. *A Queen's Messenger* returned the star to type at the end, with goodness peeking out from beneath the tarnish.

Changes of heart like the one demonstrated by the star's spy were common among vaudeville dramas. Sometimes the transformations owed to a longer play being cut with mortal wounding of situations written to take shape more slowly. Lightning changes of motive were good for thrills, too, though generally at the expense of the plausibility the theatre of the day, rife with well-made plays, prized so much.

In vaudeville as in variety, sharp reversals showed influence from the "protean" turns popular on both sides of the Atlantic. Named after Proteus, the Roman god who changes form at will, proteans paraded their versatility more than the theatre allowed them to do by playing a single role or two, or more only in walk-ons. Vaudeville and variety saw proteans head turns that showed them in several characters, or many, in some cases playing every part in the cast in odd little plays written to serve their talents. Nearly all proteans impersonated men and women and mixed comic characters with dramatic ones. Some shifted between evil and goodness, à la Millward as the spy.

She'd entered vaudeville to play against her familiar earnestness. Having touched on evil in her turn, she knew she had to retrieve some goodness if she wanted to uphold her stardom. The prospect of honest labor didn't daunt her, and many vaudevillians were known for their manic exertions. In Millward's case, there were not only the four turns a day, but also those toilsome transitions that *A Queen's Messenger* required.

She wanted to dispose Proctor to hire her again, though not straightaway. The plan worked. Her tour lasted into the summer. Tired but in better financial order, she sailed back to England. There, she was startled to find herself "disappointed in the acting" she'd revered and been proud to represent.[13] After a few more theatrical engagements in England and America, she toured vaudeville again in 1908.

This time, she only recycled *A Queen's Messenger* with a different young actor in the title role. *Variety* praised the star for her "grace and skill . . . all too rare" in vaudeville, but complained of her "utterly foolish and unconvincing vehicle."[14] At the Fifth Avenue, she and her co-star needed all the skill they could muster against conventional turns like Ethel Levey's, who'd divorced the tunesmith and budding impresario George M. Cohan the year before. Billed as a solo act, Levey's song-and-dance was held over to lighten a bill that cried out for it with Millward twisting her way through *A Queen's Messenger*. *Variety's* passing mention of Millward as a "former Frohman star" told how little she could trade on her reputation against dynamos like Levey.[15]

In 1908, however, Millward kept snaring the poor messenger, even though she won less favor for it than she'd found four years before. The money was good, again, and she was likely taken up in matters personal. Soon after the tour ended, she married John Glendinning, known as "the Terriss of the North" as a young Scotsman before touring America in warmed-over Adelphi melodramas.[16] After marrying Millward, he joined her to show turns in British variety. In fact, they tried *As a Man Sows* as a variety turn in 1911, and that fall they played it in vaudeville on a tour that carried the couple into late May of 1912.

In the 'States in *As a Man Sows*, they opened at Hammerstein's throbbing Victoria in New York City. Then they moved along the eastern circuit before venturing into the West. From the prairies to the coast and back, working all the way, she remembered feeling as if on "a prolonged holiday among glorious surroundings."[17] On the road, she won praise regularly, as from the *Minneapolis Journal* for being "one of our half dozen best actresses" on a bill opposite two blackfaced acts and Leona Thurber and Harry Madison in "patter about their shopping tour."[18] If Millward felt out of her depth, it would have made her work even harder.

Even her strenuous efforts didn't enliven her crowds enough. She wouldn't have wanted to face other audiences like the one in

Cincinnati, which, after seeing *As a Man Sows*, "did not applaud suf-
ficiently to call forth a bow."[19] Under pressure, she changed *As a
Man Sows*' the title of in mid-tour to *Reaping the Whirlwind*.[20] But as
with her second go-round in *A Queen's Messenger*, she had no other
turn at the ready and could make only cosmetic improvements to the
one she had at hand. The exhaustion she suffered on returning to
New York showed the strain she'd been under, even with such amenities as she could afford, entrained with John Glendinning.[21]

In line with her formative years on the stage, Millward had taken
a co-starring role. Glendinning's performance, however, couldn't
have been less Terriss-like in showing an abusive man. Millward, in
choosing the play, may have hoped to get out from under the weight
of her stardom or to serve the man she'd married. Her mind may
have wandered to her younger days, when she'd played helpmeets to
the heroes of more famous men.

Whatever she had in mind, she would have had a hard time
realizing in such a troubling vehicle. It was, she called it, "a grim little
tragedy" that let her play a character who, "for entirely excellent
reasons, poisoned a worthless man." In Britain, the militant wing of
the suffrage movement was bringing such pieces to the fore.[22] In
America, where militants were all but unknown, the sight of a woman
killing a man, no matter how excellent the reasons, didn't sit well.

Nor could Millward shed Terriss's ghost, if ever she really wanted
to. For the benefit of readers who didn't know her life's saddest chapter, she raised Terriss's memory continually and for years before
doing it in the memoirs she wrote in her retirement. In the year
before her second vaudeville tour, a full decade after Terriss's death,
she had sat, she reported, beside his body "four nights at the mortu-
ary," knowing that "it was thoughts of me that anchored his spirit to
earth." His spirit, she knew, needed to leave thoughts of her behind
before it could find "a plane of perfect peace."[23] Glendinning can
hardly have found perfect peace himself, standing in for Terriss with
an actress communing with the dead in the way of the late Madame
Blavatsky and her successors among the Theosophists.

Whether Millward treated with spirits, she'd called on her serious
side once too often in vaudeville. Her murderous heroine had even
fewer of the endearing qualities that had founded her stardom than

the spy did in *A Queen's Messenger*. Seriously as she wanted to be taken, she kept choosing turns at odds with what her fans remembered and what regular vaudevillegoers could abide.

When vaudeville caught her on the cusp between stardom and oblivion, she found the two tied together as closely as she felt to the dearly departed William Terriss. What had made her most precious lay buried with him. Her entrance into variety one last time, in 1913, was an afterthought. Soon after, the war extinguished any hopes she could have had to resurrect her stardom.

\* \* \*

The century had turned with Britain bogged down in the Boer War. American newspaper publisher Whitelaw Reid saw his upstart nation rivaling Britannia with an empire of its own. The Pacific "is in our hands now," he crowed, and

> we own more than half the coast on this side, dominate the rest, and have midway stations in the Sandwich and Aleutian Islands. To extend now the authority of the United States over the great Philippine Archipelago is to fence in the China Sea and secure an almost equally commanding position on the other side of the Pacific—doubling our control of it and of the fabulous trade the Twentieth Century will see it bear. Rightly used, it enables the United States to convert the Pacific Ocean into an American lake.[24]

President Theodore Roosevelt made bold to say, though not in public, that "England is on the downgrade."[25] His opinion made Henry James's praise of "the honor that sits astride of the consecrated English tradition" sound antique in the same year Roosevelt sent the Great White Fleet around the world.[26] America wanted respect and America would have it, if not in any immediate way in the realms ruled by cultured Europeans.

The first President Roosevelt claimed the right, on his nation's behalf, to an empire Americans could believe was beneficent, even when policed from offshore by a bigger, faster fleet vying to rule the waves as Britannia had done for so long. On the homefront, vaudeville had made itself the leading force in commercial entertainment.

In the years around 1900, homegrown stars from the theatre with names now all but forgotten, like Nance O'Neil, Robert Hilliard, and Clara Morris, who was born a Canadian, gave turns.

Charles Hawtrey (1858–1923) was hardly homegrown or Canadian. English as they came, he was as dependable as he was pricey. Unlike Jessie Millward, his line was comedy, shading toward sentiment. Like her, he'd been touring America when hard times fell. But the steep recession didn't stop Proctor from snapping him up, and Millward with him, to show them in tandem on some of the highest end bills yet seen. Hawtrey was making $1,250 a week (~$26,500) when only the week before Millward opened, he started his own dual engagement on the afternoon of Monday, May 16, 1904.

He took cabs back and forth between Proctor's 23d Street and the Fifth Avenue on exactly the route Millward followed when she shared both his bills the week following. The *New York Times* praised Proctor for supplying identical "scenery and accessories" to put each star with trappings before twice as many patrons as could have seen the turns otherwise.[27] The producer gave crowds what the *New York Dramatic Mirror* called, in Hawtrey, "a $2 attraction for 50 cents." It was as if vaudeville were a clearing house, offering, in the *Mirror's* words, "special inducement, with trading stamps thrown in."[28] The foreign stars made fancy trading stamps indeed.

James D. Norris has written that around 1900, Americans were defining thrift not to mean saving so much as "getting your money's worth on your purchases."[29] Theatre took the trend and ran with it. For years by this time, "two-dollar star" (around $43 now) had been the ready phrase to describe actors in greatest demand. Hawtrey was closer to two-dollar stardom than Millward was. His serious side was harder to see. He did what he could to keep it that way.

Hawtrey's choosing *Time Is Money* for his turn sidestepped seriousness altogether, as it must have seemed. The play gave him a character who lied, was caught at it, but remained charming if harried throughout, and all in less than half an hour. The star had come to fame with just such bursts of gentlemanly dismay. Proctor knew that Hawtrey would add style, and his own brand of efficiency, to the proceedings. Mrs. Hugh Bell and Arthur Cecil had given the play a title that celebrated efficiency, American-style—this in spite of the play having been written in England where Hawtrey and others had shown it.[30]

If Millward joined vaudeville intending to keep "the pressure . . . up to the topmost notch," as she put it,[31] Hawtrey wanted to ratchet things up, too. It wasn't made easy for him, unless to kick him into a higher gear, that his deal with Proctor gave him only three days to tighten up *Time Is Money*.[32] The rapid turnaround, frenetic as it was, let Hawtrey turn his own scarce time into cash.

He played the impoverished suitor of a wealthy widow. Because she loves him, she

> makes up her mind to give him plenty of encouragement, so that he will propose, as she has funds enough for both. He calls in a hansom [carriage], but on searching his pockets finds that he has not a penny about him. This fact gives rise to a series of amusing episodes in which a servant maid figures prominently, as she runs in every few minutes with messages from the cabby, who is growing more and more impatient all the while.

"Matters finally come to a crisis," the reviewer wrote, when Hawtrey's character, "Charles Graham," makes "a clean breast of the matter." Then he "borrows three shillings [~$16.50] from the widow, pays the cabman," and is left free, finally, "to proceed with his lovemaking."[33]

The hansom never materialized. It was an effect the theatre could manage better anyway, with real horses sometimes. Given vaudeville's economy of means, sound effects were left to suggest a horse-drawn cab like the ones carrying the star and his company back and forth between one and the other of Proctor's downtown houses.

Hawtrey's "Charles Graham" rang true for another reason. Sharing a name with his character let the star seem "always himself" as Alfred Sutro later proposed it for Hawtrey's epitaph.[34] Seeming always oneself, as anyone who knows acting knows, makes one of actors' hardest tasks. Hawtrey had it down pat.

Proctor's clientele would have seen a star being always himself by sharing not only a given name with the jittery hero but also the daredevil's fondness for risk. "Charles Graham," true enough, dissembled and wooed more honorably than Hawtrey was known to do, but the star's turn in *Time Is Money* claimed authenticity on another score. It was "thoroughly English" for fixing on tradeoffs among gender, money, and class.[35]

The turn also caught something decidedly American that the contemporary Dutch historian Johan Huizinga would later call "Taylorism of the mind."[36] Taylorism took its name from Frederick W. Taylor, the first so-called efficiency expert. Huizinga coined a word using Taylor's name, to describe Americans' fondness for introducing "methods of the business world into intellectual activity." Efficiency was infiltrating every corner of the American enterprise, not least the arts. *Time Is Money*, made the kind of turn that Taylor and the acolytes could applaud.

Proctor Taylorized his bills by making Hawtrey and his little cast, with Millward and hers the week following, the only parts moving between one packed vaudeville house and another. The star turns joined other modular ones, timed to the second and formularized to a fare-thee-well, on a bill of specialists fitted like clockwork into the fun-making. Haste in *Time Is Money*, like the flurry from the acts around it, gave an industrial-strength rush like caffeine did, or nicotine.

Not only did Hawtrey practice his elegant efficiency, but he made it look easy. He never struggled with shorter formats as Millward did. Nor did his character's trials depart so far from the standard turns opposite his, like Crawford and Manning's "capital black face act" at the Fifth Avenue, or the Four Donazettas' "odd acrobatic grotesque specialty" among other offerings at the 23d Street.[37] By the end of his tour, Hawtrey was praising vaudeville to the skies whereas his fellow British stage stars were turning up their noses at music halls and variety in their homeland. Vaudeville was, he concluded, "immensely superior to the corresponding accommodations in England."[38]

The star's magnanimity didn't owe only to his earnings. Feverish action of the kind he favored—English actor that he was, and with his ever-so-English ways—left audiences feeling thrifty, efficient, and refined all in one. The patrons' good humor confirmed Hawtrey's wisdom in souping up a turn for teeming Manhattan that he could carry, with its feeling of hurry, into the provinces.

For weeks after leaving New York and his four-a-days, Hawtrey was catching trains at the same tight intervals workaday vaudevillians did, daily in the City, and over longer distances from one week to the next on reaching the hinterland. Mass urban transit had joined steamships and railroads to widen performers' range and, with it, their humble patrons'. The currency of the word "vehicle" in the theatre suggested that *plays* could be ridden by stars in the same way trains and ships were, or cabs, horse-drawn or combustion-powered. Hawtrey brought a vehicle to hurry audiences already addicted to speed. He raced his way through *Time Is Money* as if it had been one of the horses he bet on. Unlike the drama queens, he pleased audiences with the sight of pains well short of mortal ones.

Few of Hawtrey's contemporaries on the stage could match him in capturing the rhythms of public conveyance, though dancers caught it sometimes when they tapped, pounded, or scraped their ways across vaudeville's stage floors. Films were showing their own mechanized rhythms. A spate of the earliest films captured factory labor in tribute to Taylorism, showing people who looked like swarming ants.

While Jessie Millward strained to meet vaudeville on its terms, Hawtrey stayed with Taylorism all the way. The advertising for his Taylorized turn might have read: "Charles Hawtrey *is* Charles Graham in *Time Is Money*." His turn didn't broach matters of life and death. But it let the star be seen working as hard as any journeyman vaude-villian did, or any factory worker who forked over the the funds to see Charles-to-the-second-power do the dance of conspicuous labor.

\* \* \*

Hawtrey and Millward hardly exhausted the attraction British stage stars held for Americans. When vaudeville recruited Lillie Langtry (1852–1929), it went after glamor, pure if not so simple. Unlike Hawtrey and Millward, and nearly everyone else on view, Langtry denied that acting was work for her at all. Distress, comical or tragi-cal, wasn't really her line either, though she felt obliged to show it sometimes, in her languid sort of way.

Her star-power was far greater than Hawtrey and Millward's combined. The story of her life was more crowded with scandal than any star's except Bernhardt's. She'd toured in greater extravagance than anyone but Sarah had, and been one of the pioneering British actresses to mount their own vehicles.

Langtry had become, for untutored Yanks, virtual royalty. In the United States she was more admired, if anything, for not having been born to the purple. Instead, it was known, she'd risen through the classes, in a manner of speaking. Before becoming an actress, she'd been one of the first "professional beauties" who now would be called supermodels. Noted photographers and painters flocked to capture her image (see figure 2) while she began to keep company with the highly leisured. She caught the eye of the Prince of Wales, who on his mother Victoria's death, lent his name, or one of them, to the Edwardian age.

The Prince didn't take long to ask Langtry into the inner sanctum. She was nothing if not game, and far from the first woman to favor him. Given opportunity, she raised her fame by lying down to share what was, even for the least puritanical Victorian, the most private of acts.

After her affair with Bertie ended, he helped her when he could. Her daughter, Jeanne-Marie, coached to call her "Aunt," may have been his.[39] He never stopped going to the theatre, though, and joined others in urging her, her marriage to the negligible Mr. Langtry wrecked and her debts mounting, to go on the stage. There, she parlayed her conspicuous, if notorious, place in British society into a long, lucrative career as star, or nearer to what came later in America to be called a personality. No one who'd seen her act would have called her extraordinary on that account. She was, however, the first star to outshine any character she played.

By the time she got to vaudeville she was well into middle age. She still inspired press releases like the one agog at the prospect of seeing "a real English lady on the vaudeville stage."[40] She was the first theatrical star to bring something larger than fame to her turns, and a good thing it was. She was so much better at fame than she was at playing a character other than herself.

Getting her into vaudeville wasn't easy. Once Hawtrey and Millward finished touring there—she to return twice more—producers raised the ante. Proctor stayed closer to home when he

**Figure 2** Lillie Langtry, after a drawing by Frank Miles made during her younger days. Note the caryatid quality Miles saw in her face, and his sense of her moving in stillness. (University Library, University of Michigan; from Langtry's autobiography *The Days I Knew* [London: Hutchinson & Co., 1925]).

hired the Canadian Henry Miller for the first weeks of what was to be Miller's only vaudeville tour, started in March 1905. Miller was still on the road the next month when retired transatlantic star Helena Modjeska was reported turning down a higher fee than Miller was getting. Later in 1905, reports had Langtry ready to work for Proctor at $2,500 a week (~$53,000), after declining to play for the measly $1,500 Miller made (~$32,000). But the deal with Langtry was never consummated.

In May 1906, she was reported ready again to enter vaudeville. It would have been under Percy Williams this time, at the same price Proctor had promised her. Williams had just seen handsome offers he'd made for the services of Madge Kendal and Ellen Terry refused.[41] Langtry's acting was hardly in the same league with the *doyennes'* of the London stage. But facsimiles of her signature on tins of Pears' Soap were only a few of the tokens that had made her recognized across America.[42]

Once she agreed to join vaudeville, Langtry, like Hawtrey and Millward, headed straight for the Fifth Avenue. There, though, instead of working for Proctor only, as Millward, Hawtrey, and Maurice Barrymore had done, she hired on with Keith, too. He'd recently bought the Fifth Avenue out from under Proctor, who'd only been leasing it. Keith then forced Proctor into managing the Fifth Avenue with him, and with that, to join forces in recruiting Langtry as the biggest trophy-turn yet.

It was to seal their alliance, in fact, that Keith and Proctor wrested her away from Williams, who'd made himself a bother to them both. Keith and Proctor's concord made Langtry into the centerpiece for the Fifth Avenue's rededication as flagship for the highest class of vaudeville. In the spirit of truce, fleeting though it was, Keith and Proctor agreed to share her out with the other moguls who oversaw major vaudeville chains in the East, in Chicago, and in parts westward. If producers in bitter competition could agree on one thing, it was that Lillie Langtry stood to enrich them all.

She was, like Hawtrey, looking to the familiar to meet unfamiliar conditions. She chose a play she knew well. *A Wife's Peril*, it was called in English, was based on French playwright Victorien Sardou's original work, several times removed. Sardou was best known for writing and staging grand historical spectaculars to star Bernhardt. Langtry had spent her career following in Bernhardt's wake.

Langtry had first acted *A Wife's Peril* twenty years before, in a version that scrapped Sardou's happy ending in favor of killing off the star's sorely tempted but ultimately self-sacrificing wife. Nearly one-quarter century onward, Langtry had Graham Hill carve out a turn from *A Wife's Peril* called *Between Nightfall and the Light*. The title was taken from a poem by Robert Browning, and the turn restored the fifty-something star to her role as the "young wife." Langtry hoped to raise favor by playing purer than her default characterization was. She'd specialized, as Bernhardt had, in what polite critics termed "soiled doves." Such characters called for whitening, even bleaching, in line with vaudeville's family-first agenda.

Langtry played the young wife accosted by

Arnold Chaloner, a close friend of her husband. Chaloner tells Mrs. Branfoy [*sic* for "Beaufoy"] that he wants her to go away with him, because he has proof that her husband loves his (Chaloner's) wife. Mrs. Branfoy refuses to agree to such a plan to even up the score, and Chaloner departs, telling her that within an hour he will kill her husband unless she meets him.

The erring husband, altogether unsuspecting,

has returned home in the meantime, [and] is confronted by his wife with the proof of his deceit, and admits that he has been weak, but begs her to forgive him. This she does, and being anxious to save him from Chaloner she puts on [her husband's] army coat and hat, steps out where the waiting man may see her, and stops the bullet intended for her husband.[43]

Mrs. Beaufoy's taking the fall ran against the star's reputation for finding her bliss in the arms of very rich men.

Langtry had introduced her second marriage, to an English aristocrat named Hugo de Bathe, into the mix. Her connubial state, she hoped, would lend respectability to the most sacrificial episode she could have chosen from the longer play. *Variety's* man in London noted, tongue in cheek, that "For dying Mrs. Langtry is to receive $2,500 per week."[44] "Beaufoy" means "good faith" in French. Langtry was showing good faith, and good value, by dying in pose.

As Keith and Proctor's dutiful employee, she graced a party they threw in her honor at their newly refurbished Fifth Avenue. The two men, uneasy partners at best, united in gallantry as they'd done by guaranteeing her massive salary. She lived up to their expectations not only by joining their first joint bill at the Fifth Avenue, but also by adding her own decorative function to the auditorium's new interior. There, amid the gilt and festoonery,

> Three shades predominate—Parisian gray, chartreuse green and old ivory. The walls are in different shades of green, and the boxes and all the woodwork in ivory and gray. The ceilings are panelled in hues of "crushed rose," blending into cream color. The draperies throughout the auditorium are of a deep Chambertin red and the carpeting a Burgundy red.

Just beyond the auditorium was a

> new lobby [which] presents a cheerful aspect in its gilt-framed panels of red and absinthe green. There are spacious reception rooms, and they are attractively treated in lavender and cream. In the dome of the theatre are eight panels painted with figures of heroic size, the work of the late Tojetti when he was at his best.[45]

The star had only to die as Mrs. Beaufoy, twice daily, to reap her windfall in the trappings of continental luxury.

Born on the Channel island of Jersey, whence her nickname "The Jersey Lily," Langtry had grown up speaking French and English. Renowned for her precious gems and Parisian gowns, she was frank in telling the press: "I worship the golden calf, and there is money in vaudeville."[46] The candor fed her reputation for living as lavishly as she could and as freely as she did. Keith and Proctor couldn't have chosen anyone to quicken interest more unless it had been *La Bernhardt* herself, or one of two native stars then in highest vogue, the *gamine* Maude Adams and Ethel Barrymore of the transatlantic bloodline.

Langtry proved a wise investment. Her elegance matched the European touches all around. Demand to see her was strong, fed by the many who hadn't been able to see her before. At fifty-four, she was aging well enough to continue on the stage for twelve years more. True, her star would dim after Edward VII's death in 1910. But vaudeville let the uninitiated catch her sooner on the cheap rather than later if at all. She was following Bernhardt, again, who'd been testing the lure of farewell tours since the 1890s.

Langtry, however, outdid the French star in sly innocence. She made it seem, for instance, as if she'd done nothing to attract attention that merely came her way, as the Prince of Wales had done according to the discreet account she gave out in her memoirs. She claimed never to have suffered from stage fright, even as a novice. She had, she wrote, "loomed so largely in the public eye that there was no novelty in facing the crowded audience." She'd known "most of the occupants of the stalls and boxes," she recalled, "and all in the cheaper parts knew me."[47] In vaudeville, the cheap seats were so many of the ones to be sold.

Langtry gave living proof, as Millward and Hawtrey had done in their own ways, of vaudeville's spending more to offer more. The producers clamoring for her services were doing what boys and men had done since her tomboy days. In adult life, she'd seen her price rise and fall with the standing of the men willing to meet it. She represented value to women, too, and easily attracted a lower-end following in vaudeville to go with some part of the upper-end crowds who'd seen her already.

Anna Marble, writing a column called "The Woman in Variety," captured Langtry's marmoreal impassiveness thus:

> Mrs. Langtry's incursion into vaudeville is accompanied by a not too ardent usage of her emotional powers. The beautiful lily, aware of the age-producing effect of temperamental expression, refrains carefully from overacting. . . . No need to ask why the lily's face is unlined, no need to question why the curves of her throat are as perfect as a [Dante Gabriel] Rossetti drawing. The answer is in the placidity of her demeanor, in the immobile beauty of her classic features.[48]

Early film acting was being called "posing for the camera." There didn't have to be a camera on hand to get Langtry to pose.

Lee Harrison, the monologist who followed her to finish her first bill, was left playing "to the departing backs" of what might under ordinary circumstances have been more patient viewers.[49] His chatter must have seemed inane to patrons who'd thrilled to the sight of Langtry's young wife dying martyr to marriage, true love, and altruism.

In an interview for the *New York Times*, conducted with her shortly before she gave her first turn, she dismissed her romances as "old bones" not to be dug up:

> "There is no need of harking back to the old days. Surely, a woman may have more than one lover, mayn't she? I believe she should have more than one. Really.". . . Mrs. Langtry was one of the first to come under the new immigration laws, which are more stringent than the old ones. "They asked me whether I had any particular distinguishing marks," she said. "I told them the only ones I could think of were a pair of big round blue eyes. They said that was all right. When they asked me about my complexion, I answered, 'Troublesome.' "[50]

Such offhanded remarks proclaimed her lack of obligation to any of her pastimes, whether it was acting, or breeding horses, or racing them, or running a vineyard, or consorting with the *crème de la crème*. She used dry humor to show that she didn't need any man, no matter how highly placed he was, including the present King of England and her latest husband Hugo, who was about to make her Lady de Bathe upon inheriting his father's title. As she'd grown older, she'd made it a habit to declare her loyalty as seldom as she could, to men, to the United States of America, to Great Britain, or to France as countries where she'd worked and hobnobbed.

The associations Langtry held with British royalty, the *boudoir*, and *haute couture*, captivated vaudeville audiences as they'd done more exclusive ones. Her seeming never to extend herself added to the spice. Until the end of her career, her greatest assets remained her face, her style, and the apparent ease with which she wore them (see figure 3). It left onlookers wanting to be her, or to have her, or to live as she did. In vaudeville, she needed only to show a tighter set of poses.

The chasm between the Lily's life and Mrs. Beaufoy's death left audiences craving resolution they were never going to get. The

**Figure 3** Langtry in a portrait shot titled "The Lily and the Rose." Her bemusement suggests why she was better adapted to comedy, though it hardly explains she insisted on taking serious, and later, topical drama into vaudeville and variety. (University Library, University of Michigan; from *The Days I Knew*.)

impassiveness she displayed in the thousands of photographs of her in circulation, left fans wanting more, always more. Some nameless desire was what she wanted to raise and control. She did it well in vaudeville, and would do it there later, again, and in British variety, too, as she'd done it so many times before, for paying crowds and otherwise.

\* \* \*

Langtry had found the public eye by posing for a series of come-hither photos of herself. These became collectibles, among the first of their kind to be reproduced and sold widely. Then, when Langtry made her stage debut in the early 1880s, she was already familiar to many by sight, and in an ideal position to exploit the advent of photojournalism that made performers like her, together with athletes and sporting figures, more conspicuous than any group was that held power of the old-fashioned kind.

Still-photographs remained the only ones until moving pictures came along. For a decade and more by then, in the mid-1890s, stars including Langtry had been turning up in photos shot in foreign or exotic places, set squarely into the middle of typeface scrolling down the page in a riot of sizes and fonts. The words surrounding the photographs skipped across the page, drawing the eye after them. Travel-shots were printed on flat sheets but they suggested movement in three dimensions.

Stars embodied movement and a kind of existential freedom in their deportment onstage. They flourished in the melodramas that grew ubiquitous in the later nineteenth century, and had become staples in vaudeville by the 1890s. One of melodrama's distinguishing features was the way it used *tableaux* to freeze actors like statues for climaxes that ended scenes and acts. Although *tableaux* were nearly as static as photographs were, they suggested motion as the freeze-frames of their day, encapsulating what had led up to them and predicting what might follow.

Photographs, like *tableaux*, suggested movement more strongly once films arrived. Films served Langtry, too, who though she'd grown too old to carry them, never lost her knack for posing. She depended on the reams of coverage she'd gotten to suggest move-ment being corseted, reined in—invisible to the camera but alive in the minds of any who watched her in person or peered at her flattened image.

Many portrait photos of the day were taken in studios, posed in front of painted backdrops like ones used on the stage. As photo-graphs of the stars grew in number and quality, actors' lives had a way of looking more staged and their performances more real. Photographs had art colliding with life. Every detail of stars' images, and in accounts of their doings, was read into performances the actors gave. Anyone who saw stars at work could interpret a performance in the light of the massive documentation of the actors' lives.

Langtry had learned that audiences welcomed redemption after entertaining fantasies of the kind she raised. As the pure vessel for impure thoughts, she capitalized on a prurience whetted by the hot-house Victorian stage-settings she commissioned. She made it easy for men, in particular, to imagine her in settings, scenarios, and states of dress like the miniaturized ones they'd bought in the rush of pornography that came with photography, and in another glut, with the advent of motion pictures. Even with that, she intrigued women as much as men, though perhaps for different reasons.

Through the first of what were to be her three vaudeville tours, Langtry insisted, it was said, on a carpet being laid from her dressing room through the backscenes to the stage.[51] If the story is true, it shows her wanting to control even the environment beyond viewers' sightlines. She also wanted, more practically, to protect a costume fit for any ice-queen, of "palest blue velvet, embroidered in gold," designed for her by the fashion house Drecoll of Paris.[52] In vaude-ville, her Mrs. Beaufoy draped the faithless husband's army coat over her matchless gown to take the imaginary fatal bullet. Any garment so rugged might as well have been sackcloth on this particular star.

But once her Mrs. Beaufoy lay mortally wounded, it was as if Langtry had discharged her obligation. No sooner did the gunshot strike the character than Langtry doffed the coat.[53] She was willing to entertain suffering, not to wallow in it.

Just as her Mrs. Beaufoy lived most fully between nightfall and the light, Lillie Langtry conjured a place where night mixed with day, abandon with control, and art with life, or some very persuasive simulations thereof. She found a turn to engage even the most benighted Yank, using the calculation that was her highest art. The ritual suicide she performed in vaudeville was the most striking star turn yet for the distance it charted between itself and the choices its star had made. Her shedding of the army coat was telling. She ended *Between Nightfall and the Light* with a death as picturesque as a butterfly's beside its cocoon. Only this butterfly rose in new light, to irresistible applause, for nothing but her.

* * *

Like Mrs. Langtry, Mrs. Patrick (Stella) Campbell (1865–1940) had tasted scandal and was no stranger to dying onstage. Unlike Langtry, she'd come to stardom before becoming notorious. After that, she'd made up for lost time.

In 1893 she'd found sudden fame playing the modish title character in Arthur Wing Pinero's *The Second Mrs. Tanqueray*. In the play, a beautiful courtesan risen to the status of society wife kills herself rather than have her past exposed. Campbell moved on to several Shakespearean heroines and, nearing fifty, was first to play Eliza Doolittle in George Bernard Shaw's *Pygmalion*, close source for Lerner and Loewe's *My Fair Lady*. Still, for all of Mrs. Campbell's later triumphs, she made her greatest impact in episodes of dangerous love.

Her particular talent set her into roles more neurotic than the ones Langtry favored. She never cultivated Langtry's detachment, either, nor found vaudeville so congenial. Her disposition didn't warm with the run of bad luck that brought her to give her first turn.

An American theatrical tour in 1907–1908 had gone so badly that it drove her into bankruptcy. Restored to England, she carried on one of her more desperate affairs, this one with George Cornwallis-West, married at the time to Winston Churchill's mother but who divorced her to become Campbell's second and last husband. When the star found herself hounded by scandalmongers and creditors, she fled to America. She wanted "to get away from England—and gossip," as she put it in her memoirs.[54] She had often needed to keep her options open, with her propensity for challenging even the most highly placed people she met.

She knew that vaudeville had paid British stage stars well. On the advice of Norman Hapgood—unregenerate cynic as to the motives of foreign artistes joining vaudeville—she used intermediaries to contact Edward F. Albee, Keith's hatchet man and house designer. Performers and rival producers feared Albee as they never did the more avuncular Keith.

Undaunted at the prospect of meeting Albee, she summoned him to her hotel room. There, she wrote later, he seemed to her to be simply

> one of those American men who make you feel "you are all right" and "he is all right". . . [He] saw me, and I told him I had an effective play, *Expiation*, and a beautiful dress, that I would play twice a day, and I wanted £500 a week [~$49,000, or ~$50,000 now, calculated against the $2,500 American papers said Mrs.Campbell was making]—a large salary . . .

Nor was she cowed when

> some other men came into my room during my interview with Mr. Albee, and they consulted together. Eventually it was decided that I should play for a week outside New York, and if I proved worth it, they would engage me at the £500 a week for ten weeks. I played, and they were satisfied.[55]

She might have been more wary had she listened to Robert Grau, who'd dealt with Albee often enough to call him "the Simon Legree of vaudeville."[56]

She had come ready to parley, and Albee could be courtly when he wished. She had an idea of how much to ask for based on the pay Langtry had gotten, which had been publicized widely. Mentioning her beautiful dress to Albee gave Campbell a way of driving up her price. She may have been enticing him, too, though that wasn't often her style as she grew older. At the same time, her formerly anorexic appearance had given way to a certain pouchiness.

Her recent setbacks had left her more tractable. Still, according to her account, she neglected to tell Albee that what she was planning to use as her turn she had already played in London, under a different title. Very likely, the dress she mentioned was left over from her embarrassingly short run the year before in the play she now called *Expiation* but had known formerly as *A Russian Tragedy*. Nor did she tell Albee of her concern, as she recalled it, that she "would never be able to play twice a day and travel on Sundays."[57] He would have found it hard to ignore her charms. But he wasn't about to give her something without getting something in return.

Albee's condition that she try her turn outside New York City was something that none of the other most precious Brits had been asked to do. Perhaps he saw dwindling profits in British stars, or supposed that none of Langtry's countrywomen could match her appeal. Whatever his calculations were, he agreed to pay Mrs. Campbell, contingent on the success of her tryout, £500 a week. It was the same fee, less inflation, as the $2,500 Keith and Proctor had paid Langtry in 1906. Albee kept tabs on salaries and kept his minions busy monitoring turns in obscure places and then bringing them to him for tweaking. None of this fazed Mrs. Campbell, in prospect at least.

In vaudeville, she found the routine more forbidding than any group of mortal men could be. Her character had to "kill a man twice a day and shriek," she wrote in pained recollection. She resented the strain. Worse, she recalled, was that the killing and shrieking "had to be done from the heart" because Americans, for all their foolishness, "see through 'bluff.' " Vaudeville's claims to host a "Great tragic actress" had been hard to live up to, she complained, because her turn was so lurid.[58]

Whatever apprehension she carried into vaudeville didn't keep her from beginning her tour auspiciously enough at Percy Williams's Colonial in New York City. Keith and Albee had probably sent her Williams's way, not so much to saddle him with a difficult star as to offer a favor of like kind, not that there was anyone like Mrs. Campbell. Patrons who lined up to see her first turns, on Valentine's Day 1910, wouldn't have found hearts and flowers awaiting.

Like Jessie Millward, Campbell played a Russian, this one named Sonja. "Expiation" was a measured title for a piece that showed unsavory intrigue with a lethal outcome. The action unfolded a cycle of viciousness set by German playwright Adolph Glass in

a room at the governor's home in Petrovolak, Russia. The governor is just such a heartless, bloodthirsty tyrant as the reading public has become familiar with through stories of Russian atrocity, and as the curtain rises a youth is brought before him accused of being caught in the garden in the act of stealing up to the governor's window and taking a shot at the Czar's good man. Paul Vanoff, the youth, is chained to a pillar in the room, is ill-treated by the governor, and is finally led off to be tortured.

Sonja chances to meet the wretched man in the hallway. Stunned to recognize him as her brother, she "leads the governor on to the account of how he killed a certain Nihilist, and the woman then learns for the first time how her husband died and who murdered him."

She is hardly in a position to show horror or rage. Instead, she determines to take the governor's life in payment for the lives of husband and brother, and accordingly gets him to show her how he chains men to the pillar. First she allows him to chain her up and then playfully tells him that she wants to "have her revenge." He laughingly submits to "the joke" and once she gets him securely bound she breaks out into a tirade against him, tells him who she is and why he is bound, and then she shoots him.[59]

The sadomasochism was set in relief by nonspeaking acts on her bill that were both vigorous and wholesome, including Jetter and Rogers's roller skating to open the show, and Hugh Lloyd's rope jumping that "overstretch[ed]" things a bit once Campbell had taken her leave.[60]

British stars were known across America, as French ones were, for straddling propriety. Some of Mrs. Campbell's appeal, and Mrs. Langtry's, and in a warmer way Jessie Millward's, owed to the thrill of pear-shaped tones and thickening hourglass figures in scenarios of unstayed abandon. In Campbell's case, *Variety's* man positively gushed over the dress she'd pitched to Albee, a "wonderful gown of black satin, over which is a coat of cut steel to the knees. The skirt is banded with an edge of steel, the coat having a border of sable fur."[61] Mrs. Campbell must have liked the metal. She certainly used the steel as a portent of the savage control her Sonja wielded at the last over the man who'd sent her men to cruel deaths.

But all of the star's finery, with her turn's kinkiness and the money she made in glad handfuls, couldn't ease Mrs. Campbell's regret on leaving New York. She made weeklong stops at Keith-Albee houses in Philadelphia, Boston, Cleveland, Toledo, Indianapolis, and Cincinnati. Somewhere between the east coast and Chicago, where the western circuit began, she jettisoned the actor playing the doomed nihilist and replaced him with her son. Alan "Beo" Campbell, in company with his wife, then joined his mother in grooming a one-act play he'd written called *The Ambassador's Wife*. The star intended to alternate it with *Expiation*, or if things went well, to use it to replace *Expiation* entirely.

Beo may not have been a millstone around his mother's neck, but neither was he a steadying presence when she needed one. The fatigue from rehearsing his play while performing *Expiation* twice a day took its toll. As she put it later, in her florid way,

> One day—I forget in which town—it was time to get up and think about the morning performance [*sic*]. I found I was unable to make any effort to move. My maid rang the telephone for the Hotel doctor—I tried to speak; it was impossible, I could only cry. "No more acting; away to Canada . . . and stay there until your nerves are mended," said the doctor.[62]

Her account rings with the same extravagance she applied, often splendidly, to her acting. Margot Peters, the most thorough and engaging of her biographers, has noted that the ten weeks Campbell remembered needing to recover from the breakdown was something more like ten days.[63] It was lucky for the star that she was so accomplished in applying hysteria to her work.

When she went back on the road, she turned high-handed. A press agent sent to watch her rehearse Beo's play in Chicago recalled having

> to handle these stars from the legitimate careful like. Now, here's Mrs. Campbell, probably the greatest woman on the stage. She doesn't understand vaudeville . . . She's used to being the whole thing . . . if she wants quiet and nobody in the house when she rehearses, then you bet that's the way it's going to be.[64]

In this instance, her neuroticism owed as much to motherliness as it did to her erratic professionalism.

Whatever impressed the press agent didn't keep the *Chicago News* from panning *The Ambassador's Wife*. With Beo playing a doomed man, again, and as his mother's character's "discarded lover" this time,[65] the turn was, the critic wrote, a "feeble effort" and more so for being "sandwiched between The Four Floods, Acrobats Extraordinaire and a brilliant group of trained seals."[66] It was deplorable, the reviewer went on, that Campbell was taking money "while her son experiments as a sketch writer." "All of which may be very fine for everybody concerned," as sharp came the barb, "save the audience."[67]

Young Beo was surprised.[68] His callowness kept him from realizing that his mother was using the Chicago Majestic to try out a piece she wouldn't have dared expose in London and probably not in New York. Still, her earnings in total amounted to what now would be nearly half a million dollars. Mrs. Langtry may have found the golden calf in vaudeville, but Mrs. Campbell drove the beast to market, slaughtered it, and sold it down to the gilded scraps. Her labors on her son's behalf showed concern, at least, for someone besides herself. She must have stirred Albee's fancy, too. Sixteen years later, in 1926, he was reported ready to help her tour again.[69]

Her troubles, and the notice they got from the British press, confirmed fears among her compatriots that touring North America could prove dangerous to the sensitive lot that British stars were. H. G. Rhodes, who was not a star but knew some, thought that distances common to travel across the United States and Canada left actors "nomadic." He noted, cozy-like, that any actor who lived in London could expect a place "of his own the year round" where he could "bring up his children" with "all the comforts that come from having one's own kitchen and one's own fireside."[70] For some time, British trade papers had been printing querulous obituaries of native actors who'd died while touring North America. The death notices blamed merciless travel and boorish audiences for killing genuine artistes, literally as well as figuratively.

Bringing culture to the former colony south of Canada was vexing for other reasons. *Era*, from its headquarters in London, printed an editorial on "The American Playmarket" listing qualities the writer saw as peculiar to an upstart nation:

> The American in his judgment of art is quicker and keener, but more superficial than the "Britisher." The pursuit of wealth is the main business of every American's existence; and he consequently does not take his amusements seriously. His taste is the reverse of narrow; he is willing to "sample" any sort of goods, on the condition that he is not asked to invest earnestness.

"On the other hand," the editorialist generalized,

> the things in which the Americans are interested, the themes which their dramatists use for the material of their plays, are often of secondary importance to us. . . . The British public refuses to believe in commercial tragedies [on subjects related to business].[71]

Or so ran one man's opinion. Americans simply couldn't appreciate artistry that the British took for granted. Vaudeville, viewed in this light, only left viewers hungrier for sensation and more numbed to quality. *Era* wasn't alone in attributing the enthusiasms of stateside audiences to an unthinking pursuit of what happiness money and goods could bring.

Among the biggest British stars after Maurice Barrymore to join vaudeville, Millward and Hawtrey gave more for the money by trying harder in their different ways. Mrs. Langtry slathered on the *noblesse oblige*, and Mrs. Campbell committed herself to emotional pyrotechnics and what would have looked like sleaze in the hands of any native actress. If Millward and Hawtrey felt distaste for audiences they played to, they didn't show it. Langtry often played the patrician, beyond the class she'd been born to. Campbell ended by lamenting her lot in vaudeville. She had nothing sour to say about it while she was there, at least in public. It's not farfetched to imagine Beo Campbell getting an earful from his mother that ran longer than any verdict the critics pronounced on his play.

It wasn't only expiating on demand that took Mrs. Pat out of vaudeville. Flush with funds as she was when she left it, she paid off some of her debts. With her finances eased and her peace of mind restored, as much as it could be in her case, she returned to England where variety had become respectable enough to have her give turns there within the year. By then, in the summer of 1911, Millward, Hawtrey, and Langtry had preceded her.

The British stage's pioneers in vaudeville entered variety to perform for what looked like a rabble, still, to sages on both sides of the Atlantic. But even when the tastes stars met were unschooled or degraded, they scarcely fazed stars in need of funds. With nations and empires on the minds of many, extreme sacrifice continued to hold as much fascination for Americans as it did for the more reserved Britons. Greater stars were soon ready with turns more loaded in sacrifice.

# 3. Growing Pains, 1910–1913 ∾

*Beware of sad endings.*

Harvey Denton, "The Technique of Vaudeville" (1909)[1]

Queen Victoria's death in 1901 left Sarah Bernhardt (1844–1923) the most famous woman in the world. She'd shown herself to be a force of nature since the late 1860s, not long before France was routed in the Franco-Prussian War. She'd seen her nation humbled with the loss of Alsace and most of Lorraine, and depleted by the indemnities its conqueror exacted.

As France became a smaller place, and a poorer one, Paris stood more than ever as host to the arts, the performing arts as much as any. Bernhardt began international touring after a decade of living with France's *malaise*. She quickly made herself one of her country's most dependable exports. Even after years on the road, she was keen to win new fans. Variety and vaudeville were filled with hearts to be won and money to be made. It wasn't the sort of challenge she was in a position to refuse.

France's native entertainments included *café concerts*, which were seamier equivalents to British music halls. Never for a moment did Bernhardt consider performing there, or in music halls, either. Beyond France, she'd learned, variety and vaudeville were recruiting dramatic stars by paying them dearly. The only people who lost in the exchange, it seemed, were the workaday performers who got a smaller percentage of the take after the great ones had taken their cut.

Bernhardt had made lots of money. She'd spent lots of it, too, which had kept her working hard. The dramatic subjects she favored, the deeper she went into her career, were suffering, or France, or both. If she couldn't defend her country by force of arms, she would call up sympathy for it in every way and place that she could. Since France couldn't appear, she would stand in for it. This went over nicely in the nations feeling crowded by German expansionism.

One of those nations, of course, was Great Britain, even with its royalty intermarried with the very newly fledged German monarchy. British relations with France had improved gradually since the end of the Napoleonic Wars and in another increment with the Franco-Prussian debacle. A toothless France called up sympathy within its bitterest historical rival. In 1879, Bernhardt's huge following for her first appearances in London encouraged French performers to follow her. Soon, hundreds of them were crossing the Channel to find lower markets to go with the higher ones in London and around and about.

Alongside French performers and native Britons, Americans could seem fervent but clumsy. In 1907, B. W. Findon wrote what all but a few of his fellow Britons were too polite to say: that American influence on the native theatre was pernicious. "What influence," Findon demanded,

> is this irruption of American plays going to have on our native drama? . . . The American plays which have been presented in our London theatres represent comfortable mediocrity, a smiling belief in the capacity of playgoers to accept machine-made articles, which depend for their success chiefly on the skill of the stage manager [i.e., director].[2]

Findon was speaking for others who thought of Americans as all raw energy, incongruous if not in themselves then in what they liked.

In 1904, Max Beerbohm, one of London's leading drama critics and half-brother to the illustrious Herbert Beerbohm Tree, bridled at what he saw as Americanisms on the stage of the Duke of York's Theatre. Beerbohm berated Charles Frohman of New York's Theatrical Syndicate for injecting into an otherwise conventional evening at the theatre,

> two ebullient gentlemen in purple coats, and two ladies in black and silver, singing comic part-songs. They withdrew ere the curtain rose on

the light comedy, and were not seen again. But they had the obvious air of being the thin end of the wedge.

The thin end of the wedge had Beerbohm predict that

> in the immediate future Mr. Frohman will "present turns" in the course of the *entr'acte* [intermission]. A little later there will be "turns" in the course of the play. The Duke of York's [Theatre] will at length be devoted, like so many of the other theatres, to musical comedy. That would be a score for the music-hall managers. But it would not be a useful score. Leave "turns" to the music hall, and the music hall will the likelier cease its clutchings at drama.[3]

Disquieting as Beerbohm found the vaudevillizing of English drama, Yank influence came under fiercer scrutiny when vaudeville's Benjamin Franklin Keith bought an underused London theatre. He planned to operate it, by report,

> after the fashion of his New York and Boston houses, with what is called "continuous vaudeville." The entertainment begins at midday, and is incessant till midnight, though the "stars" have appointed times much as they would have [in London] . . . and intervals are effected, during which the building clears, by the performance of specially unpalatable artists, or "chasers," as they are vividly described.[4]

London's culture mavens needn't have worried in the short run. Keith was thwarted when his infrequent visits gave the London County Council an excuse to deny him a license to show his noisome continuous vaudeville.[5]

His British counterparts filled the breach. Oswald Stoll had been transplanted from Australia to England's north country as a boy. A tireless speculator in entertainments, he was not to be deterred. After operating music halls in the north and in Wales, he'd come to London to manage Edward Moss's provincial chain.[6] In 1904, on his own, he opened the mammoth London Coliseum and advertised continuous performances like the ones he'd seen in vaudeville in Manhattan.[7] Before long, he'd hired the American expatriate actress Mrs. James Brown Potter (*née* Cora Urquhart) to dress some of his bills. A "professional beauty" in the style of Mrs. Langtry, Mrs. Brown Potter was still striking in her mid-forties. She had found a second career dispensing beauty secrets and advice on looking young. As recently as 1900, she'd won Londoners' momentary allegiance by giving patriotic recitations at the Empire Varieties to complement Mrs. Herbert Beerbohm Tree's ringing out "The Absent-Minded Beggar" at the Palace.

Whatever memories Mrs. Brown Potter stirred didn't carry her far at the Coliseum in June 1905. Then recently divorced and only nominally Mrs. Brown Potter any longer, she was careless or arrogant in recycling a piece that had left Londoners barely lukewarm a few months before. Nor had she rid herself of signs of gross American-ness. Such crudities, in combination with her pretension, made her look less, even than Langtry, like an actress at all. In 1899, not long before Mrs. Brown Potter would set to demonizing Boers, Chance Newton heard her speaking onstage with "an 'Amurrican' accent that one could cut not only with a bowie-knife but with a bludgeon." "She should be called not so much a siren of Scylla or Charybdis as Calypso of Coney Island!," he exulted in Greeks-meet-moderns alliteration.[8] Mrs. Brown Potter surfaced at the Coliseum again in January 1906, briefly, in a turn called *Love's Apotheosis*. Stars more in vogue steered clear of variety for two years more, even as three of them—Langtry following Hawtrey and Millward—went prospecting in vaudeville.[9]

In 1908, in London, an economic slump revived the bitterness that lingered after a strike the music-hall and variety performers had called the year before. The performers' action had disposed Stoll and his rivals to bully the malcontents. They hired actors, including stars, as a warning to every regular performer. The strike's more extended legacy came with making the Coliseum a fixture owing to the cheap prices Stoll could charge there given its enormous seating capacity. Over the next few years, Stoll kept hiring native stage stars to fill the Coliseum's farther reaches. Other variety producers in and around the West End followed suit. Constant bidding for major actors made the dickering for them more spirited, especially for debuts.

London's theatre managers also helped variety, unwittingly, after Stoll and his fellow managers had broken the strike. Facing a balky economy, the theatre's leading managers, some of them London's biggest stars, banded together. The protective organization they formed lacked the grander scale of America's Theatrical Syndicate. But in London, the chief managers' cozy brotherhood incensed the rank-and-file. It also provoked every manager facing ruin to give a name to what looked like greed at the top.

Precisely these conditions, which loosened ties between working actors and the stars who needed able and abundant support, brought more stars to the Coliseum and other variety halls nearby. Stars took to giving turns in resort towns on England's south coast, or in the dingy industrial cities to the north. Everywhere stars went, an elevated clientele followed them, or simply turned up.

When Laurence Irving joined variety in 1908, he was noteworthy for being younger son of the late Sir Henry Irving, who was the first actor to be knighted. The senior Irving had refused to enter variety even as he'd neared the end of his life in dire straits. After Sir Henry died in 1905, his contempt for music halls kept many who'd admired him clear of variety, including every star of current standing.

Laurence Irving was still up-and-coming when he hit the Coliseum in February 1908. He appeared together with his wife, Mabel Hackney; and it was she, in fact, who took the title role, hands on hips and feet well spread, in *Peg Woffington*, about life and cross-dressing on the eighteenth-century English stage. The Irvings did well at the Coliseum, and the next year crossed the Atlantic for a theatrical engagement. When that ran out, they didn't find much of a welcome with a vaudeville turn called *The King and the Vagabond*. Their being British dramatic actors wasn't enough, by itself, to bring success in vaudeville.

As much as Laurence's father had sniffed at the music halls, the son entered variety by praising it. Baiting his father's ghost, he pronounced himself broad-minded. "I recognize in the step I have taken nothing derogatory," Laurence said,

> either to myself as a man or as the son of a famous father. The attempt to resent or grieve over the fact of my wife or me succeeding an orthodox comedienne or preceding a troupe of acrobats savours to me of artistic snobbishness and bigotry.

Variety and the music halls were already crammed, he said,

> with the most persevering, self-reliant, energetic people in the world.
> And I am expecting to gather any amount of useful information whilst
> I am amongst them; as already I have experienced every consideration
> from them, even under the circumstances of their turns being somewhat
> curtailed that I might spread myself out to my heart's content.[10]

Stoll's hiring would-be stars such as the Irvings spurred his rivals to
action. Within a month, Alfred Butt—his name lent itself to jokes so
conveniently that convenience became part of the joke—hired
Canadian dancer Maud Allan to show "The Vision of Salomé" to
audiences at the Palace including "at least 80 per cent ladies" at the
matinees.[11]

Stoll wanted to keep the upper hand in hiring considerable actors.
He made a standing offer of £500 (~$49,500 in early twenty-first-
century currency) to any star willing to play a week at the
Coliseum.[12] Among the ones he courted was George Alexander, who
with Tree had replaced Henry Irving in playing host to the most
fashionable theatregoers in London.

An economic slump caught Alexander out on provincial tour.
Things were going badly. In Birmingham, he complained to a friend
of "the worst week's business I've ever seen." Then he asked for
advice:

> Stoll has offered me £500 a week for a month at the Coliseum in our
> "off" season. Why? I can't flatter myself for a moment that I should draw
> anything like that amount to his treasury, and I know he has offered the
> Kendals [eminent stage actors, husband and wife] £700 [~$69,000] on
> the same terms. Again, why?

Alexander's chum had been managing theatres in Birmingham for
years. He told the star,

> I can only give you my own opinion, for what it's worth. I know
> Mr. Stoll to be a very shrewd man. He never does anything he hasn't
> thought out. . . . I think that possibly Mr. Stoll would like to show you,
> and all the other West End "stars" he can rope in, to his music-hall

patrons at prices from 3s. 6d. [shillings and pence, now around $17.50] to 1s. [in 1908, around $5 now], under circumstances which, on the enormous stage of the Coliseum, would certainly prevent you from appearing to anything like the advantage as in your own theatres, and so undermine your market value in the eyes of general playgoers.[13]

Alexander heeded his friend's warning. He held out against variety for the time being.

Less well-established actors and managers couldn't afford to. Seymour Hicks was running no fewer than three London theatres when he gave his first turn at the Palace, in December 1908, in a very slight comedy called *The Fly-by-Night*. The play treated early aviators in the news, and its title referred viewers, in a punning way, to the gall Hicks had shown by contesting Alexander and Tree for the West End. Others who followed Hicks in giving turns included familiar faces such as Herbert Sleath's, Ellis Jeffreys', Allan Aynesworth's, and Herbert Waring's, early in 1909.[14]

The end of summer saw Sir Edward Moss join his former employee, Stoll, and Alfred Butt in recruiting stage stars and other stylish acts. Among the first Moss hired was Fannie Ward, an American who lit up the bill that opened the London Hippodrome as a variety house in August 1909. Ward was a more wholesome, sprightlier version of Langtry, as much a personality, and later a marvel of agelessness, as she was an actress.[15] Sharing Ward's first bill was Charles Hawtrey, in variety for the first and only time in *Time Is Money*, his trusty vaudeville turn. Other stars joining variety before the holidays had been there before, including Seymour Hicks at the Coliseum, Mrs. Brown Potter in the provinces after tanking in vaudeville, and Irving and Hackney on tour around England, Scotland, and Wales. Arthur Bourchier, another actor-manager weighed down with obligations, came to the Palace with his wife, Violet Vanbrugh, during Christmas week in 1909. They acted in *The Knife*, a melodrama that qualified Henry Arthur Jones as the most prominent dramatist yet to write a turn expressly for variety.

More momentous news came, with the Bourchiers at the Palace, that Sarah Bernhardt would favor the Coliseum with her presence there in the fall of 1910. *Era* reported her hesitating as other theatrical stars had done before her, but giving way on hearing that "many of our leading English actors and actresses have appeared, or are to appear, at our music halls."[16] Word of her decision spread quickly, drawing interest from native stars who hadn't tried variety but found in her the best reason to try. Within weeks, Lewis Waller, a matinee idol of heroic demeanor and spine-tingling voice, was giving a solo turn at the Hippodrome playing against type as a suicidal writer. Then he headed off to the Coliseum with a cheerier offering that had him, alone again onstage, spouting patriotic verse in his more familiar style.

In April 1910 at the Hippodrome, the French star Gabrielle Réjane beat Bernhardt into variety by half a year. Better known in London than any foreign star except Sarah, Madame Réjane showed, in line with continental touring practice, two offerings, and she spoke both of them, consistent with another custom, in her native language. The first piece, *Lolotte*, had an actress outwit a baroness for the actress's lover. Many among Réjane's unusually fashionable gatherings were reported retracing their steps to the Hippodrome a couple of weeks later to catch her second turn, in Sardou's more substantial *Madame Sans-Gêne* that showed a friendship between a humble washerwoman and Napoleon Bonaparte. In mixing the hazards of love with the pitfalls of power, Réjane was treading ground Bernhardt knew well and would revisit.

Whatever following Réjane attracted couldn't match the one awaiting *la grande Sarah*. Ellen Terry, who'd been Henry Irving's leading lady, called Bernhardt "more a symbol than a woman" and meant it as a tribute.[17] Wherever Bernhardt had performed over the last thirty years, she'd spoken French and impersonated figures from her nation's turbulent history, including patriotic heroines and even the odd hero. She'd heard "The Marseillaise" played in her honor wherever she'd gone. On tours outside France, she'd acted characters whose glamor and sexuality conformed to prevailing notions of French abandon. She'd toured Britain often enough that theatregoers there considered her their own, her Gallicisms notwithstanding.

Preparing to show her first turn, she spoke as though she were coming home, not only to Londoners but to those who'd seen her on provincial tours or had never seen her at all. She credited London for giving her "what celebrity I have."[18] Her specialty, everyone knew, lay in some of the most mortal action around. She was ready to become the novelty, again, displaying the same brands of suffering she'd been showing for decades.

\* \* \*

Bernhardt preferred bigger crowds to smaller ones. In 1909, the year before joining variety, she toured French towns by auto, stopping in the larger towns to perform and waving her way through the smaller ones en route. Smaller gatherings meant lighter proceeds. Her ambition still burned.

Her stardom stood at a crossroads, and other stars' with hers. Some of the first generation of stage directors were reining stars in or declining to cast them at all. This didn't pose a problem for her, who'd staged her own productions or chosen directors who would do her bidding. Still, any stage star her age—not that there were others of such magnitude—seemed antique in a theatre squeezed by popular entertainments from below and from above by a fledgling *avant garde*.

Aging stars, with Bernhardt front and center, saw their operatic styles counted against them with the taste for more level speaking that photographic realism brought with it. When a show failed, its star failed in greater or in lesser measure even when, as was generally the case with new plays, the writer took the blame. Two failures in a row could dim the brightest star. Three flops running spelled disaster. Stars made easy scapegoats.

Stars under pressure appreciated the features of variety entertainment that clearly favored them. Bills of turns conceived and produced independently of one another gave many stars greater discretion than they were used to. The briskness required of turns ruled out an acting *ensemble* on the scale the theatre's progressive wing had been implementing, if not to stars' disadvantage then to their lesser role in larger productions. Some stars also felt that they made natural attractions in variety entertainment because, since the 1880s, variety and vaudeville had been showing short plays for turns, though more comic ones than serious. In the serious vein, melodramas as turns gave stars, in brief, the same advantages as in the theatre at greater length: the spectacle of good triumphing over evil and of love winning out, with laughter to chase the tear in the eye. Stars had made themselves stars in exercises like these. Not one actor of note was a stranger to melodramas, though in more and more of them that didn't end necessarily with the survival of the lead character. The more eminent the actress, the more often she had played heroines in melodramas, or heroes in the cases of leading men.

Stars knew full well that whatever money they made had to come with strings attached. Stationed in featured slots toward the end of the bill, stars expected control over what they showed so long as they kept it short. They faced a disadvantage in being shown together with other acts with interests of their own to protect. Star power could be dimmed again, in relative terms, by the singular appeal of any noteworthy act before or after theirs, or by the impact of the other turns in aggregate.

In the theatre, stars stood, literally now and then, on the shoulders of large supporting casts. They wore rich costumes and moved among handsome furnishings that left viewers feeling transported. But no turn, however grand, was allowed time to draw in patrons accustomed to being won, or at least engaged, from the outset. It was a tough demand on actors used to grand entrances built by being delayed, discussed, and anticipated as full-length plays allowed.

In turns, stars had to hit the stage running and take the crowd by storm. Their turns had to be timed out and trimmed as standard acts were. On the good side, the trials stars' characters suffered could be intensified for being brief. Relief from high drama on the bill was never more than minutes away.

Bernhardt knew that it would be people in the Coliseum's cheapest seats who needed the quickest introduction to the pleasures of pain. She gave out a stream of democratic pronouncements. She was cultivating, "without the slightest disrespect," what even her interviewer and translator called

"le petit public." They belong to the class which cannot afford to pay anything considerable for their entertainment. It is conceivable that many of them do not understand the language that I speak, and possess very little knowledge of the piece in which I appear. But really that seems to make practically no difference to the strained manner in which they follow the action, or the appreciation they show of every effect made by the artist.[19]

She was wise to consider the little people. She was on the small side herself when it came to physical stature.

No one could have called her earning power *petit*. In variety, she made £1,000 a week, or what now would be about $97,000 for spending an hour a day onstage over a week's time. The roundness of her fee was reported widely, from London's tabloids to the city's *Times*, to provincial newspapers in cities where shortly she would be touring, to journals in more out-of-the way places where most readers weren't expecting to see her at all. It may have occurred to some of them that her weekly salary made a fine yearly income for a family of middle station.[20]

Long international touring had trained her to act for audiences who knew little French, if any. In variety, as she'd done in the theatre as necessary, she had English synopses for each turn included in the printed program. She used pantomime, or silent acting, to embellish the French she spoke. The sound of her voice thrilled in the way a trained singer's can, and conveyed nuance to those who couldn't follow her from word to word. She'd put on weight, and photographs don't show her leaning so much into the camera, but set at the center of groups giving her their undivided attention.

She took charge of other images. In an early instance of multimedia marketing, her signature endorsing Icilma Toilet Preparations—the Fluor Cream, the wet shampoo, the dry shampoo, solidified Icilma Water, and the tooth powder and soap—appeared on the Coliseum's souvenir programs under a carefully cropped photograph of Bernhardt wearing a crown. The bits of her on view, in the flesh and elsewhere, were more miniaturized and numerous than before. She'd reached the godhead of celebrity, when images multiply as if by themselves.

When it came to acting, her sheer will mattered more than ever. She'd settled into showing scenes or single acts from longer plays, serving up a series of what were, in effect, highlights from her repertoire. She still could apply high energy in moments, making up in flourish what she'd given up in length. She still struck poses to mark climaxes, in quintessential melodramatic style.

Framing climaxes by posing for them had worked well for her outside France and in silent films. Apart from transcending language, her late style clipped along at a rate that precluded boredom. In these respects, it catered nicely to those many who had never seen her before. She came to variety expecting to attract a sizeable number of patrons who hadn't seen her younger self, and wouldn't be comparing it with her present form. *Stage* reported her entrance into variety as if it were a referendum. Having "conquered the classes," she wanted "to win the suffrage of the masses."[21] "Suffrage" and "suffer" were sounding more alike with the campaign for votes for women heating up.

Shows of suffering had anchored Bernhardt's acting for years, but age was visiting more of its own true suffering on her. It was not only that she'd grown brittle and added poundage. In 1905, she'd reinjured a leg doing Tosca's suicide leap when a mattress hadn't been properly placed to catch her fall.[22] Since then she'd compensated for her lameness by leaning her way around the stage on furniture and other actors.

Over time, she'd woven her own chronic pain into characters already distressed from their being hemmed in or trapped. The more confined her characters were, the better position she put them in to triumph in the end, often by dying a noble, highly wrought death. This didn't play out as defeat, but as liberation.

She'd always performed more than one play on tour as was standard for continental stars who took to the road. Playing more than one character gave patrons a reason for coming back. Like other stars, Bernhardt chose any set of roles she toured to be able to modify or calibrate responses to it from one performance to the next. In variety as later she would do in vaudeville, she always played several turns as she went. She squeezed each one of them for the last swoon and pang.

Her settling on the second act from the relatively unfamiliar *L'Aiglon* (The Eaglet) to open her first Coliseum engagement puzzled B. W. Findon. *Devoté* of variety that he was, he doubted whether

Madame Bernhardt realises the peculiar characteristics of the Coliseum clientele. It is a kind unto itself, and at least two-thirds will probably make her acquaintance for the first time. [Edmond] Rostand's play made no great appeal to English audiences when it was produced at [Herbert Tree's theatre] His Majesty's, and but for the reputation of its author [who'd written the better-known *Cyrano de Bergerac*] I question whether it would have maintained its position in Paris.[23]

Bernhardt's aim was historical as much as artistic, and sidelong enough to elude Findon. She used *L'Aiglon* to conjure Napoleon's ghost. The memory of him was potent still, especially across Britain.

Impersonators of the Little General had stalked across British stages since the Battle of Waterloo. Napoleon's image in the preening silhouette, the hand tucked into the cummerbund, or the cocksure tilt of that impossible hat, stirred up old antagonisms. Nearly a century after the Emperor had left the scene, Bernhardt entered it in his name.

She would use Napoleon to turn any lingering Francophobia to her advantage, and France's. She kept the element of threat largely in check by playing Napoleon's diminutive son, the nineteen-year-old Duke of Reichstadt. Rostand had written the role for her a decade before, but her playing the manchild may have seemed more daring ten years onward, with her nearing seventy and the battle for women's suffrage fully joined. This is not to suggest that *L'Aiglon* flattered the grown men it characterized. It may have aroused uneasiness on that score, too.

The turn began with the Duke under house arrest, his moods shifting wildly as he fends off flatterers and the weasels of his world. Reichstadt has a keener sense of slights than of danger, which makes a serious failing in someone at the mercy of intrigue. He is as ineffectual, in his headstrong way, as in the full-length version for being kept in the custody of men who treat him as a troublesome adolescent. Only a few of them wish him well. The prize he keeps in mind is France, to which he's forbidden to return.

Captive in Vienna, the seat of Hapsburg power and the source of France's subjugation, he's confined to a cosseted existence in

the Palace of Schönbrunn . . . surrounded by spies, but the Count Prokesch, his friend, is restored to him. The boy pours out his soul, and confides his hopes and fears to the faithful Count. To distract his mind Prokesch leads the Duke to study tactics. But, alas! the very toy soldiers they use are Austrian [enemies of the French]. No! Some faithful friend has painted the dolls with French uniforms. What splendid memories the puppets recall! The Duke hastens to reconstitute his father's triumphs.

Evil lurks in the insinuating person of the Austrian statesman Klemens von Metternich. On finding Reichstadt at play, Metternich orders the toy soldiers

taken away. The [Eaglet's] anger is stayed by the encouraging whisper of Flambeau, "Hold, monseigneur! I will paint more." This veteran of Napoleon's, ostensibly a spy, has attached himself to the person of his master's son. Metternich is followed by Marshal Marmont, whom the Duke detests for his treason to the fallen conqueror, but from whom he seeks to hear stories of his father's triumphs.

His soldier-set impounded, the boy hears a dismissive account of his father's glories. He's incensed when the traitor Marmont begins to belittle Napoleon, and

flings scornful reproaches at him, calling him "Misérable." "Others betrayed him too," pleads the Marshal, "but when they saw him again they were his slaves. I never met him again—but to-night I am his because he stands before me." And he falls at the Duke's feet. Flambeau, carried away in narrating his great commander's exploits, explains his presence at Schönbrunn. "Am I forgotten in France?" says the Duke. "Never," cries the veteran. "See this pipe, this plat, this pouch that bear your portrait!"[24]

The tokens were key, and that there were three of them. The most electrifying moment came when the Duke raised his father's ghost in fury at the slimy Marmont. This might have seemed more menacing if France's diminished state hadn't been so patent in the person of a small, lame woman with a golden voice. The German-speaking powers could afford to leave the Duke to twiddle his (or her) thumbs while they drew new lines across the map of Europe. Bernhardt left British patrons with their pride at their forbears' part in removing Napoleon from the world stage.

Her turn didn't end with the Duke's death as the full-length play did, and as many who saw her would have come expecting. Still, audiences responded warmly to Bernhardt's showing France as reduced, decorative, feminized, harmless in the guiltless, guileless person of Napoleon's son. The only threat to be taken from the abbreviated *L'Aiglon* lay in power-hungry Teutons scuttling after Napoleon's empire. Even the least worldly viewers could see that Reichstadt was no match for Metternich and the Hapsburgs whose heirs, everyone knew, lay presently in close alliance with imperial Germany.

Bernhardt's small, aged, womanly person drew viewers to France's side against the German juggernaut. The fatherland gave the star's nation and Britain, for the first time in centuries, a prime enemy that was not the other. A Russian balalaika orchestra and Bioscope newsreel carried international flavor deeper into the bill. Bernhardt's eaglet couldn't fly, but with her to stretch his wings, he lifted imaginations toward the Alps overlooking France, and Vienna, and at greater distance, the Second Reich.

Rich as *L'Aiglon* was in geopolitics, Bernhardt exchanged it after two weeks for *Tosca*, a melodrama with an ill-starred heroine who falls into the snares of a corrupt, lascivious aristocrat. This villain imprisons the man she loves and has her listen to the poor man's torture. Bernhardt's turn from the middle part of Sardou's play— source for Puccini's more famous operatic version—ended with the heroine stabbing the evildoer to death. As with Reichstadt, the star chose not to show Tosca's death as at the end of the longer play. Her first set of turns would be the only one, in variety or vaudeville, that didn't show one of her trademark mortal endings.

The next fall, in 1911 at the Coliseum, she more than made up for her deathless rounds the year before. She played doomed women in the middle part of *Théodora* and the end of *Fédora* (both written for her by Sardou) and in turns taken from the inquisition scene in Émile Moreau's *Le Procès de Jeanne d'Arc* (The Trial of Joan of Arc), and the final act of *La Dame aux camélias* (The Lady of the Camellias a.k.a. *Camille*) by Alexandre Dumas the younger. Camille was the only character who isn't dangerous to anyone but herself, succumbing to consumption and finishing in deathly rapture in the arms of her beloved.

Fedora takes her own life with poison. Of the two characters who survive, namely Theodora and Joan of Arc, death lays a cold hand on each, with Theodora killing a man who she fears will break under torture and reveal her lover's identity, and Joan of Arc seen only interrogated though destined, as the curtain falls, to be tortured and burned at the stake. Bernhardt wanted to haunt viewers whose ancestors had conducted Joan's interrogation and carried out the grim sentence they'd pronounced.

As for Fedora, Bernhardt had been known from the 1880s for the writhing suicide-by-poison she performed once her character has been denounced by the lover who believes, in error, that she's plotted to have him killed. As Theodora, Empress of Byzantium, Bernhardt met the desperate captive's request that she kill him, by taking "straight aim at his heart with her hairpin." This execution, one critic noted, came "in a very different manner to that employed by" Tosca the year before, who'd used "a table knife for dispatching the villain" while chanting the French for "Die, die, die."[25]

These were some high-stakes outcomes, including Joan of Arc's dying for love of France. Death lurked at every corner. When Bernhardt's characters didn't die or face death, they dealt it out using distaff implements for weapons. Her Camille, the courtesan reformed, was milder for dying grateful instead of murderous, coughing her life away for the only man she's truly loved. This lady of the camellias joined every other one of Bernhardt's second set of turns in exposing, as one historian has put it, "some aspect of the heroine subjected to torture."[26] With no male character like the eaglet for the star to play, there was less to break up the torment. Queen Victoria had gone to her reward, but Victorianism was alive in the masochism Bernhardt radiated.

Stoll chose other acts to ease every woe. Albert Chevalier was like Sarah the creature of show business, even narrower in his cockney specialty than Bernhardt was with her shows of death. Like her, he was known for reaching high and low for his following. Joining him and Bernhardt, playing *Théodora*, was impressionist Cissy Loftus in imitations of native star Mrs. Patrick Campbell, Italian tenor Enrico Caruso, and Bernhardt herself.[27] The week Sarah first showed her turn as Camille, Will Evans turned up in "his funny concoction 'Harnessing a Horse,' " with the beast animated by two men, front and back.[28] In variety, though never so much as in vaudeville, Bernhardt played on bills that jerked audiences between the ridiculous and the sublime, from the horse's ass to *la grande Sarah's* agonies.

She kept associations between herself and France in play. Camille and Joan were figures from French history as the Duke of Reichstadt had been the season before, in spite of his name. The plays containing Camille and Joan were set in France, and among Bernhardt's 1911 turns *Jeanne d'Arc* called up France most lovingly. Written to celebrate Joan's having passed another step on the way to being canonized, the play was the freshest one the star had tried as a turn. As Joan, Bernhardt blended her seasoning with flashes of youth, as when Joan is asked to state her age to the English tribunal. "Dix-neuf" said the star, drawing gasps even from patrons not sure of the French for "nineteen."

Showing Joan's martial prowess might have made her more fearsome than the Duke of Reichstadt and more threatening at a time when Joan was becoming a figurehead for the women's suffrage movement. But Bernhardt's Joan was mainly the victim of aggression, and that at the hands of the English. As *Era* reported the turn:

> The dauntless saviour of France is arraigned on a charge of blasphemy at the instance of the Earls of Bedford, Winchester, and Warwick. Strong in her faith, Joan tells the simple tale of the devout little *bergère*, who hears the voices of the saints while tending her flocks at Domrémy.

The shepherd girl

> relates with glowing pride the determination derived from inspiration— the inspiration that changed a timid maiden into a warrior undaunted and undismayed. The whole trend of her life had been changed by these mysterious voices, and the mission from on high had been entrusted to her on account of the sufferings of her country.

She warns her inquisitors that "the hated yoke of England [is] nearing its end. In another seven years the perfidious tyrants would be driven out of her beloved France." The critic admired

> the ringing tones of Mme. Bernhardt's voice [which he]ld the house
> in thrall, and the spell is not broken until the curtains slowly close in
> upon the spectacle of Joan stretched unconscious upon the table, where
> she had been placed for the purposes of torture, which we are happily
> spared.[29]

The image of the heroine's body set for torment played fast and loose
with the archive. It was picturesque enough to let audiences finish
the episode in their minds.

The next fall, in 1912, the star found other vehicles for wringing
sympathy. For six weeks at the Coliseum, and on a third tour
through provincial variety, she played title characters in Act 3 of
Victor Hugo's *Lucrèce Borgia*, in Act 2 of Jean Racine's *Phèdre*, and in
the final act of Émile Moreau's *Elisabeth, Reine d'Angleterre*
(Elizabeth, Queen of England). Dangerous love figured in each one
for showing a character torn between passion and duty. Phaedra is
enamored of her stepson, and Lucrezia Borgia protects a young
man her overbearing spouse thinks is her lover but who is really
her son. Queen Elizabeth has her eye on a man young enough to be
her son.

To these three Bernhardt added a woman of the world, who, like
Joan, loves no man so much as France. Written for her by Henri Cain
in collaboration with her son and only child, Maurice Bernhardt, the
one-act play *Une Nuit de Noël sous la terreur* (A Christmas Night
under the [French Revolutionary] Terror) had Sarah playing a
camp-follower, or *vivandière*, named Marion. She travels with the
revolutionary army selling food and drink to the soldiers.

Stoll had made plans to celebrate Bernhardt's sixty-eighth birthday with several events.[30] This may have seemed to some a curious
initiative for him to take at a time when the star's latest leading man
and, rumor had it, her lover, argued at least twice daily against her
decrepitude. Lou Tellegen, Bernhardt's sculpted co-star, was a Dutch
actor young enough to be her grandson.

If there was less to Tellegen than what met the eye, there was more
to Bernhardt's plan in using him. The single romantic character he

played, as Phaedra's toothsome stepson, is horrified on learning that such an old woman, not to mention his father's wife, craves him. This Phaedra, like the star's Lucrezia Borgia and her Queen Elizabeth, shifted attention firmly from love to its liabilities.

Audiences could see danger elsewhere on the bill. The Bioscope newsreel for Bernhardt's third week at the Coliseum showed glimpses of British Captain Robert Scott and his party racing to beat a Norwegian team to the South Pole. Scott's body, frozen solid with several of his comrades', wasn't found until November, after Bernhardt had left the Coliseum for the provinces. Bioscope's "Speed Demon" showed other intrepid men in racing shots of automobiles opposite Bernhardt's Lucrezia Borgia. George Robey's appearance as "clown prince" of the music halls supplied more of the lighthearted than Scott did, or the race drivers with their derring-do.

Bernhardt took care with what she showed. She may have been hoping that Tellegen's chiseled line could substitute for her panther-like movement, long gone. It's not clear whether she saw her relationship with him, whatever it was, as foolish or risky, or that she wanted audiences to see it that way. In any case, Tellegen's haughty demeanor and the narcissism he found it easy to radiate threw her characters into higher relief. She played out danger in every romantic attachment, illicit or not, and gained sympathy thereby, even from patrons who may have judged her own life harshly. Rumors of the star's love-interest aside, her roles in 1912 resounded with resignation on the personal side and British interests on the political one.

To *Stage*, it was clear that Queen Elizabeth I was Bernhardt's means for appealing "favourably to an English audience."[31] Far from the nineteen-year-olds, Reichstadt and Joan, Elizabeth was a well-worn sixty-six, barely younger than the star was. The Queen has had bad luck in being smitten with, in *Era's* account,

the fascinating Essex, who does not requite her affection, having won the love of the beautiful Lady Howard. The jealous Queen finds them together, and learns that they intend to elope. At first she gently reproaches Essex for his infidelity, and begs him to remain staunch to her. When, however, he tries to screen Lady Howard, Elizabeth loses all self-control, and insults him before the whole Court, whereupon Essex forgets himself so far as to draw his sword half from its sheath.

Fiery Essex has made a fatal mistake. The Queen is scarcely in a position to ignore it when

a cry of horror is raised by those who witness this scene . . . Essex, in Lord Howard's custody, is conveyed to the Tower. He is arraigned, condemned to death, and executed, the historic ring that would have saved him having failed to reach the Queen.

Elizabeth moves in simplicity and resignation, as a woman

who has loved and lost, but as the sovereign of large achievements and great wisdom she puts aside the momentary weakness, and in slow, impressive, and dignified phrase becomes once more the sovereign of an Empire, nobly served by soldiers, sailors, and statesmen, whose lustre is still undimmed. But the hand of Death is upon her, and, falling forward on her face she passes away. The play ends with the sentence "La Reine est morte!" [the Queen is dead].[32]

The star's expiring Bess ranked acting with statecraft, celebrity with royalty, and in a much more cordial way than Joan of Arc did, France with Britain. "The Ambassadress of France to the remotest corners of the earth" was later the way May Agate described the star whom the young British actress had supported in *Elisabeth*.[33] The much-admired Ellen Terry, who was nearly the same age as Bernhardt, called her French counterpart "Queen Sarah" and herself a "devoted subject." In the spirit of reciprocity, British audiences celebrated Bernhardt's birthday while she celebrated their history.

Her fourth and freshest turn in 1912 was *Une Nuit de Noël sous la terreur*, which treated the French Revolution at its bloodiest. Unlike other turns she'd shown, it removed her entirely from love and obligations of state. The *vivandière* was a working-class woman with a heart as golden as Camille's and a past less besmirched. The action unfolded, according to *Era*, in

> *La Vendée*, where so much blood was shed in support of the Monarchy. The anxious mother, who is hourly expecting to hear of her fugitive husband's capture, is attracted towards *La Vivandière* (Marion) by the friendly attitude of the latter, who invites her to assist her in preparing the vegetables for the Republican soldiers' meal.

A humble woman, this Marion, salt of the earth.

> The audience sees, through the *vivandière's* knowing eyes, that the Countess has been quite unaccustomed to peeling potatoes, and her air of high breeding and refinement rouses the suspicions of "the child of the regiment." Under cross-examination the Countess confesses that she is not the peasant woman she appears to be, and throws herself upon her questioner's mercy.

At first the *vivandière*

> seems inclined to call in the soldiers, but relents. Presently the Count [played by Tellegen], flying for shelter, comes into the cottage, and is hidden by the friendly *vivandière*. A search party arrives, but there is no necessity to hunt for their quarry, for he surrenders himself to the commandant, who, after questioning him, condemns him to death. But the Count has an unexpected ally in the *vivandière*. She threatens, she cajoles, she pleads, and in a burst of righteous wrath disowns comrades who dignify assassination with the name of war. Eventually, the stern sentence is recalled, and the hated aristocrats are at liberty.[34]

Maurice Bernhardt and his collaborator had given Bernhardt a piece to show France more distressed than her character was. The star's task was to leave patrons with little choice other than to wish for the mercy on the victims that the *vivandière* showed, finally. Bernhardt's billmate Albert Chevalier used his assortment of cockneys to ingratiate himself as Bernhardt was doing it, from the bottom up.

She made her last swing through variety in the final fall before the war. Her displays of suffering didn't find so much favor. She'd lost Tellegen to America when he'd stayed on there after the end of her first vaudeville tour. Back in variety without him a few months later, she set out to expunge him.

But with less time to prepare, or more fatigued, perhaps, after a long tour in vaudeville, she chose four of her six turns from familiar ones including *Théodora, Une Nuit de Noël, Jeanne d'Arc,* and *Phèdre.* Her two fresher roles came in another new one-act play her son had written with Henri Cain, called *La Mort de Cléopâtre* (The Death of Cleopatra), and in Act 2 of Rostand's *La Samaritaine* (The Woman of Samaria). It was in the latter that she opened at the Coliseum.

It was sixteen years since she'd given the full-length play its premiere in Paris. The title role featured an ecstatic spirituality not unlike Joan of Arc's, and a past redeemed like Camille's. The Samaritan, once a prostitute, has found her true calling from seeing Christ preach. Bernhardt planted the Nazarene's image not by showing Jesus onstage, because it wouldn't have met the requirements of any turn within her grasp. But she spoke for him, and with every ounce of authority she had.

The Samaritan has led an abandoned life, but her conversion

is dealt with in stirring fashion. The scene is the market place of Sichem. Photine, the Woman of Samaria, arrives to tell in glowing words of her meeting with [Jesus] the Nazarene at Jacob's Well, and of her complete subjection to his eloquence and charity.

The star used "animated and fervent speech" to win the assembly

to her side, and the people who have come to jeer remain to sympathise with the Christian creed which Photine expounds. . . . [T]he audience stood bareheaded while the "Marseillaise" and "God Save the King" were played [after the curtain call], the actress bowing gracefully all the while.[35]

Even the panoply, though, and the heroine's piety, and the hoped-for accord between Catholic France and Protestant Britain, weren't enough to ease *La Samaritaine* into a longer run, much less a tour.

The Lord Chamberlain, more than halfway through his second year of vetting plays to be shown as turns, had objected to an opening scene that would have shown the apostles John, Peter, Andrew, and James in the midst of "a crowd of hawkers, fruit-sellers, and provision dealers."[36] Bernhardt patched in a less vendor-heavy replacement that had one of Photine's former lovers overhear a conversation laying out her sordid past.[37] In its corrected form, the turn was approved, but the Lord Chamberlain had Stoll on alert. To "prevent any shocking of devout playgoers," as *Stage*'s critic put it, the producer had his house orchestra play stately music during the intermission before Bernhardt's turn.[38] *Samaritaine* was left to finish the bill, with no turn to chase it.[39]

Stoll was doing everything he could to protect the star and her vehicle for a benefit to serve his pet charity, which was a French hospital near the Coliseum. He'd invited George V to attend the event, and the King had accepted before declining as controversy grew around Bernhardt and *La Samaritaine*. The King changed his mind again, but only after gaining assurance that Bernhardt would replace her biblical turn with the classic, de-Tellegenized *Phèdre* for what Stoll never stopped calling the "Good Samaritan" benefit.[40] Showcasing Bernhardt for charity let Stoll play the Samaritan himself. The anthems that capped the turn joined formerly warring nations in Christian, anti-German brotherhood.

When it came to Christianity, however, the star's ecstasy as the Samaritan may have called up too much of the Catholic—and the Jewess—for some of the Coliseum's sterner protestants. Even after *La Samaritaine*'s alteration at the Lord Chamberlain's request, and before the turn's removal from the benefit at the wish of the King, it became the only one of the star's opening turns that didn't run for a second week at the Coliseum. To follow it, then, her son's and Cain's Cleopatra never caught on so well as their French-Revolutionary play had done the year before, or as Bernhardt had done with an earlier dramatization of Cleopatra on her first trip to London more than thirty years since.

Because the star's godliness didn't please, or not enough, her last pre-war repertoire ended by looking tired, whatever controversy there was to spice things up. Her son's writing gave credence to the idea that his mother's acting ran parallel to her life; but his being an only child whose father she never named posed an inconvenience for a woman intent on impersonating a vicar of Christ.

The negative responses may have confused the star, who'd spent decades bringing Christianized tales of sacrifice and redemption onstage (see figure 4). She had, it was known, been born of a Jewish mother, and this may, among the narrower-minded, have drained her Samaritan of sanctity. Even Albert Chevalier couldn't save the day. It's easy to imagine him and other performers assigned to her next bill sighing with relief on learning that Bernhardt would shift the week following into *Théodora*, who had only to kill a man.

The week after that, when Bernhardt revived Joan of Arc, the wondrous juggler and future film star W. C. Fields turned up on the bill. Bill Fields was American, and as such, a sign of the times. But whatever levity he brought to the proceedings couldn't redeem *La Samaritaine* and the shopworn turns to which Bernhardt resorted when it failed. The star needed darker times before she could shine again. War would give her the chance, when she played an angel of mercy, after playing several angels of death.

* * *

Bernhardt's first turns had French and British stars fairly lining up to follow her. But each of the actors' efforts, with her own, made the next star's appearance a little less momentous. Variety, like vaudeville, bowed to novelty. Fresher faces weren't hard to find.

Bernhardt's countrywoman, Jane Hading, was beyond her youth, too, but new to variety when she followed Bernhardt with her own study in tormented motherhood, called *Madame X*, at the Hippodrome. The same fall, in 1910, Yvette Guilbert, a worldly wise French *chanteuse*, shared Coliseum bills with Bernhardt. Gabrielle Réjane, having preceded Bernhardt into variety, gave turns again in 1911, and in 1915 with the war on.[41] Réjane knew how to nudge laughter toward pathos, and endow love outside marriage in wistfulness. As Bernhardt did, she built her followings from the upper and lower ends to bulk up her considerable base in the middle.

Among British stars to follow Bernhardt was Lillie Langtry, in a cutting from the play known formerly as *The Degenerates*. Written at the peak of Mrs. Langtry's notoriety in the 1890s, *The Degenerates* yielded a shortened version called *The Right Sort* for a provincial tour

**Figure 4** Sarah Bernhardt in Edmond Rostand's *La Samaritaine*, trading in the sacrificial (Harlan Hatcher Library, Special Collections, University of Michigan; from *Theatre Magazine* [New York], January 1906.)

that brought Langtry to the London Hippodrome late in 1910.[42] John Martin Harvey was a more able actor, though hardly as celebrated when he gave his first turn as King Konrad, who ruled "an imaginary region" called Polavia, on the variety bill that opened the new London Palladium on Boxing Day 1910.[43] Just after the New Year, Lewis Waller followed appearances at the Hippodrome and Coliseum the year before with one at the Palladium to replace Martin Harvey on the bill.

Harley Granville Barker, another star with a triple-barreled name, held forth at the Palace in February and March of 1911 in four different turns as the jaded title character in *Anatol*, a bedroom comedy set in decadent Vienna. One of Granville Barker's excerpts had his wife Lillah McCarthy as its co-star, who was nearly the attraction he was. Within weeks after Réjane's second engagement at the Hippodrome, in July 1911, Mrs. Patrick Campbell made her variety debut in *The Bridge*, a drama of intrigue like the one she'd played in vaudeville the year before. Stars knew how to exploit a winning formula, as Bernhardt did again when she carried a chunk of her variety repertoire into vaudeville in the fall of 1912.

Native star Lena Ashwell had made her variety debut at the Palace in the fall of 1911. Later that fall, Irene Vanbrugh, the most popular West End actress of her day, gave her first turn in November of 1911 at the Hippodrome. The next month, Harcourt Williams brought *How He Lied to Her Husband* to the Palace to give George Bernard Shaw his baptism in variety. Arthur Bourchier and his wife, Irene's sister Violet Vanbrugh, returned to the Palace later that December.

The parade of star turns helped persuade London's County Council to grant licenses to let music- and variety halls show fully staged plays, so long as the plays were as short as the ones Bernhardt and other stars were showing as turns.[44] The council's action in November 1911—Ashwell's and Irene Vanbrugh's turns may have been straws that broke the camel's back—forced the Lord Chamberlain to extend his oversight to every dramatic turn set for production at any one of the two dozen leading variety halls around London.[45] The Lord Chamberlain started exercising his broader purview in January 1912, and a few months later was suggesting improvements to Bernhardt for *La Samaritaine*. The expanded censorship wasn't only repressive, but approving in a bureaucratic sort of way. The Lord Chamberlain's implicit endorsement, along with producers' lavish incentives, drew more big stars into variety.

Actor-managers stood as some of London's greatest attractions, and among them were the men who'd fought hardest to preserve the theatre's claim to the Lord Chamberlain's exclusive attention. Once they had made their peace with variety, the preeminent actor-managers took pride in challenging the Gallic stamp that Bernhardt and her countrywomen had put on variety.

Leading the holdouts was Sir Herbert Beerbohm Tree (1852–1917). Recently knighted, indefatigably sociable, and keenly ambitious, he'd worked himself into position to stand for Britain in something of the way Bernhardt stood for France. Like her, he'd expanded his portfolio away from the stage. He was known for charitable work as open-handed as his wife's was,[46] and for using his chummy dealings with journalists to uncanny advantage—though not the theatre's, or so said the few who expressed the envy he inspired. Tree had German, Jewish, and Slavic ancestry to go with a sturdy English pedigree on his mother's side. His bloodline, and the breeding it brought him, would shape his punctilious Henry Higgins at the premiere of Shaw's *Pygmalion* opposite Tree's weighty co-star and sometime nemesis, Mrs. Patrick Campbell, who played the first-ever Eliza Doolittle.

Tree's talents suited a generation that had watched the Empire reach its zenith.[47] He embodied the empire to glorify it, to serve it, and to memorialize it, whatever was required. Britain's empire, of course, needed things beyond what Tree could provide. But if the power that drove the empire could be made to seem benign, Tree was the man to do it.

His wife's reciting Kipling as the Boer War turned ugly had given him a nearer view of variety. His dealings with the Palace stayed cordial after Mrs. Tree had come and gone there. Ten years on, he may have needed money or been caught up in one of his extramarital adventures when in January 1910 he packed the newly titled Lady Tree off to her own variety engagement in Liverpool. Later that year, his profession designated him to escort Bernhardt, fresh from a Tosca at the Coliseum, to a reception in her honor.[48] Both occasions had

Tree tiptoeing around variety. Still, Bernhardt's success in it, with Tree's gentlemanly acknowledgment of it, couldn't cut the *Times* loose from the view that "the variety stage is not a place on which any sane dramatist would attempt the serious discussion of moral problems."[49] Actors who took themselves as seriously as Tree did needed to apply themselves to matters of weight. Perhaps because his private life was not so private as was convenient for him, he was eager to embrace, in the realm of art, the sacrifice empire required.

He'd ended 1911 by playing a misbegotten Macbeth as the first of a nasty string of failures at his theatre. The setback didn't daunt him, much, or dampen his prospects in variety. If anything, the Scottish play left him needing the nearest thing he could find to a sure thing. His press coverage in variety, he knew, would be heavy. And so it proved to be, with headlines heralding the "First Knight on the Halls."[50] His salary wasn't given out as widely as Bernhardt's had been; it would have seemed crass to native actors and worse to non-actors. As was known to only the relative few, Tree made either £750 or £1,000 a week, which would be about $71,500 or $95,000 in current value.

Newsworthy as his debut at the Palace was, where some of London's best-dressed audiences were known to gather, Tree was hardly the first star to try variety. He made it seem so, though, even as he followed Bernhardt at the Coliseum by fifteen months and his wife on the same Palace stage by something close to twelve years.

Tree had been around long enough to know how well patriotism could tug at heartstrings across lines of class, gender, and age. Just as Kipling had served Mrs. Tree during the Boer War, so did the Nobel Laureate serve Sir Herbert in what were less urgent times for the nation though more trying ones for the star. Tree had Kipling's *The Man Who Was* on hand from commissioning a stage adaptation of the short story nine years before. He'd starred in the play at his own theatre, which was called His Majesty's after Edward VII had succeeded his mother on the throne. In 1912, with the pleasure-loving Edward two years dead, it was the men's turn to suffer and be silent.

The hero of *The Man Who Was* has undergone torture, imprisonment, and utter isolation. He is, or was,

Austin Limmason, once an officer of the White Hussars . . . [who'd been] captured by the Russians at Inkerman [during the Crimean War], and through the machinations of an unscrupulous enemy . . . sent to Siberia. After twenty years he escapes, and finds his way through dense forests and by way of the sea coast to Peshawar, in India [now in Pakistan], where his old regiment is quartered.

Limmason's twenty-year imprisonment was in line with the premise of *The Count of Monte Cristo* and other prison-and-vindication stories that stirred imaginations in the day, and

> The climax of Tree's turn came when his character finds himself in the regimental mess-room, where his former brother officers are assembled, [and] his memory is restored by the sight of the trophies which adorn the wall, chief of which is the tattered standard which stands over the mantelshelf . . . [whereupon] the stricken officer is received with open arms, only to die just as he has reached home.[51]

The broken man's rapturous death wasn't so different from Camille's in the throes of love. Transported states were made to look as if they were the way to go.

Owing, perhaps, to the fanfare Tree had gotten for going on the 'halls, the star made a greater impression as Limmason than he'd done in the theatre. *Era*'s reviewer, for one, was riveted by the star's gradual way of establishing

> the identity of the escaped prisoner. . . . The first glimmerings of return-ing reason were eloquently indicated, while the fleeting bursts of passion when the martial spirit asserted itself commanded the admiration of all. Extremely touching, too, was the meeting with the long-parted brother and sister before the tragic end.[52]

Tree wasn't using muteness *à la* Bernhardt, to compensate for speak-ing a foreign language. Like Bernhardt, though, he wanted to call up associations that were deeper than words would allow. To match the scale of Limmason's dumb passion, Tree brought a supporting cast to the Palace that numbered sixteen, and grandly costumed they were. They further improved a well-appointed set that threw the tatters the star wore into higher contrast (see figure 5).

Tree's custom was to give a little speech to mark noteworthy events, and he followed his own practice on Monday evening,

**Figure 5** Herbert Beerbohm Tree in *The Man Who Was*. Tree's showing the backwashes of power qualified him as Britain's leading imperial actor after the Boer War. His tableaus of suffering spoke as loudly in variety as they did on the legitimate stage. (Harlan Hatcher Library, University of Michigan; from Hesketh Pearson's *Beerbohm Tree: His Life and Laughter* [London: Methuen, 1956].)

January 22, 1912, just after the curtain had fallen on his first turn. He was standing in Limmason's rags when he addressed the audience and said something very like this:

> Ladies and Gentlemen.—I have nothing to say except to tell you how delighted I am to have made my debut—(laughter and cheers)—that I have broken, as it were, the bread of variety for the first time to-night. I have frequently been invited by the enterprising manager of this theatre, Mr. Butt,—to whom I tender my hearty thanks—to appear on these boards, but I always said, "No; so long as the law [treating the licensing of plays] is as it is I shall not do so." The law has been changed, and I am glad to be among the first to recognise it cheerfully. I hope in this I have been consistent, if not in obstinacy at any rate in wisdom. I trust the new stage of things will lead to a wider appeal of the drama and make it better for us all. I thank you most heartily—indeed, I should be wanting in appreciation did I not do so—for the kind enthusiasm with which you have welcomed me to-night.[53]

He took another bow or several in farewell. He'd kept the discussion deftly but firmly on himself. He felt no need to mention Bernhardt or any of his other distinguished colleagues, including his wife, who'd given turns extending back into the previous century.

As it happened, Tree shared his first bill with Harcourt Williams, whose turn in Shaw's *How He Lied to Her Husband* had been held over since late November. *The Man Who Was* got a flyer of its own,[54] whereas Shaw's play had to share print-space with the other turns on the printed program. Tree may have helped foot the Palace's publicity, to see to it that his efforts would be set in the best light.

Those efforts show a man looking over his shoulder. The last thing Tree wanted was to invite charges that he was cheapening the theatre. He was attracting enough criticism as it was. The same year he joined variety, W. R. Titterton accused him of lowering

> the convention of Shakespeare . . . to the formula of musical comedy. But he has lacked the courage of his convictions, and though he has introduced colour, choruses, dances, and topical gag, and though he has cut the text to suit the palate of the public, he has omitted to provide himself as chief humorist with comic songs.[55]

Titterton had Tree pitching Shakespeare the way a clownish, drunken master of ceremonies might have done to the rankest music-hall audience in days of yore.

Stung, it seems, the star apologized for himself afresh the next fall, while he was leading a provincial tour that took *The Man Who Was* to variety houses at Glasgow, Manchester, Liverpool, and Brighton. Writing to his daughter Viola, he claimed that he'd wanted only to put polished drama in front of some who'd never seen it. He was gratified, he told her, that

> by my present tour I shall have reached a vast number of the masses (32,000 in Glasgow alone) with whom I shall henceforth be a household word: that is something—and it is the people that I want to get at—for they most want me—I mean, one does good to them—whereas one is a mere entertainment to most of our fashionables . . . Some day I would like to take Shakespeare to these places—having no other entertainment on the same night—and cheap prices.—That would be a fine thing to do.[56]

Such wishfulness was the star's latest attempt to mollify his eldest and most severe daughter. She'd been upbraiding him since learning that he would show himself at the Palace.

She'd let her feelings be known outside the family. Just days before Tree's debut at the Palace, one of her friends had seen Viola "furious over this music-hall affair." She couldn't abide her father's taking a job that seemed so futile to her, "even financially," as she'd said, "since it is not assured income but only like a sum won gambling, which he will have spent or lost in six months."[57] No matter that he provided for her grand society wedding later that summer. The newlywed was hectoring him still in the fall, when he returned to variety not long after giving her in marriage.

Answering her from Liverpool while on tour with *The Man Who Was*, he revisited the circumstances he'd faced in prospect of paying for her nuptials when losses at His Majesty's had been mounting. "It would have been terrible to have gone bankrupt," he pleaded, "and there is my duty to you all—so don't despise the humble means."[58] He told Olivia Truman, the most attentive of Viola's friends, that he'd been offered £4,000 (~$380,000), probably to have been paid at the rate of £1,000 a week, to appear at the London Alhambra in the fall of 1912. He was depending on Olivia to relay the details to Viola.

Actually, Tree had chosen to take *The Man Who Was* on the road only after learning that the Alhambra wanted to bill him dead opposite Bernhardt and her round of birthday galas based at the Coliseum. As he would have known, the Alhambra lacked credentials in higher culture, or the pretensions to them, that the Palace flaunted, and the Coliseum in more modest ways. Tree made it seem as if his sacrifice in joining variety had been all for Viola. He could tame large crowds more easily, it seems, than he could pacify this high-minded daughter.

Celebrity at the level he'd reached had become a highwire act for him as much as it was for Bernhardt. He attracted crowds so large and lived so much of his life in public that he couldn't help letting people down from time to time, and he never liked that. The demands on him were hard even for Viola to understand, having grown up in his shadow and her mother's.

Like Bernhardt, Tree invoked "the people" from whom, in variety, he felt a sense of kinship that touched him. Showing the flag was his way of showing them common cause. Taking a page from Amy Roselle and Maurice Barrymore, he played a character so abject as to let no one take offense. *The Man Who Was* was timely *and* nostalgic with the Empire already pressed sorely enough in many of its outposts.

Tree's defensiveness wasn't only to soften his daughter. While showing *The Man Who Was* in Glasgow, he wrote a letter to that city's *News* defending himself against an acid report on his turn that the journal had printed. He noted, in a spray of snarky glosses, thus:

> Your contributor seems to me at fault, both as to logic and as to facts. I will deal with the latter first. *The Man Who Was* is not "a potted [i.e., abbreviated] play"; it is acted just as it was written. It seems to me to be a complete little work of art in itself, and is exactly suited to the audiences of a variety theatre. So far from being injurious to the drama, I believe the result of this and kindred representations will be in time to create a taste for the theatre on the part of a public which has hitherto been largely ignorant of, or indifferent to, its claims.

Not content to anatomize, Tree launched into an exhortation. "Let us of the theatre," he wrote, "do our best to create a taste for the drama among music hall audiences,"

> and they will in time develop a love for the theatre, and so be drafted into the regular army of its supporters. The music hall has been steadily improving in the quality of its entertainment, and the infusion of the dramatic element has, I venture to think, contributed in no small degree to this result. We live in democratic times, and I for one hold it a privilege to go forth to the masses bearing them the message of the drama— and so to extend the franchise of my audiences to their profit—and to mine![59]

For all his apparent confidence, Tree had more to lose from joining variety than Bernhardt did.

Granville Barker was contesting him for the right to head a national theatre dedicated to the works of Shakespeare. The younger man, to gather money and loyalists, had ventured into variety at the Palace the year before Tree did. But Granville Barker was entirely un-Tree-like for feeling, as he would express it later, that his "present loathing for the theatre is loathing for the audience."[60]

Tree, of course, loved nothing so much as audiences who loved him back. The more such gatherings he found, the better he liked it. As *Era* noted, he couldn't afford to be too choosy where his followings came from, because

> the difference between the audience which pays to see *Macbeth* and the audience that delights in a variety entertainment is in the capabilities of sustained attention and temporary abstention from drinking and smoking. If the class which possesses these capabilities decreases, and the other class increases, it will simply mean that a number of theatres will have to be turned into music halls.[61]

It's unlikely that Tree thought variety- and music halls could eclipse the theatre, even after his sorry showing in *Macbeth*. But he found a way to honor the theatre, and variety, by packing more significance into *The Man Who Was* than any star other than Bernhardt could have done.

Tree's next sortie into variety came with the war a year old when he revived, in brief, his role as Svengali in *Trilby*. Adapted from George du Maurier's tale of a girl mesmerized into opera stardom by an outcast Jew, the play had helped Tree build his theatre. In *Trilby's* chopped version, years later, Tree's Svengali suffered a heart attack without much ado, before calling "for help of the God he disowned" and then dying.[62] This was about as sacrilegious as ever things got at the Birmingham Grand, in this case against frolics like Sam Barton's on his bicycle, Frank Le Dent's juggling, and the Martini Trio's vocal and instrumental stylings.[63] Against this assortment, Tree showed dispossession and death in *Trilby* much in the way he'd done in *The Man Who Was*, which at least had left patrons warm with thoughts of empire.

When Tree himself died of a heart attack two years later, someone who'd known him remembered that he'd been "admirable in the expression of that irony which is the revenge of the beaten or the refuge of the helpless."[64] In stardom, he'd gravitated toward men-who-were instead of to ones who'd won their ways through life in the intoxicating way he had.

With the Empire fraying at its edges and the nation tempting war or tasting it, Britons liked to rally around the underdogs they fancied themselves to be. Tree's Limmason epitomized what Seamus Deane has called, with Irish irony, Britain's "chivalric, gentlemanly behavior towards inferior races."[65] Britain's consummate imperial actor embodied the chivalric, gentlemanlike Briton when he agonized his way through *The Man Who Was*, as earlier and later he agonized as the entirely unchivalric, un-British Svengali. For all of Sir Herbert's attempts to distinguish himself from Bernhardt, he met her at the mute point of her finest suffering.

\* \* \*

The British Empire had London turned into a crossroads. Where many roads met, native entertainers were left to vie with foreign attractions. As 1912 began with Tree at the Palace, continental revues on the high side, and American ragtime on the lower one, swamped the capital. Imported acts stood among the pleasant if slighter outcomes of empire.

Variety and vaudeville had built empires in entertainment grand enough to attract the theatre's greatest stars. But in the way of capitalism, expansion had to give way to contraction. After Bernhardt and Tree, there were no bigger stage stars to be drawn into variety; and her entry into vaudeville in 1912, like Tree's into variety earlier that year, put the two entertainments on the same footing. Not much later, the cinema would leave its own stars with less incentive to join or rejoin variety or vaudeville, or to try the stage if they never had, or try it again if they had done so already. Still, in 1912 no one could have guessed that variety or vaudeville would never shine so bright.

Opportunism and thrift, so to say, on variety's part, drew a number of major actors to giving turns after Tree's. Lillie Langtry did it, and Lena Ashwell, Irene Vanbrugh, and Cyril Maude over the next few months. In June, the Queen joined George V for an evening at the Palace, its name befitting the royal couple. They watched the first variety bill summoned by royal command on the same stage Tree had graced five months before. Bernhardt's appearance at the Coliseum and on tour that fall coincided with Tree's short provincial tour in *The Man Who Was*. Charles Hawtrey, Seymour Hicks, and the Bourchiers were all in variety at the same time Bernhardt was in the fall of 1913, none of them for the first time either.

When Sir George Alexander became the second knight to play the 'halls, he did it, like the Trees, at the Palace. But in January 1913, Alexander couldn't raise headlines so blaring as the ones Tree had brought the year before. Tree's half-brother, Max Beerbohm, had written a turn for Alexander called *A Social Success*, about a man suffering "from the boredom of being lionised by expectant mammas and young married women."[66] Alexander may have thought that world-weariness would disarm anyone who faulted him for giving a turn. *A Social Success* also let him play the man of standing he'd made himself not only in the theatre, but in fashion, gentlemen's sports, and city politics in London.

*A Social Success*, perhaps for showing more of the snob, lacked the wider appeal of *The Man Who Was*. Even the £2,400 (~$233,000 now) Alexander earned for his month at the Palace couldn't dig him out of the hole into which his costly staging of *Turandot* at his

St. James's Theatre had pushed him.[67] Despite Alexander's other social successes, he was showing signs of losing touch with what had made St. James's London's most fashionable house from the late 1890s until the early 1910s. His declining health soon ended his run in city politics. The bidding for stars continued, but not at the same feverish pace.

The week after Alexander gave his first turn, one of Britain's vaudeville pioneers, Jessie Millward, began a tour in *The Gray of Dawn*. The play had been "such a sensational success in America" that she'd secured its English rights in hopes that "the opinion of London audiences will prove to be an endorsement of the verdict of their American cousins."[68] As in vaudeville, her turn gave her an aging, downtrodden version of her proud maidens, the latest one cursed for loving a criminal. Millward was showing how fully she'd embraced things American. But her fondness for Yankee fare served her little in 1913, with so much of the purely American stuff to be had in London and beyond.

As in vaudeville, Millward played a character crowded with emotions: "sweetness in rejecting the love of the honest man . . . terror when she is surprised by Terry after he commits the murder . . . fierce love . . . and her assumption of 'bluff.' "[69] Appealing as it was to the chameleon in her, Millward's turn of grimmest grays was only one of the ones to leave E. M. Sansom wondering at how such a "plethora of dramatic fare . . . flooded the Variety stage during 1912." "Many of the condensed dramas" approved by the Lord Chamberlain and County Council had been, Sansom wrote,

> excellently done from all points of view, but many of the others were quite the reverse. Old plays with a humour that was out of fashion, and a number of characters that were more or less unintelligible to 1912 audiences, found their way to the music halls.

Sansom then claimed to have joined others in departing variety in irritation that after "a programme made up of two hours of drama at a minimum, the customer might still be left looking for his best amusement." The best amusement, he added, was to be found at "the picture palace."[70] The number of picture palaces was growing, and many of the newest ones held more people than the older ones had.

Picturesque acting of the kind stars showed in their turns may have helped quicken the demand for films. In any case, films flourished borrowing a formula from melodrama that had them mix slapstick with moralizing in the old, full-blooded style. The word "Chaplinesque" would soon be coined to capture the potent blend of pratfalls and pathos. In 1912, though, no one was left to wonder why the theatre and other tony entertainments continued to leak performers into variety.

One of those performers, shortly, was to be Herbert and Maud's eldest child, Viola Tree, who began a provincial tour in November 1913. *Era* noted, with respect, that she'd "reached the music hall stage through the legitimate theatre and the concert platform."[71] Her parents had allowed her this path, if not encouraged it. If ever a father had been proud, it was on the night Tree's Viola made her London debut playing *Shakespeare's* Viola in her father's typically lush staging of *Twelfth Night*.

By the time Viola followed her parents into variety, refinement didn't seem so precious even to her. The next year, disastrous events would force famous actors to new lengths altogether. By the time the Great War ended, Britain's imperial mission would stand compromised more grievously than France's was in culture's quieter fold. American films became the source of greatest celebrity. They have remained so ever since, though never without being contested.

\* \* \*

The same year Tree beat the royals to the Palace, H. G. Hibbert, gazing across the Atlantic at North America, was certain that music halls had endowed vaudeville with the best of itself. "What first impresses the student of the variety stage," wrote Hibbert, was that

> twenty years ago, what in America is called vaudeville had no distinction, and little importance. It grew, in emulation of the English music halls, borrowing our artistes and other material freely, but in the course of time, it has repaid with interest—for the commerce of the two countries is in no respect more remarkable than in variety art.[72]

Hibbert's chauvinism came in reaction to what *Era* was calling "the year of the American boom," when something like 130 acts would find their ways into music halls and variety.[73] When it came to the commerce in popular culture, America was leading the way.

Against this onslaught, British chauvinists from high and low praised music halls for relying on sturdy homegrown fare. Turns by Tree, Bernhardt, and other stage stars had the same Titterton who belittled Tree, denouncing "A deliberate attempt . . . to capture the Halls for the well-to-do." This stratagem, Titterton warned, compromised "almost the one democratic institution left in modern England."[74] Other reactionaries took Titterton's side, defending nearly anything that marked or mirrored class distinction. Stuffy aristocrats joined freethinkers in calling for class to be cried out in the old ways in newer venues. A body of opinion arose, in the face of change that struck many at every level as too rapid, that favored upholding at least some of the traditional boundaries between the classes and the institutions they supported.

In North America, meanwhile, vaudeville could claim to offer something for everyone. It had taken its name from a French word with a whiff of the cosmopolitan. "Class," though, was a word used commonly in the United States to describe something that could be acquired. "Classy" people were ones with skill, grace, or accomplishments, no matter what their origin. Words like "classy" and "vaudeville" bespoke an ideal of classlessness that left high-end British fare seeming hidebound and pretentious. Randolph Bourne would shortly ridicule the British nation for being "stupid, blundering, [and] hypocritical." The French meanwhile, he thought, were generous, gregarious, and broad-minded.[75] Other Americans joined Bourne in praising the French people and their history for sharing their nation's revolutionary heritage.

Such generalizing overlooked a spirited debate in France itself. In the 1830s and 1840s, Auguste Comte had founded the field of sociology on the premise that groups were more important than individuals were in forming and changing societies. Comte's views never gained consensus in France or elsewhere, but they brought a backlash against his egalitarianism, such as it was. One of the sharper responses came in 1895 with Gustave Le Bon's book, *La Psychologie des foules* (The Psychology of Crowds). Le Bon believed, as one who's studied him writes, that "from the moment when the moral forces on which a civilisation rested have lost their strength, its final dissolution is brought about by those unconscious and brutal crowds known . . . as barbarians."[76]

Pulling no punches, Le Bon compared the workings of crowds with the rash acts of women and children. He attacked the theatre and other performing arts for encouraging crowds to respond viscerally to images. Images as opposed to words, he wrote, brought out devolutionary tendencies among the least intelligent in any audience and, by extension, in the society that had produced the audience. Le Bon was afraid that the persons lowest in status were most susceptible to the simplest stimuli and the most savage, too.

In the same year *La Psychologie des foules* went into print, Le Bon's countryman Paul Bourget brought out *Outre-Mer: Impressions of America*, warning that wherever "universal suffrage is the rule, it becomes necessary to speak to the people by means of pictures." The people most influenced by pictures "see everything as a whole, and naturally like coarse and striking things."[77] Nor was Le Bon's influence relayed only through French partisans like Bourget. Theodore Roosevelt, incorruptible president of the New York City Board of Police Commissioners, may have had his doubts about the wisdom of universal suffrage. He felt clearer about crime, though, and so did many of his peers in the American aristocracy. Roosevelt had Le Bon's book on his shelf within a year of its publication.[78]

Crowd-, or more accurately, mob-theory wasn't the only critique of democracy. Over the previous generation, proponents of "neuromimesis" had argued that emotions spread among crowds in the same way infectious diseases did.[79] Because women were the weaker sex, the theory held, they risked hysteria simply by going to theatre, much less by working there or in other places where crowds gave off unruly emotions and noxious germs. The French sociologist Gabriel Tarde reported hearing a Russian viewer explain, after seeing Bernhardt's Camille expire in Moscow, that

at the most dramatic moment, when the entire audience was so silent you could have heard a pin drop, Marguerite Gautier, dying of consumption, coughed. Immediately an epidemic of coughing filled the auditorium, and during several minutes no one was able to hear the words of the great actress.[80]

If the witness spoke true, Bernhardt was mixing tuberculosis, the weaker sex, and public performance into one pestilent brew.

If the neuromimeticists were right, Bernhardt was spreading hypochondria and hysteria, or worse than that, disease. Anyone who paid to see her had to share the air she breathed to shape the glorious sounds she produced. If she was spreading sickness and encouraging malingering, variety and vaudeville must be doing it, too. If the lower classes, especially the men, were infectious and ungovernable, mingling with them was dangerous. Women of means were told that they stood at risk for not having been exposed to more of the pathogens and seedy characters that might have toughened them up.

Meanwhile, pressure toward universal suffrage for men wasn't easing, least of all in the most industrialized nations, which were also the most militarized. Warfare, like industry, called for sheer numbers. France's losing the Franco-Prussian War had Bernhardt on a mission to promote French solidarity. She believed that the least sophisticated weren't only to be charged for the privilege to see her, but inspired and unified thereby. When she sailed to America, vaudeville-bound in late November 1912, she expected to edify many more people than she'd seen on any of her tours of variety, perhaps all of them taken together. Her landing in New York Harbor drew another round of the media frenzy that had moved Henry James to call her "the muse of the newspaper."[81]

While musing in interviews, Bernhardt struck a more exclusive note than she had in Britain. To call up competitive urges among her prospective patrons, she told the *New York Times* that she would have to see whether stateside crowds could appreciate her acting as much as Londoners and tourists did at the Coliseum.[82] Nearly in the same breath, she credited audiences in the 'States for being "a different type from the English public" in doing "everything on a large scale."[83]

With scale in mind, she expanded her repertoire to a half dozen turns, more than she'd used across any variety season to that point. *Camille, Théodora, Tosca, Lucrèce Borgia, Phèdre*, and *Une Nuit de*

*Noël sous la terreur* were all of them pieces she'd shown in variety. The last turn was soaked in humanitarianism, and much rarer for this star, in comedy.

She didn't take up her engagement in New York directly, but traveled West and stayed for several months. The tour took her farther than she'd traveled overland in recent years. She began with two weeks in Chicago, anchor of the Orpheum circuit. Then she made stopovers in St. Louis, Milwaukee, St. Paul, and Minneapolis; into Canada at Winnipeg, and on from there to Edmonton, Calgary, and Victoria; back into the United States at Bellingham Bay in Washington, southward to Seattle and Portland, then to one-night stands in the California farm towns of Chico, Stockton, and San Jose; set down in San Francisco before showing up in Oakland and Fresno for shorter runs; to Los Angeles, Salt Lake City, and Denver at wider intervals, followed by short stays at Colorado Springs and Pueblo, Colorado; laid over in Lincoln, Nebraska, with a split week that took her from Omaha to Kansas City, before starting an eastern leg at Keith's Hippodrome in Cleveland and heading into New York and the newly open Palace near the heart of Times Square (see figure 6). At the end of her three-and-a-half weeks at the Palace, she'd made what would now be about $3.3 million, which still in 1913, just barely, came free of the income tax that became the law of the land that year when it was ratified as the Sixteenth Amendment to the United States' Constitution.

Lou Tellegen traveled and acted with Bernhardt for what turned out to be the last time, and he was photographed beaming arm-in-arm with her as often as he had been on her third tour of variety, and his first. He looks more relaxed in photos taken away from the stage than in the ones taken on it, where he may never have felt quite balanced against her force. She looked dead game, onstage and offstage.

Playing through California's Bay Area in February 1913, Bernhardt caught a darker side of American life on an expedition to San Quentin Prison. On Washington's Birthday, in what had become a standard courtesy from touring stars, she faced a non-paying audience that filled the prison yard and was reported to have included a score of women and five men under capital sentence. She chose *Une Nuit de Noël sous la terreur* for ending with every prisoner freed from

**Figure 6** Sarah Bernhardt framed in a Palace Theatre program from 1913. Note the way that vaudeville appropriated Bernhardt's image by containing it and figuring her as *faux* royalty. (Reprinted by permission of the Theatre Collection, Museum of the City of New York.)

the Bastille. San Quentin's inmates, standing in the exercise yard in their striped-pajama uniforms, applauded the sight.[84]

Her five other turns showed characters loving at their peril, or dying, or both. Except for the *vivandière*, Bernhardt's repertoire allowed little hope other than for a noble death and a better life to come. The star traveled in luxury, but her staying on the road for so long at her age, and the publicity she got for doing it, underscored the rounds of sacrifice she was showing as many as fourteen times a week, complete with her dying-swan curtain calls. Now and then she would let a photographer catch her looking haggard.

Excepting the *vivandière*, her characters skirted the cemetery as closely as they'd done in variety in the fall of 1912. As in Britain, constant reminders of the star's mortality created a sense of scarcity even while she was taking the stage twice a day. Vaudeville adopted a reverential tone in tributes like the one inserted into the Palace's souvenir program:

> Notwithstanding the fact that the greatest contemporary authors, artists and impresarios had given their very best service to the younger child of the stage [i.e., vaudeville], the announcement that the world's greatest actress, Madame Sarah Bernhardt, would be seen in the "two a day" brought first an echo of universal surprise and then a flood of appreciation.[85]

Vaudeville made the world's greatest actress its most shining star, brighter than she'd been in variety with knights of the realm and the royal family to contest her place in the constellation.

In vaudeville, she stood at the head of a group that since the late 1890s had included British stars Maurice Barrymore and Millward, Hawtrey, Langtry, and Mrs. Pat; native notables at the ends of their careers like Ned Harrigan and Clara Morris, and suchlike Europeans as Czech *emigrée* Fanny Janauschek. There had been Nance O'Neil, Walter Hampden, and Douglas Fairbanks (Senior) nearer the beginnings of their careers; Robert Hilliard, John Mason, Robert Mantell, Arnold Daly, Henry Miller, James K. Hackett, and James O'Neill at various points along their journeys; and two of Maurice Barrymore's children, Lionel and Ethel, soon to be followed by their brother

John, in vaudeville for the first time since his youthful outings with his father in the closing days of Barry's career.

The list of stars had prepared the way for Bernhardt to make $7,000 a week, or what now would be around $140,000. Her retinue of twenty-five included the photogenic Tellegen, with the rest of her entourage and some fine sets and costumes to "banish the vaudeville atmosphere," in the words of one critic who'd been properly impressed.[86] Her contract gave her $2,000 (~$39,000) more a week than she'd made in variety, with another $2,000 on top of that to cover what *Variety* called "incidentals" that probably included some or most of her production costs.[87]

The fuss and the fees raised doubters. Bernhardt's reputation had vaudeville loyalists questioning her novelty when they couldn't dispute her drawing power. *Variety's* chief editor, Sime Silverman, wrote at the beginning of her tour that, in his purist's eyes,

> The weakness of the big time is possibly exemplified by Mme. Bernhardt . . . [who earns] an impossible salary, a foolish salary whether it draws business as Bernhardt must draw (as a curiosity to the American people) or whether the prices are raised to meet the expenses. In either case the public will be disappointed, if not by the increased money they must pay to see the great star, then by the next week's bill—for what can follow Bernhardt?[88]

What indeed? The question made Silverman nervous.

The men who ran vaudeville milked the occasion by raising prices as Silverman supposed they would. Keith and Albee at Manhattan's Palace were last to do this, and the greediest, when they set the standard cost of their most expensive seats at $2 (~$40)—the same figure that had capped the legitimate theatre's ticket prices since before the turn of the century. *Variety* scoffed with the headline, "Palace $2 Vaudeville a Joke: Double-Crossing Boomerang."[89] The paper blamed Bernhardt for making the bills around her weaker. Silverman had an axe to grind and didn't have far to look for the grindstone.

Bernhardt had let it be known that she found blackface in poor taste. Her insistence on the right to approve turns on her bills, and to disallow blackface, robbed audiences of some of the standard humor. With her consent, a string of singers, many of them classical, were assigned to the slots around hers. The singers, all of them seasoned and most of them women, joined a number of what then were called "living statues" to lay on the refinement that Bernhardt represented. When her Lucrezia Borgia was followed by Bessie Wynn, for instance, who'd come by her braying style in barrooms, Wynn was followed by the tantalizing Robbie Gordone, posed in series with other sound-bodied young women to look like Greek or Roman statuary. Gordone's turn was much like the positively reliquary "Seldom's Poems in Marble," which had ended Bernhardt's first Palace bill to cap the *vivandière*.[90] *Variety*, in reaction, noted that the only turn with Bernhardt's and Gordone's to truly fit "the Palace as though built for it" was W. C. Fields's "high art pantomimic comedy juggling."[91] Fields was well known by this time for the *faux*-hobo look he'd cultivated to blur his own artfulness and, in this case, to protect himself against the overload of gentility on his bill.

Some of Bernhardt's harsher critics implied that her handpicking other turns showed her insecurity.[92] If this was true, it meant she wasn't giving more for the money no matter how many roles she played over a week's time, or a month's. It was harder for her to give more for the money—she knew it better than anyone— when prices to see her were so high as to match the theatre's ticket scale. Silverman and *Variety* wouldn't let the cost of hiring her go months after she'd left the Palace, when they disclosed that vaudeville's newest showcase hadn't made "a dollar though Bernhardt drew as much as $22,000 [~$440,000] one week." The Palace "is reported between $50,000 and $60,000 behind to date" (~$1–$1.2 million). Before she'd arrived, entire *bills* had been paid less than she'd gotten, as *Variety* claimed with authority.[93] But the carping couldn't change the fact that Bernhardt had confirmed Keith and Albee's control of what quickly became their new showcase and the seat of big-time vaudeville that housed their offices in the Palace building that stands even now within hailing distance of Times Square.

Keith and Albee used Bernhardt to show how grandly they could rule the big time. Their iron-fistedness marked an end to the most frenzied bidding for the services of stage stars. Actors' prices never got so high for giving turns as Bernhardt's were along her first tour.

\* \* \*

She altered her approach to vaudeville from the one she'd taken to variety. She performed in French again, but gave over plays that linked her most narrowly to French and English history: *Elisabeth*, *L'Aiglon* and *Jeanne d'Arc*. With no historical turn to show, she took on a more mythic profile for Americans who preferred to see the past reenacted, briskly, to reading about it in books.

Reviewers stateside generally sketched out her plots more quickly than British reviewers did for variety. Americans' lesser interest in plot left Bernhardt more the attraction and her fatal endings more insistent. As star of the highest order, she blotted out everyone around her, whether it was other performers on the bill, or Lou Tellegen as her candy-man co-star, or Jean Racine's Phèdre, which had by then been a classic role on the French stage for more than two hundred years. She didn't need to blot out blackface for having eliminated it already.

For every difference between her and Tree, the stars moved in parallel. He was known as a linguist and for traveling across Europe. He vacationed regularly at the German spa at Marienbad, where British high society congregated during summertimes first to join Edward VII, and then to commune with the king's spirit until the war. Bernhardt's tours, trans- and multi-continental, marked her as a traveler without peer except among the most imperial royalty. Much of the publicity she got, and Tree, showed the range of their movement onstage, on tour, and on the emotional journeys their characters took on the way to giving more for the money.

Both stars tapped the audiences' desire for vicarious travel. She moved farther back, and more often than he did, into the past. At relatively low prices, with enhancement from arts of the make-believe, even the least worldly viewers had Bernhardt to escort them to ancient Greece, to Constantinople during the Byzantine Empire, to Florence in the high Renaissance, or to France at various points in its history. In Britain, some varietygoers who'd gone on imaginary trips with her had Tree to take them around the Cape to India, or later during the war, across the perilous Channel to the Bohemian quarter of Paris to recall a time before German armies were dug in along French borders and German submarines could be spotted offshore. Vicarious travel, tricked out as drama, was better than no travel at all for the many who'd never gone far.

Besides the stars' wanderlust, Tree and Bernhardt shared a flamboyance that makes current specimens of stage realism seem pallid and tight. Together with the *panache* that many other turns exhibited, the leading dramatic stars left a record that confirms Peter Davison's sense that the music halls' greatest contribution—the same would apply to vaudeville—lay in keeping "alive the fanciful and absurd during a period when . . . the film, by its very nature, *seemed* to present the world as it actually was."[94]

Tree and Bernhardt made films that showed, or seemed to show, the world as it was. Onstage, they perfected the kind of frontal, solitary, wide-eyed, still, and silent moments that films made into close-ups. The stars were throwbacks in the melodramatics they flooded their turns with and passed on again through their films. The stars' affiliations with history—and for Bernhardt with Britain's history woven into France's—confirm Eric Hobsbawm's opinion that traditions have needed "inventing" to ease the uncertainties of modern life.[95] Bernhardt as France's greatest star, and Tree as Britain's most imperial one, invented tradition in the stories their characters suffered through. It was the cleanest apology they could have made for the considerable influence they wielded—for actors—and the massive adulation they enjoyed.

As persons with Jewish ancestry at a time when, and in places where, assimilation was obligatory, the greatest stars blended countries, ethnicities, and religions in themselves and in everything they did. They radiated stateliness—and a statelessness with it—that set them beyond the limits of any costume or setting they could have devised, or any history they could have invented. They made it look as if they practiced statecraft by posing as artists of pure motive. Pricey as they were, they were cheaper to hire and easier to command than the countries they stood for. They were bargains in their way, who strived always to seem more so.

The next phase for Bernhardt and Tree came, as for other stars, under conditions that dwarfed the antic stage. The most famous actors weren't turned into profiteers, exactly, through the agitation the suffrage movement brought, and after that, the war. But unrest followed by calamity left stars more than ever as the alchemists for modern times, turning shows of suffering into gold.

# 4. Suffer the Women, 1910–1914 ⌒

*At the capital of the British Empire, women have been smashing win-*
*dows, scattering flames and acid: at the capital of the United States,*
*women have been building pageants, scattering the creative fires of beauty*
*and reason.*

Percy MacKaye, "Art and the Woman's
Movement" (1913)[1]

In 1910, what then was called "woman suffrage" stood in danger of losing much of the sympathy it had attracted. Sarah Bernhardt, for so long independence personified, learned to be cautious in voicing support for votes for women. Asked just before her first vaudeville tour for her opinion of London's radical suffragettes, she "exclaimed tragically," according to the *New York Times*, that

> "They are fools!" and asked what the suffragists were doing in America. On being told that they contented themselves with holding parades and meetings, the French actress said "That is the way the women began in London and were held up to ridicule. Perhaps they will come to adopt the same methods here later as they are using now in England."[2]

Protests were one thing and guerilla actions were another. Moderates like Bernhardt believed that women could claim higher ground by asserting what many, men and women, took to be the women's native nonviolence against others, at least, besides themselves.

The din from London made activism in the United States seem tame. A little controversy didn't have to be a bad thing for stars, and a dash of notoriety could come in handy when careers needed a jolt.

But bitterness and factionalism couldn't hold large audiences for long, and variety and vaudeville were known for wooing patrons, not haranguing them. Stars would often back away from controversy when they felt an audience stiffen. Nevertheless, several of the world's best-paid workingwomen determined to do what they could for suffrage. Their initiative was most visible in London, where they could turn their turn fame to advantage while upholding their convictions.

In 1908, the Actresses' Franchise League (AFL) formed squarely at the seat of empire, or at least the fringe that stood nearest Leicester Square. Among the League's cofounders and honorary vice presidents were four stars: Irene Vanbrugh, Lena Ashwell, Lillah McCarthy, and Lillie Langtry. These actresses didn't have much in common otherwise, but they stood shoulder-to-shoulder for suffrage.[3] Each star took her office as something more than honorary, though they acted on their sense of obligation in different ways. At the least they wanted more rights for themselves and for women who idolized them but weren't in the same position to shape opinion.

Famous actresses weren't so different from workaday ones in the lack of control they felt over their careers. For a quarter century and more, the mavericks among women had been Bernhardt and Langtry, admired for their independence even as moralists decried their personal lives. Elizabeth Robins, one of Britain's earliest proponents of Ibsen and the drama of social critique, wrote that not even actresses "who by some fluke had proved their powers had any choice as to what they should act."[4] An oracular Bernhardt complained of being forced to play

three subjects and three alone, no matter how many variants one may mention. They are love, maternity, and sorrow. Most women know the first, a large proportion experience the second, and as for the last, no woman escapes it. When you have covered these subjects, you have run the gamut for women.[5]

She'd taken roles playing men as often as she had, she said, to escape the tribulation that came with playing women. She'd endeared herself to suffrage groups by playing Joan of Arc at a time when many suffragist sisterhoods were adopting Joan for their mascot or patron saint.[6]

Interest in a woman who'd lived so long ago showed how few women in history, and fewer heroines from the dramatic canon, avoided the maudlin or the masochistic. AFL members found it troubling, too, that most women's-rights plays had been written by men. The League responded by urging its members to take up their pens. Over time, the strategy brought more suffrage- and women's-rights plays to the fore. The AFL performed them, and older plays, in and around London, mostly. By far the largest number of the League's members lived there or nearby. They were ready to act in concert when they could agree on a plan. Showing plays made a plan the entire membership could applaud.

For all of the plays the AFL sponsored and the manifestos the larger movement churned out, the actresses declined, collectively, to endorse either the moderate suffragists or the fire-eating suffragettes. Moderates far outnumbered radicals in the theatre as elsewhere. There were many women, including actresses, who opposed suffrage for themselves and other women. All but a few actresses had, in the way of the times, been brought up to oblige or to seem obliging, and found the chance to show their knack onstage. Many actresses who'd conducted their careers by obliging were put off enough by activism to refrain from joining the Actresses' Franchise League. Most AFL members communed primarily with their colleagues anyway, because it was convenient and more civil, usually, than the public debate that grew around an increasingly divisive topic.

In variety, women stars saw quickly that, they could stage their turns outside the patriarchy that actor-managers ruled. Variety had its own patriarchy, of course, but that one allowed women, stars and others, to write plays or adapt them, or dress the turns and themselves at their discretion. Once the League got underway, it sponsored events that had actresses taking roles they'd never have played otherwise, in pieces too partisan to survive a commercial run. Although it was inconvenient that most plays treating the rights of women had been written by men, some of the men, a few with considerable reputations, lent their voices to the Cause. Best known among them was James M. Barrie.

Remembered now for writing *Peter Pan*, Barrie had a gift for fitting choice roles to fine actresses. One of those roles—besides Peter Pan—was Kate in his one-act play, *The Twelve-Pound Look*. The piece opened in London in March 1910 among an evening of short works.[7] The play, as would have been clear to anyone who saw it, children aside, advocated women's rights to divorce and separate property. But *Look* was loaded with irony, and with too many polemics to suit those who'd come to soak up some of Barrie's patented blend of fantasy and fun. *Look*, and the other plays with it, did not run for long.

Barrie had also missed Irene Vanbrugh (1872–1949) at *Look*'s premiere. He'd written the leading role with her in mind, as he'd done with other leading roles before it and would do with other ones afterward. Vanbrugh had rehearsed *Look* expecting to open in it. Within days before the first performance, she'd taken ill. Lena Ashwell, who played more forcefully, replaced her.

The show had to go on and go on it did, with Ashwell playing the former Kate Sims. The lost opportunity didn't trouble Vanbrugh much at a time when she was having of one of the finest careers among the generation of actresses to follow Ellen Terry. It would be Vanbrugh's adaptability, and moderation, that drew her into variety and kept her there through a period when the struggle for suffrage turned increasingly acrimonious.

\* \* \*

Any actress, activist or not, would have recognized *The Twelve-Pound Look* as a spin-off from Henrik Ibsen's *A Doll House* (1879). In what became one of the landmark plays of the nineteenth century, the protagonist is shown having led a dutiful and almost entirely exemplary life as a daughter, wife, and mother. At the end of the play, she leaves her husband and three children after learning how deeply she's compromised herself in her need to please. *A Doll House* has its final curtain fall as Nora closes the door on her stricken husband and their former life including the sleeping children. The ending raised controversy, and not just among playgoers. The sound of heavy doors slammed shut haunted viewers, or infuriated them, across Europe and the Americas from the 1880s.

*Look*'s heroine does as Nora Helmer might have done several years on. Kate has escaped a loveless, childless marriage to a thriving if self-absorbed businessman named Harry Sims. She visits him for the first time since leaving him several years before, as *he'd* assumed, to find another man or to run away with one. Harry has since taken a more docile wife. Kate faces him just after he's been knighted for his worldly success.

Kate deals in the material realm, too, telling him how she'd taught herself to type before leaving him after earning £12 by her labors (around $1,150 in the early twenty-first century). Sir Harry doesn't take the news well at all, clinging to the possibility of that other man. The play shows him growing grumpier and alarmed, at the last, on seeing his current wife, so recently become Lady Sims, coveting a typewriter of her own.

*The Twelve-Pound Look* is bittersweet. Kate is attractive and quick-witted. Lady Sims is dull if companionable. Sir Harry is a blustering fool. The play holds many laughs, mostly at his expense. Kate laughs, too, often from a sense of life's odder outcomes. *Look* never refers to suffrage directly, but neither does it cloak its sympathy for a character who has worked for pay, been divorced, and found a standard for success beyond marriage and privilege.

The "twelve-pound looks" Sir Harry gets from Kate and Lady Sims as the curtain falls show women he'd considered possessions gazing back at him, levelly and unafraid. *Look* advances an ideal of companionate marriage by showing the signs of its absence in everything Sir Harry says and does. For all the laughter, it must have seemed to some who watched it as if they'd tasted a bitter pill. Others would have liked it for ending more mercifully, and quickly, than *A Doll House* did with its three full-blown acts.

For several years by 1910, star actresses had been giving turns that saw their characters reject or divorce spouses, or deceive, betray, or even kill men with cause. Husband-, vengeance-, and mercy-killings by women in turns from Bernhardt, Jessie Millward, and Mrs. Patrick Campbell among others, didn't support votes for women explicitly. But the plays raised issues that suffrage had made more sensitive. Plays that showed women killing men, for any reason, called up greater anxiety after suffragettes began destroying public and private property across London and thereabouts in the summer of 1909.[8]

Shock at these tactics was instant, strong, and widespread. It made variety producers wary, and stars with them. Other performers, not least the comics of both sexes, stayed fairly free in making jokes at the suffragettes' expense. The humor ran uneasily, though, as it often does in the shadow of profound change.

Irene Vanbrugh certainly knew how to win laughs onstage. She'd proven it by playing Gwendolen Fairfax, the more citified of the two sharp-witted girls, for the premiere of Oscar Wilde's *The Importance of Being Earnest*. But Vanbrugh wasn't going to play a suffragette or make fun of one so long as she had anything to say about it. Her success in other plays by Barrie, together with *Look*'s brevity and oblique reference to suffrage, recommended it for variety.

In late October 1911, a year-and-a-half after it had opened without her, Vanbrugh made *Look* her first turn. When she had a respectable run in it at the London Hippodrome, she took it five months later to the Coliseum at Oswald Stoll's request. Her first week there, she was joined on the bill by Sir Edward Elgar conducting his own composition, "The Crown of India."[9] In the halls of mirth, at least, women's rights were vying with some of Britain's most hallowed institutions.

Nearly forty years later, Vanbrugh would remember that in the theatre, for lacking her presence, *Look* "had not influenced the box-office." But when she'd taken the play to the Coliseum, almost directly across the street from the theatre where it first had run with Lena Ashwell in it, Irene recalled its making "a most sensational success."[10] If she was exaggerating, it wasn't by much.

Vanbrugh's approach called up sympathy for *Look*'s uncompromising heroine. The star played a Kate who was purposeful throughout, but with what one reviewer saw as

no suggestion of hardness, no hint of embitterment consequent upon Kate's unfortunate experiences of matrimony. Rather is Kate a woman triumphant in her freedom, regretting nothing—except perhaps to find her former husband still weak in the weakness which comes from financial strength and success—and possessing abundant pity for her who has taken her place. It is essentially a womanly study, and one which is thoroughly convincing.[11]

The "womanly study" showed the Sims wives sticking together against poor Sir Harry. Variety audiences, with women and girls particularly well represented at matinees, took the turn not only with good humor but also as vindication, not least from the sight of Sir Harry's last helpless gesture.

*Look* held its appeal right through events that might have sunk another turn or another star in it. In January 1912—two months after Vanbrugh offered the play at the Hippodrome and two before she took it to the Coliseum—suffragettes clashed with police outside Parliament. The first of March saw more than two hundred suffragettes jailed after they had smashed windows across London. Then, with their numbers depleted, they sustained a campaign of milder civil disobedience around the city. If these events affected Vanbrugh, they didn't keep her from bringing *Look* to the Coliseum within a week after the windows were broken. Her acting left audiences in good spirits, Kate's steely resolve notwithstanding. She didn't look like a window-breaker, apparently.

The next year, with tensions running higher, Vanbrugh took a softer approach. She'd played Barrie's one-act *Rosalind* in the theatre, and at the Coliseum she played the title character again, a retired actress and

> pretty picture of the popular ingénue, who is really "forty and a bittock" and is revelling in the restfulness of middle-age, warning her youthful admirer against falling in love with one so much older than himself, and suddenly resuming her sprightliness and juvenility and dashing off to town to repeat her former triumphs [on the stage].[12]

Barrie had his middle-aged star ask the young admirer, not purely in sweetness, whether he'd noticed that "there are no parts . . . for middle-aged ladies."[13]

There were plenty of parts for Irene Vanbrugh. Her Rosalind's fey charm could hardly have been more different from the other Vanbrugh sister's solo turn on the same bill, showing Lady Macbeth's troubled sleepwalking.[14] Violet Vanbrugh was herself an honorary vice president of the AFL, but while she sported Lady M's medieval gear, she didn't try to match her younger sister dressed "artistically" as

Rosalind, as bohemian suffragists did to show their free spirits. For the next week's bill, Violet exercised womanly license of an even more disquieting kind with her turn in *The Woman in the Case*. It showed "depravity of the higher grade" in Violet's character's murdering one man and nearly framing another for the crime.[15]

As for psychopathology in women, Violet's tabloid Lady Macbeth had fared better in the provinces than it did on reaching the Coliseum. In London, to judge it by its short run, the Scottish turn only left patrons who'd been spooked already by reports of violence, or the sight of it, more skittish, Stars like the Vanbrughs, in turns ending with poetic justice, could denounce the violence, or as Violet Vanbrugh did, enact it before submitting her character to the consequences. In tandem at the Coliseum, the Vanbrughs showed the moral compass that the suffrage movement liked to claim.

In May 1913, between Irene's two variety runs in *Rosalind*, she was asked to speak

> in favour of the vote [for women] at a big rally in Drury Lane Theatre organised by the Actresses' Franchise League to bring the importance of the movement home to a wider circle of the dramatic profession. I consented only under the definite assurance that it was on constitutional lines that the meeting would be held and that under that assurance Mrs. Henry Fawcett and other prominent members of the right [moderate] wing had consented to be on the stage with us . . . to preclude any speeches being made in favour of the militant method.[16]

Enough AFL members attended the rally to fill the stage of the Drury Lane Theatre, whose size was matched only by the Coliseum's in London. Irene's husband, Dion "Dot" Boucicault, feared the worst.[17] She brushed off his concerns, and her own better judgment, perhaps, to join the assembly.

When her fellow AFL Vice President Lena Ashwell rose to speak, it was to denounce employers guilty of "sweating" or overworking women in menial jobs. Facing a radical surge, Mrs. Maud Arncliffe-Sennett, herself an actress, producer, and by the scale of the day, moderate, struggled to find common ground by telling the throng that she couldn't defend militancy, but that "with Heaven's help she would never repudiate" it.[18]

At this point, Irene Vanbrugh took the floor, or rather the stage. According to the paraphrase in the next day's *Daily Chronicle*, she said she had no "sympathy with militant methods and with the terrible disorder that they had brought about." "There was a deplorable state of disorder," she'd gone on, and all of it "caused by the action of the militants." She was heated and sorrowful in the same breath, saying that she knew "she had played an unsympathetic part" but felt obliged to "say what she felt."[19] She remembered getting more upset when Ashwell replied that "while she appreciated my wishing to clarify my own attitude, it was not possible for the AFL to dissociate themselves from both sides in their campaign."[20]

The dispute over tactics may not have been the only bone of contention between Vanbrugh and Ashwell. When Irene had played *Look* at the Coliseum, it was with Arthur Playfair, who'd been Ashwell's first husband, acting Sir Harry. Something about Vanbrugh still rankled Ashwell more than twenty years later, when she wrote in her autobiography that she would have been "altogether too humble" not to mention that Vanbrugh hadn't been "half as good" a Kate as she'd been.[21] It must be said, in fairness, that such meanness was uncharacteristic of Ashwell.

Events beyond the stage may have aggravated whatever divided the stars. The AFL rally came just days before Emily Wilding Davison, who on a staircase while in custody the year before had thrown herself into the stairwell, died when she ran in front of the King's racehorse at Ascot on Derby Day. Davison's death was more shocking for happening in full view of the royal party and the thousands looking on. Vanbrugh's willingness to play "an unsympathetic part," even in heated times, was uncharacteristic of her as well.

Contentious as the meeting grew, it didn't keep Vanbrugh from variety and her advocacy in the fall of 1913, a few months after the mass meeting. Calling on Barrie for a third turn, she secured material less objectionable than even the tranquilizing *Rosalind* had been. Barrie had his own eye fixed on popular audiences. He'd written *Half an Hour* expressly as a turn for Vanbrugh, and given it a running time to match the title.

The character Barrie handed Vanbrugh was Lady Lillian Garson, miserable in her marriage and fed up with her life as a pampered woman. She plans to leave Lord Garson, who is nastier by far than *Look's* pompous if dimmed-down Sir Harry. When Lady Lillian's lover dies just as he's about to spirit her away, she's forced to return to her husband and deceive him as to her whereabouts and actions. She can't leave him, she fears, because he is her only means of support. If Kate in *Look* hadn't been so self-reliant, she might have followed Lady Lillian, the cow-like Lady Sims, and every real woman chained to an overbearing or abusive man.

It was clear to one reviewer that *Half an Hour* touched on "Feminism when . . . the doctor exclaim[s], in response to [Lady Lillian's] 'I cannot work!' 'Shame to all men that it is so!' " It was a line, the critic noted, "that would surely cause an extra heart beat or two in a modern Suffragist audience!" Barrie had made his hand-maiden more ingratiating by shielding Vanbrugh from having to speak the most charged lines. He arranged that she be "exquisitely gowned" to deliver what the same sympathetic critic called the "cultivated calmness, the agitated self-interested deceit and the final effrontery of her Lady Lillian."[22] The gown catered to Hippodrome audiences known for being more fashion-conscious than the Coliseum's regulars were.

If the plain frock Vanbrugh had worn as Kate called up the dowdy suffragettes, Rosalind's clothing signaled an independent soul. And liberated as Rosalind was, *Half an Hour's* downcast heroine sports her stunning apparel while being reduced to "self-interested deceit." Even patrons the least well-off could feel luckier in love than Lady Lillian was. She seemed sadder when measured against her husband's nearly absolute control in dressing her as if she were a doll.

While Irene sketched out the terrors of life among the swells, sister Violet was touring the provinces in *Her Wedding Night* by Alicia Ramsay. This play showed a character recently married off for her dowry of £250,000 (over $24 million now) reconciled with a clumsy but honorable aristocratic husband.[23] The Countess Fotheringham, like Lady Lillian, knows that money can't buy happiness. Unlike the Garsons, she and her husband find their way to a marriage of equals when he meets her tears with tenderness.

Violet Vanbrugh never had the good fortune to fall in with a play-wright as her sister did with Barrie. And it was Irene who later paid tribute to other men for helping her when she'd reached an age at which even the brightest stars had been known to dim. She'd appreciated her husband especially, she remembered near the end of her life, for setting aside his dim view of the suffrage movement to stage her in the turns that led her successively from Kate's impoverished liberty to Lady Lillian's luxurious enslavement.[24]

Irene also felt beholden to Oswald Stoll for having told her that *Look* would "be an interesting thing for you to do" in variety.[25] In offering his opinion, Stoll must have supposed that she could call on Barrie freely, to give her the play wherever she wanted to show it. But when she had gone to petition the playwright, she'd been so nervous, she recalled, that she balked before finding the courage to ask him for "something I want so badly that I am frightened." Barrie coaxed it out of her: Stoll's offer and Dot's stipulation that

> I could accept it only if [Stoll] would allow me to play *The Twelve-Pound Look*. I . . . felt it would be thrilling to present that play in the very best way possible with Edmund Gwenn [later a familiar character actor in films] also in his original part [as the hapless Sir Harry]. I told him that the salary that I had been offered had been a handsome one, but I would not let that weigh with me unless I could do something that was worthwhile.

Barrie ended by blessing the venture, but not before saying,

> "Well, I don't like to refuse you anything, Irene, but I will not be responsible for this production. Dot will have to do the whole thing and my author's fee would be £50 a week" [~$4,800]. I felt very happy and Oswald Stoll was delighted with the suggestion; it was exactly the sort of turn he had hoped for.[26]

According to her own account, Vanbrugh had needed no fewer than three men to make the break into variety and a new phase in her career. A recent suffrage historian, appraising Vanbrugh's deference, has called her "a flower . . . nourished by its 'foundation' in 'generosity.' "[27] Surely, the dutifulness the star showed Stoll, Boucicault, and Barrie nourished the generosity, and the paternalism, that each man showed her in his own special way. Their attentions left the younger Vanbrugh sister far from Kate's lonely indomitability at one extreme and Lady Lillian Garson's voiceless desperation at the other.

The star's life stood closer, actually, to Rosalind's as the most care-free and expressive of the characters Barrie wrote to exploit Vanbrugh's range, and his own. The sequence of her turns from the author of *Peter Pan* showed not only how differently women's rights could be construed, but how lightly proselytizing could be let fall from a performer so favored. Some men, apart from her familiars, may have been brought to favor—against their wills, perhaps, and only for a moment—the rights of women as Irene Vanbrugh presented them.

It's tempting to see moderate suffragists such as the Vanbrughs as hopelessly compromised, the creatures of whatever charms they possessed. But Irene Vanbrugh's choices through the height of the suffrage debate show the struggle for women's rights finding, now and then, a resourcefulness that hid itself howsoever it could.

\*    \*    \*

Lena Ashwell (c. 1871–1957) was never so eager to please. Neither did she warm to the role of Kate as much as Irene Vanbrugh did. In fact, Ashwell barely acknowledged *Look* in her autobiography as one of three plays she'd done "after closing my [1910–1911] season."[28] But whatever thanks she'd gotten from Barrie for replacing Vanbrugh on short notice, and from AFL members for her activism ongoing, it didn't help her when it came to braving two bastions of the male establishment.

She entered one of those strongholds seeking some favor from the decided anti-suffragist Sir Herbert Beerbohm Tree. She made what only later she realized was a tactical error by showing up to see Tree with a copy of W. L. Courtney's *The Soul of a Suffragette* in her hand. No sooner had she set the book down than Tree, known for his affa-bility, picked up the volume and, in her words, "with a magnificent gesture of contempt flung it into the far corner of the room."[29] He must have feared, as Irene Vanbrugh and her handlers did, that the Cause had grown too divisive to yield any dividend. Lady Tree, in the matter of suffrage, seems to have exercised a wifely reserve, attending, as she had to, to the fallout from Tree's perennially roving eye.

Ashwell never curried favor in the circles Lady Tree reached courtesy of her philanthropy. Neither did Ashwell lead Irene Vanbrugh's charmed career, perhaps because she'd been tested in ways that had left her radicalized. She'd been divorced and remarried when it wasn't common, with Langtry the stage's most conspicuous and cautionary exception. Ashwell was also heading a theatre as Tree was when she went to see him. It was in her position as manager of London's Kingsway Theatre, in fact, that she was invited to join a suffrage delegation that entered another male preserve to meet a more prominent Herbert even than Tree was . This was none other than the prime minister, the right honorable H. H. Asquith.

Ashwell's visit, in company, to 10 Downing Street came in June 1910. Days before, 10,000 suffrage supporters had marched through the streets of London in ranks two miles long.[30] They had Asquith's attention, in a way. However, the delegation's audience with him didn't go well. As Ashwell recalled it, the event

> was irresistibly comic because it was so tragic. We were just a very ordinary little group of women, received by the flunkeys as if we had a strange odour and had been temporarily released from the Zoo. We were ushered into a room where rows of chairs faced a door at the end. As we sat patiently waiting a head was thrust around the edge of the door and stared contemptuously at us; then the door was shut, but presently the other door, by which we had entered, was opened and again this hostile person surveyed us—Mrs. Asquith, the wife of the Prime Minister!

Not every lady of privilege supported suffrage.

The Prime Minister joined the assembly shortly. He spoke only "a few polite phrases" before coming to the point. He told the women that

> so long as he was Prime Minister he would give no facilities for the discussion of the [suffrage] Bill. A clear voice from the back of the room called: "Then you must be moved." With his thumbs in the armholes of his waistcoat and a spreading movement of his chest and abdomen, his head well thrown back, he said firmly, I will not say defiantly, "Move me." And, like a gentle refrain of the Litany, the deputation replied, "We will."[31]

The list of Ashwell's turns would sound a less gentle refrain than the one Asquith heard that day, and less euphonious than the one Irene Vanbrugh floated courtesy of James M. Barrie.

Ashwell gave her first turn at the Palace in October of 1911, the month before Vanbrugh gave her very first *Look* at the Hippodrome. Ashwell's appeal had never matched Vanbrugh's nor ever would. Neither did Ashwell court popularity as Vanbrugh did. She chose Alfred Sutro's caustic *The Man in the Stalls* as the vehicle for her variety debut. The play had a title that referred to the most expensive seats in theatres of the day. It had a plot that reeked of privilege, and it had a trio of upper-crust characters not to be "classed in the category of 'nice,' " as one reviewer put it.[32]

The star wasn't known for playing nice. Nor did she expect any turn to make much of a difference. Later, she included variety among the "many hateful things" she'd done to keep the Kingsway open.[33] In the way of hateful things, *The Man in the Stalls* showed intrigue among a playwright, his wife, and her lover who is also the husband's best friend. Ashwell's Betty controlled the *ménage* by being cleverer than what another critic called an "obvious fool" of a husband and the "unmitigated cad" who was the lover.[34]

The turn was one of a recent crop that showed men behaving badly and women making fun of them for it. *The Man in the Stalls* went *The Twelve-Pound Look* one better by adding a second man as foil to the star's acid-tongued character. The role was a type with which Ashwell was "quite familiar," to let her "bring out with strength and subtlety the heavier as well as the lighter phases."[35] The Arawa Maoris dropped a tincture of the exotic to be mixed into the bill with Ashwell's venom.[36]

A few months later, in late February into March of 1912, she gave two more turns treating the plight of women, and called on the playwright Cicely Hamilton for both of them. Hamilton was an actress, writer, and charter member of the Actresses' Franchise League. She'd already written *The Pageant of Great Women* and seen it staged with an all-star cast that had included Ashwell in a supporting role.[37] Ashwell had produced other plays by Hamilton at the Kingsway and liked them well enough to ransack them for a turn or two. The first cutting came from *The Constant Husband,* showing two women involved with a very inconstant man. Romantic triangles were in vogue in plays of the day, and these were written in clever and multiform variations.

Triangles were not unknown among London's smart set, either, owing somewhat to the difficulty of divorce. With gossips on the prowl, Ashwell wanted to show a certain kind of marriage as a sham that discerning women could use to suit themselves. It was clear to one critic that the star, playing Justine Ronpell, spoke for the playwright whose opinions "do not err on the side of flattery . . . making her feminine characters the more entertaining, and [giving] her pretty wit . . . full play."[38] It was left to the star, of course, to claim the prettiest wit and give it fullest play.

*The Constant Husband* shows two women unite against the philanderer. Ashwell's character tames her rival by confiding to her that

> it is not the first time that Mr. Ronpell has taken a lady to the Continent, and has written good-bye to [Justine]. . . but after a few weeks he had always returned home, amenable and affectionate, greatly to her annoyance, and to the interference of her business in Bond-street. She hopes that Mrs. Beaumont [the "other woman"] will make a permanent job of it this time, and in leaving, offers her husband's new love her cookery-book, which she declares has been alone responsible for Mr. Ronpell's previous returns.[39]

Only a few suffrage supporters were advocating that women be granted the same liberties that men had. But women were raising their voices against men for abusing what freedom they had. *The Constant Husband* sounded the same note by ridiculing the faithless man relentlessly, from its title dripping with sarcasm to Justine's stinging commentary.

Mrs. Ronpell has found her independence by managing a clothing shop on Bond Street along one of London's best-stocked retail districts. Ashwell, as manager of a theatre known for its genteel decor, made nice casting—until the window-breakers took to the streets just days into her run. Bond Street wasn't far from the Palladium where she was playing Justine. Some among the weekend crowd walked through shards of glass to catch her bill.

*The Constant Husband* drew praise before any windows were broken. But the suffragettes' action, and the virulent reaction to it, took Ashwell by surprise. She'd run up against Vanbrugh before, who'd happened to be playing *Look* when both actresses had toured turns through Glasgow. Back in London, she needed a prime attraction to compete with a bigger star in a role Ashwell had played to less acclaim.

Backing off slightly, she called on another Cicely Hamilton play. *Diana of Dobson's* had Ashwell speak "the forceful, if somewhat rough, eloquence of Diana Massingberd." It was obvious to one who'd been on hand that the star was determined "to please a popular audience" at the Palladium that stands even now, but then was in only its second year of existence.[40]

The shortened play begins in the women's dormitory of a large London clothing store. Shop girls are getting ready for bed.[41] The sight titillated some ticket holders enough to raise complaints from a few who were sitting nearby. "Some of the clever lines fall on barren ground," *Stage*'s critic reported ruefully, "because of the irresponsible tittering of those who find amusement in the undressing scenes."[42]

The sight of girls in nightclothes charged the turn's opening moments, but *Diana of Dobson's* moved quickly to matters of weight. The conditions many working-girls and workingwomen faced were so spartan that the play didn't need to take license to show that

> the shop assistant at Dobson's drapery establishment has to work and exist on five shillings a week [~$24] minus fines, and that, suddenly finding herself entitled to £300 [~$28,500], [Diana] considers herself rich beyond the dreams of avarice. She will live through one perfect hour of life, with hope enlarging all the space beyond; and, shaking the dust of Dobson's from her shabby shoes, she goes out into the world to taste its luxury, to enjoy the delights of elegant toilettes and refined society, and to feel at last that she "lives."

Diana's resolution and plain good fortune leave the other girls aghast at her "insubordination." But because she is the

> daughter of a doctor, [and] has to go out to work in consequence of the poverty of her mother[,] Diana, though she lives laborious days, has a

strong sense of humour and is quite a sport. When Miss Pringle, the manageress of Dobson's, upbraids her for the defiant attitude she has assumed, she replies, "Damn Dobson!" and down comes the curtain.[43]

The unladylike language might not have been allowed in vaudeville with Keith and Albee presiding.

The star's boldest stroke was in representing working-class women of the kind refined suffragists, and many retailers, ignored or took for granted. If the turn was intended to captivate men and some of the less worldly women and girls who would see it, it effaced images of grim-faced women, wearing drab clothing and practical shoes, carrying brickbats. Ashwell cut the turn short of ending as the full-length play did, with Diana striking fire in the heart of a young aristocrat she meets on her dream holiday in the Alps. Cicely Hamilton had written a happily-ever-after ending for Ashwell to stage at the Kingsway. The star used the shorter version to underscore Diana's independence.

Three-and-a-half years later, fully five years after appearing in *The Twelve-Pound Look* at its premiere, Ashwell revived Kate for a turn in the fall of 1915. She needed money to run her theatre under wartime measures offering incentives to theatres for showing attractions to please soldiers stationed in London or on leave there.[44] In *Look*, at the Coliseum this time, she played the workingwoman as Kate, and in her own person, by earning money to hire women for backstage- and technical jobs at the Kingsway.[45] More women went to work outside their homes with the war on, taking jobs less interesting than the ones Ashwell needed to fill with a war draining manpower.

Years later, and with votes for women won, Ashwell blamed her flair in unsympathetic roles for cutting short her time in the lime-light. The characters she'd been best at, she recalled, had been "women who were unfortunate, who had 'fallen,' and what poetry they had was well hidden."[46] Satire and social critique had taken her only so far, she felt. The end of her time as a star, with her frustration that so few of women's complaints had been redressed, kept her from claiming more credit.

But by advocating women's rights as strenuously as she did, Lena Ashwell took her support for the Cause beyond the halls of power and the dens of privilege. She always scorned variety and never changed her mind on that score. But principle kept her giving turns to earn the money she needed to put her principles into practice. Variety was never a noble or satisfying endeavor as far as she was concerned. It was the means to an end.

*   *   *

Among AFL vice presidents, Lillah McCarthy (1875–1960) fought as hard for suffrage as any. She'd come to fame by playing roles as willful heroines in plays by George Bernard Shaw. She'd played Justice, the leading role in Cicely Hamilton's suffrage extravaganza, *The Pageant of Great Women*. She'd played Kate in *The Twelve-Pound Look* after Ashwell, but before Irene Vanbrugh used variety to make the part her own. McCarthy was playing *Look* in the theatre, in fact, at the very time Vanbrugh was showing it more often, and to larger crowds, at the Coliseum.

Nearly a year before, McCarthy had played *Look* to a very small group indeed, in a much more exclusive setting. This was not what might have been expected of her, whose politics stood closer to Ashwell's than the Vanbrugh sisters' did. On the other hand, McCarthy was better connected than Ashwell or any other actress was to some of London's most powerful men. It was McCarthy's interest in a powerful man, and his in her, that carried the actresses' campaign for suffrage nearest the source of power.

At 10 Downing Street, on June 30, 1911, McCarthy acted *Look* at the earnest request of Prime Minister Asquith, heading the then-flourishing Liberal Party. He'd invited her for the pleasure of his guests of the evening, George V, crowned the week previous, and the new Queen. The command performance came just two weeks after 40,000 members of various suffrage societies had gathered in London to press Parliament to enact a measure allowing women to vote.[47] The prime minister was attending more to niceties.

He certainly knew McCarthy, and of her prominence in the Cause. He was hoping that she could help him impress the royals and appease her fellow suffragists among London's artistic crowd. Showing her off in *Look* would let him play the honest broker.

He was counting on McCarthy's friendship, at the least, who after she and Harley Granville Barker separated during the war behaved in ways that raised rumors that she was or had been Asquith's lover.[48]

Because she knew Asquith well enough to hope to influence him, she aimed to argue her case to him directly. She was like Lena Ashwell in doubting whether *The Twelve-Pound Look* could speak forcefully enough under the best of circumstances. On the other hand, if there was ever a best of circumstances, it would have been a command performance for the prime minister and royal couple.

None of the principals left an account of the evening. Years later, McCarthy recalled finding herself alone in the prime minister's office while waiting to rehearse *Look*. There, she'd seen "baskets of papers and . . . a blotting pad" among other things that were

> the austere, solid ornaments of the Prime Minister's desk. Fervour for the cause took hold of me. I felt like a Joan of Arc of the ballot-box. Martyrdom or not, the occasion must be seized. I opened a box of grease paints, took out the reddest stick I could find, and wrote across the blotting paper, "Votes for Women." I went out of the room exultant.

The thrill of her naughtiness didn't last long:

> [When] the rehearsal for which I had gone to Downing Street was over, Mr. Asquith came to me. We had tea together. He asked: "Why do you think women should have the vote?" By Heavens, I told him! I poured out arguments in no unstinted measure. He greeted them with a quizzical smile which, whilst it did not discourage me, forced me to wonder whether the weight of my arguments was as great as their volume.[49]

Her convictions, she saw, weren't going to weigh heavy with him no matter what her influence was, or her charm.

McCarthy, like Lena Ashwell, had tracked power to its lair—not that either of their efforts did much to advance the cause of suffrage in the short run. But no actress, saving Bernhardt, could have found such a golden opportunity in variety, in which the women in attendance and the women entertaining them not only couldn't vote, but had little access to those who could help them do so. Working-class men who frequented variety *did* vote. There must have been many of them who wouldn't have favored greater rights for ladies of higher rank like Lillah McCarthy, and with her, a fair portion of the membership of the Actresses' Franchise League.

By the time McCarthy played *Look* at the prime minister's beck and call, she'd done variety herself, four months earlier, in February 1911. She'd chosen a turn, or had her husband choose it for her, that hid a deeper agenda. At the Palace, opposite Granville Barker, she fleshed out a piece called "The Farewell Supper." It showed an episode from Arthur Schnitzler's full-length play *Anatol*, which was about a womanizer facing comical consequences for the abandoned life he's led. McCarthy played a bohemian dancer named Arimi, who is as promiscuous as Anatol, her sometime lover. She and Granville Barker shared a bill with Maud Allan, who was famous for dancing the head-hunting Salomé, but this time was moving to the more stately strains of Edvard Grieg's "Peer Gynt." Also on the bill was Vesta Tilley, variety's leading male impersonator, who made fun of men by imitating them in ways that weren't the highest form of flattery.

The reputation McCarthy had won in Shaw's plays left the *Times'* critic amused at the "delightful perversion" of her "most valuable stage qualities."[50] Her Arimi was loosely strung and looser-living. Another reviewer described the character's "wonderful hat and dress, [which gave her] all the charm of a fair sinner without any of the coarseness." Now and again, McCarthy would toss in "a touch of vulgarity."[51] Her wonderfully hatted Arimi drew more laughs, and more from the belly, than her celibate Kate can have raised in politer circles.

Shaw would never have lowered himself, or McCarthy, to writing a role like Arimi for her. But he would have known that sexual promiscuity was another channel suffragists explored in quest of true equality. Whatever Lillah McCarthy may have known, or thought, or done, she never lost her soft spot for masterful men.

In the same month that she and Granville Barker were cavorting their ways through *Anatol*, a suffragist named Lottie Venne played the London Hippodrome. Venne was not so well known as the AFL's vice presidents, but had performed often at organization meetings.

As a veteran of variety, she knew a thing or two about tastes there. She chose Percy Fendall's *Mrs. Justice Drake* for her latest turn. It showed what a reviewer called "one of the results of giving women the vote" in the form of a

> fantastic study in anticipation. The action is placed a few years ahead, when, for the humourous purposes of the author, there will be absolutely no men administering justice in the country.

Presiding over the utopia was

> Mrs. Justice Drake, the lady Divorce Court judge, [who] during the progress of an action for the restitution of conjugal rights, which is tried in her own drawing-room, informs the Court that she has done away with the tedious practice of listening to counsel's opening speeches, and in the particular case which she is adjudicating decides to hear the defendant's side first.

The defendant, one Mrs. Bunter, courts the judge's leniency by complaining to the court that she doesn't want to perform "wifely duties" with her husband any longer.

Having brought this euphemism to the bar, she falls to gabbing with the judge about perfumes. Mr. Bunter, meanwhile, is

> attracted to the judge, and she confessing "sorrowfully that she is a child-less widow". . . an outrageous flirtation between the two is interrupted by the entrance of Mrs. Bunter. [The wife's] abuse settles the matter, and though it has not been asked for, the lady president of the Divorce Court grants a decree *nisi* [enabling divorce], and is escorted from the Court by the delighted Bunter.[52]

The Court may have lacked the majesty of Lillah McCarthy as Justice personified in *The Pageant of Great Women*. But *Mrs. Justice Drake* was funny for being absurd. Men liked it, too, which was sel-dom a bad thing, though it may have grated on suffrage supporters when men's favor owed to the wrong reasons.

Fantastical as Lottie Venne's turn was, it called on two matters that were as dear to educated suffragists as the right to vote was: namely a woman's right to decline sexual relations with her husband, and an unmarried woman's right to invite sexual relations without losing face. The lady judge's juridical interest in "conjugal rights" gave her legal grounds to satisfy herself with Mr. Bunter should she choose. In any case, her reading of the law put sexual intimacy at her discretion as much as his, and the soon-to-be-former Mrs. Bunter's, at the wish of the court.

Pairing Mrs. Justice Drake with Mr. Bunter promised a time when sex would cease to be an obligation, or a manipulation, or a domination, or the battering that Mr. Bunter's name suggested. This dull menace couldn't keep the courtroom of *Mrs. Justice Drake* from seeming remote from power enough to free laughter. The sight of Lottie Venne, bewigged and presiding, raised laughs because men could consider it as something that never would happen, or not in that way. They were half right.

*    *    *

For all of Lillie Langtry's notoriety, her commitment to suffrage owed to a lifetime of adventure laced in with control. She'd been a theatre manager, horsewoman, and divorcée, and her not altogether painful experience had taught her the merits of equal property and handier divorce. To promote the vote as a preliminary to those and other causes, she joined her fellow AFL vice presidents in variety to support women's rights. To that end, she helped write a pro-suffrage turn she showed in her homeland. After that, she became the only league vice president to tour vaudeville, and in *two* turns that spoke to the rights of women.

She started off tamely, politically speaking. Sydney Grundy's leering *The Degenerates* had given her one of her signal successes in the theatre. For her first go at variety, in 1910, she had the piece shortened and retitled an almost prissy-sounding *The Right Sort*. Her recovering degenerate saved a friend, "an erring wife" as one critic put it, from blackmail at the hands of a "would-be betrayer."[53] Another reviewer offered, in cautious praise, that "the little serious scene between the two women [was] sincere and free from bathos" and "the comedy element . . . delightful."[54] Turns that mixed laughter with suspense promised success. Any variety crowd come to see Langtry, many of them for the first time, would have come eager for the sport she provided, in her measured way.

After opening *The Right Sort* to considerable fanfare in Birmingham, she brought it to London directly. There, she met the wrath of theatre managers in shock after Bernhardt's first turns. The managers found in the Francophilic Langtry Bernhardt's nearest image. No sooner did the star arrive at the Hippodrome than the theatre men challenged *The Right Sort* for violating a gentleman's agreement that any full-length play needed fifteen years after its premiere before being made into a turn.[55]

Under threat of legal action, as in vaudeville in 1906, Langtry revived the turn she'd shown in America.[56] *Between Nightfall and the Light* restored her to the wife who gives her life to save an erring husband. But Langtry's sacrificial lambs can't have sounded as plangent as her idol Bernhardt's did. When the Lily's audiences needed relief, they got it from Kenneth Douglas and Grace Lane among the other turns, in a sketch called *A Pair of Lunatics*. In it, a man and a woman couple meet while visiting an asylum but won't start courting until each is assured that the other is of sound mind.[57]

Langtry was shrewd to show altruism on her character's part, just as she'd done in vaudeville. Her choices may have seemed odd to many who wouldn't have seen her as a model of selflessness. On the other hand, in turns such as *The Right Sort* and *Between Nightfall and the Light* the star could suggest that even characters she played wouldn't favor their own interests as slavishly as men did.

She had stood for independence long enough to play against her reputation. Despite her basking in her currently married state, no one was going to forget her past, no matter how many obligations her characters met or hazards they faced.

Nearly a year went by before she showed her next turn. She spent some of the interim cowriting a turn with Percy Fendall, who'd written *Mrs. Justice Drake* and given it to Lottie Venne the year before. Langtry and Fendall called their play *Helping the Cause*, and she began showing it in February 1912, a few weeks before the window-smashing.

The turn's stark setting certainly challenged the star's reputation for the highlife. *Helping the Cause* also had a byzantine plot that demanded strict attention from the reviewer who wrote after its opening in Manchester:

> Lady Victoria Vanderville, a militant suffragist, is brought in for a fortnight, in default of paying a fine of five pounds [~$480] for having broken the window of a police station, at the instigation of the lady president of the "Non-Yielders" to do something, somehow and somewhere, for the good of the cause. The cold and inhospitable cell is obviously no place for a person like Lady Victoria. The hard, low bed, the iron washstand, the comfortless bench, and, worse than all, the implacable wardress, Mrs. Cross, are a contrast and an offence to the susceptibilities of the charming prisoner.

The charming one accepts

> the situation, in the spirit of the cause, and . . . lay[s] siege to the affections of the male officials. The rough handling of a policeman provides a reason for sending for the doctor to examine a bruise on her arm. Mrs. Cross is all for unsympathetic discipline, but the clash that takes place is unquestionably in favour of Lady Victoria; and so the ill-tempered wardress is forced to remain outside the cell while the doctor attends to his patient.

When Lady Victoria flirts with the young doctor, the prison warden makes his move. She recognizes him

> as Sir Martyn Mangels, with whose wife she is acquainted. Sir Martyn explains that his wife has just run away with his chauffeur. That lays him open to the wiles of his present charge . . . [and when he] invites her to dinner . . . his rival insists on being there too as the lady's medical adviser. Lady Victoria and the governor [i.e., warden] are comfortably engrossed in conversation on a couch when the acrid Mrs. Cross looks in to announce some business for the governor to attend to. This turns out to be a document from the Home Office, instructing the immediate release of Lady Victoria Vanderville.

Home Office or no Home Office, Lady Victoria decides that she wants to stay in prison in devotion to the Cause. To get rearrested, she

> commits an assault on the officials and begins to overturn the appointments of the cell, declaring herself ready to abide by the consequences. She is promptly taken charge of, her dress is changed into the prison costume, and the curtain finally falls upon her standing martyr-like . . . in her grey robe, with a halo about her head and a yard or so of oakum hanging round her neck . . . [The play,] to judge by the reception accorded to the first performance, has a successful career in view.[58]

Jail-time was made to seem like highjinks. Every warder except the battleaxe Mrs. Cross fawns over Lady Victoria, who conquers everything before her except the prison walls. And even after all that, the sight of Langtry's character standing martyr-like as the curtain fell might as well have dressed the star in sackcloth. The spectacle Lady de Bathe made, dressed in gray prison garb at the last sight, showed fashion and privilege shed for the Cause.

The turn held up nicely in Manchester, where agitation for suffrage never reached the feverish pitch it did in London. When she took *Cause* to Stoll's Coliseum the next week, the bill around her featured other distinguished attractions such as Herbert Sleath and company in a play called *The Third Degree*, and Oscar Straus conducting the Viennese Orchestra. Langtry's efforts, meanwhile, anticipated suffrage-inspired turns in plays soon to be shown elsewhere, with Lena Ashwell getting ready to show *The Constant Husband* at the Palladium and Irene Vanbrugh set to bring *The Twelve-Pound Look* into the Coliseum on Langtry's heels.

Emmeline Pankhurst, suffrage's most radical firebrand, had things on her mind other than famous actresses queuing up to support women's rights. Thinly disguised as "lady president of the 'Non-Yielders' " in *Helping the Cause*, the real Mrs. Pankhurst issued her edict that "the argument of the broken pane of glass is the most valuable argument in modern politics."[59] Then she led two of her confederates to breaking windows at 10 Downing Street. The incident shifted the terms of engagement, but not enough to shake

Langtry's confidence that her good humor and civility could crown any occasion.

At the Coliseum, she succeeded well enough. When she took the turn to the Victoria Palace across town, she didn't charm nor did her *Helping the Cause* amuse. The play's producer and AFL stalwart, Mrs. Arncliffe-Sennett, wrote of missing "the feeling of tolerance in the audience with which I had become familiar when I first produced the little play." "The window-smashing," she wrote in English understatement, "undoubtedly brought a change in the public attitude."[60]

The star was hardly known for being a non-yielder. Still, she stayed with *Cause* right through a provincial tour that lasted into July. She may have felt committed to it for having helped write it. She may have expected *Cause's* rollicking tone to count for more away from London, or hoped that audiences outside the capital might harbor greater goodwill. In any case, within a matter of weeks the window-breaking faded into memory against news of the suffragettes' fresh offenses against property and the public order.

Langtry's doggedness in the face of adversity may have surprised some. Her looks could be deceiving. She'd needed to be tough to live the life she'd led, to stand up to the censure she'd borne and still, nearing sixty, remain in position to speak to public policy, however whimsically. She was statuesque still, inscrutable as ever in her aging, ageless beauty.

\* \* \*

Only months later, in early fall of 1912, Langtry crossed the Atlantic to launch her second vaudeville tour six years after she'd shown her first turn. The agitation around British suffrage was getting coverage in the 'States, and she arrived expecting to meet with interest, if not warmth, in *Helping the Cause*. In her favor, as in the English provinces, was the fact that the backlash against suffrage never mobilized itself anywhere across America as it did in London.

Whatever concerns Langtry brought with her owed largely to the competition she expected to face. Ethel Barrymore, the biggest native star yet to join vaudeville, was set to hit the Orpheum circuit in *The Twelve-Pound Look*. Bernhardt was planning to join vaudeville at the end of the year, though not in any turn that could be linked conclusively to women's rights. With Edward VII dead, Langtry was more on her own than she'd been at any time since she'd gone on the stage. She didn't shirk the challenge.

She opened *Helping the Cause* in New York at the Colonial in September 1912. Instead of provoking audiences as the play had done in London, it bored many who saw it. *Variety* reported that at her opening, she'd drawn less than a full house. This was, it sniffed,

> barely making good for Mrs. Langtry. The theme of her present sketch, to the average New Yorker, is foreign. The militant suffragette we don't know, so much of the satire is wasted. In London, where these progressive little women do anything from incendiarism to caving in the dome of a Prime Minister, the piece was funny. . . . With the satirical side lost, it becomes merely a farce and not a good one at that for America.

The problem *Variety* found didn't lie with Langtry, *per se*:

> She's a wonder, and didn't even begin to look old alongside the Doctor who appeared about twenty-two. The company is competent. It is simply a question of drawing power with Mrs. Langtry, and it isn't likely she can maintain the even break of the early week's business at the Colonial.[61]

Her failing to break even in Manhattan, for her first half-week, didn't bode well. She was still in only her second week in *Cause* when the *Brooklyn Eagle* reported a crowd receiving the turn "coldly" at the borough's Orpheum. On the same bill, John Wade did nicely with his blackfaced, bone-sucking turn in *Marse Shelley's Chicken Dinner*. The Avon Comedy Four showed well in *The New School Teachers* with the school year just underway.[62]

Things got worse for Langtry even as other acts on her bills held to form. In Pittsburgh, in early November, she made it through only her two Monday shows before Harry Davis, who managed the Grand, announced that she'd fallen ill and wouldn't be able to fulfill her engagement for the week. Some reports had local audiences taking offense at *Helping the Cause*.[63] Other accounts had Langtry canceling her own appearances, but that seems unlikely given her attachment to the play. She may have been seeking publicity or saving face when she continued to show up at the Grand for show times, twice a day as her contract stipulated, to claim installments against the balance of the $2,500 (~$49,000) Davis owed her for the week.

In London, the version of these events that *Era* put together reads as though taken from Langtry's mouth, or one of her friends':

> Lady de Bathe (Mrs. Langtry) has received condolences from her friends in England on her "bad treatment in the States." She does not know what they mean. As a matter of fact she is having such a successful tour that Martin Beck [for the West Coast Orpheum circuit] has asked her to prolong it till the end of March.

Even this account suggested that things hadn't gone entirely well. Langtry's tour, *Era* continued,

> has not been without adventure. She "bestruck" a lunatic in Pittsburgh—a real lunatic who had been twice in a private asylum. His madness took the form of not wishing women's suffrage to be discussed in the theatre even in the burlesque manner; but as the popular actress got her salary just the same her spirits were not affected.[64]

Colorful as the tale was, events proved that Harry Davis was no lunatic. He was also London-born, and so may have taken greater umbrage at Langtry's gall.

In Cincinnati, which was her next stopover, Langtry was at the point of shifting from *Helping the Cause* into *The Test*, which was itself a retitled version of *Between Nightfall and the Light* that had been her first vaudeville turn and her second one in variety.[65] She ended by showing *Helping the Cause* in Cincinnati, but things can't have gone swimmingly there, because she changed into *The Test* the week following at the Chicago Majestic. She played *The Test* to only middling responses until February 1913. Then, on reaching the Orpheum in Los Angeles, she shifted into *Mrs. Justice Drake*, the play Lottie Venne had introduced in variety two years before.[66]

In Southern California, Langtry almost certainly would have accepted a film offer if one had come up. But films weren't ready to hire her as mistress of ceremonies, and still less as comedienne-in-chief at this point in her career. She finished out her tour playing the lady judge. Audiences in Los Angeles saw a turn loaded with what one local reviewer called "prankish situations arising from the regime of the suffragettes."[67]

Within weeks after she left vaudeville the next month, a Michigan state referendum to approve granting the vote to every American woman was rejected by a margin of more than 100,000 among the men who'd cast ballots. This came as a blow to people hoping to add an amendment for women's suffrage to the American Constitution. If the cause of American suffrage needed help, it wasn't going to get enough of it from the Jersey Lily. It wasn't for her lack of trying.

*    *    *

A few months after Langtry finished her quixotic tour, Olga Nethersole (1863–1951) entered vaudeville. She was British, but her reputation was, like Langtry's, greater in the 'States than in Britain. Nethersole's greatest success had come in 1900, when she'd played the temptress in an American adaptation of the soft-pornish French novel *Sapho*, by Alphonse Daudet. The dramatized version had the star laying leechlike "Nethersole kisses" on the leading man on her way to becoming "the most notorious actress on the American stage." For playing Sapho—a picture of tortured heterosexuality as opposed to her Greek namesake from the Isle of Lesbos—Nethersole was charged with public lewdness in New York and acquitted after a sensational show trial.[68] After that, she carried on in *Sapho* to packed houses for another six weeks.

Thirteen years after the *cause célèbre* that was *Sapho*, Nethersole used a cutting from that play to begin her only vaudeville tour. Her turn cooled the piece down, avoiding its raciest moments and all Nethersole kisses. This helped sanitize an excerpt that showed the title character banish her wastrel of a husband for refusing to accept her child by a former lover. Sapho (a.k.a. Fanny Legrand) ends by choosing the child and motherhood over the man and her marriage, such as it is. The turn would have seemed wrenching but responsible to all but a few looking on.

Opening night for the tabloid *Sapho* came in New York at the Palace in early October 1913. Things went far better for Nethersole than they had for Langtry in *Cause* the year before. *Sapho*'s first-night audience called the star in front of the curtain fourteen times. Their enthusiasm exceeded what the more familiar acts on the bill got, including Nethersole's countryman Harry Tate's with his walkabout in *Motoring*, and two "club maniacs" named Lynch and Zeller, who'd just added an electrified rubber chicken to their juggling act.[69]

Nethersole's thunderous reception in *Sapho* may have emboldened her. At Keith's Philadelphia for her third week on tour, she introduced *The Last Scene of the Play*, based on a recent English novel treating divorce. The star wanted to alternate the piece with *Sapho*, something the way Bernhardt had done, more lavishly, by shifting among six turns the year before. In vaudeville, where "more" generally meant "better," actresses who couldn't show as many turns as Bernhardt did could make up for it, as Nethersole did, by chewing the scenery.

*The Last Scene of the Play* cast the mid-fortyish star as a young bride, shades of Langtry in *The Test/Between Nightfall and the Light*. But Nethersole's strenuous blushing didn't carry far into the turn before her character discovered, on her wedding night, that her husband has detectives hot on his trail for murdering his previous wife. After some hair-raising complications, the bride kills the man for what Jessie Millward called "entirely excellent reasons" in the similar turn she'd shown two seasons before.[70] In *The Last Scene of the Play*, reasons for killing the husband were excellent enough to leave a London reporter praising the piece for being "a vital argument in favour of a repeal of the English divorce laws."[71]

Vital or not, or too narrowly English, again, *The Last Scene of the Play* won little favor in the 'States. Nellie Revell, in the *New York Telegraph*, called it "tedious" for giving the villain more than the star's character had to do.[72] Another critic, for the *New York Review*, reported that an audience at the Colonial had hissed the turn. The "English Militant Suffragette" author was to blame, the *Review* suggested, for trying to "excuse wife murder."[73] This made a curious phrase to apply to an outcome that had Nethersole's character taking a *husband's* life.

There was a bit of levity on the bills to balance the hysteria Nethersole was laying on. In Boston, as she shifted between *Sapho* and *The Last Scene*, she shared bills with two up-and-comers, including Sophie Tucker, famous later as "The Last of the Red-Hot Mamas," and young Buster Keaton of the Three Keatons, in a sketch that had him getting buffeted, all in fun, between his veteran-vaudevillian parents.[74]

It would have taken a stretch of the imagination for Nethersole to claim that reactions to *The Last Scene of the Play* were misogynist. Vaudeville crowds were known to applaud women performers for mentioning their divorces onstage, or for saying that marriage was not a bed of roses.[75] *The Last Scene of the Play* was entirely unfunny, however, and its jarring ending brought a sharper outcry than Langtry had raised in *Cause*. Audiences took Nethersole's second turn as badly as they'd taken Jessie Millward's heroine using poison as a last resort. For some who caught Nethersole in *The Last Scene*, the reasons could never have been excellent enough to justify a woman's murderous act, even in the realm of make-believe.

It may be that the applause Nethersole raised in *Sapho* everywhere she went made reactions to her other turn easier to bear. Perhaps the polar responses she faced convinced her to keep challenging groups she thought needed it. This would have been un-star-like of her, but she was ready to stop feeding the beast.

Indeed, the hostility that *The Last Scene of the Play* aroused brought out the star's combativeness. With members of the press, she criticized Americans for being troubled by third-hand, and as it seemed to her, biased accounts of the suffragettes. Speaking to the *New York Times*, Nethersole wasn't joking when she said that "women could come off victors in a battle with the entire English Army if they were trained."[76] She criticized the United States' government for threatening to bar Emmeline Pankhurst from the country. Nethersole recounted a conversation she'd had with Pankhurst herself, who'd told her that "the militant methods are not suffrage . . . they are politics."

Nethersole took this as gospel. She told the *Times* how "wonderful" it was that during all the unpleasantness around suffrage, "the militants have never killed a single person." "They are the only ones who have suffered," she noted indignantly. "It is quite different" in America, where, she said,

> The women are treated differently, and they are going to get the vote, but in England they must fight for it. You do not know about many of our laws, you do not know about the inequality of our divorce laws. A woman may not get a divorce for what a man may divorce his wife without opposition. I am on the Divorce Reform Committee in England, and how could I help being a suffragist?[77]

The notion that suffrage supporters were the only ones to have suffered repeated an argument British suffragists were using to praise their countrywomen who'd been jailed and then force-fed when they'd gone on hunger strikes. One wonders how common what now would be called eating disorders were among the most zealous of suffrage's partisans, or how much force-feeding resembled torture.

To ennoble the martyrs, Nethersole spoke with the kind of right-eousness that had set teeth on edge in her homeland. Statements like hers left American suffragists impressed, stars and all, at the depth of their British sisters' resolve. This still wasn't enough to keep all but a few American women, in show business and outside it, from avoiding fury when they could. American stars, in the way of Irene Vanbrugh, would compromise when it came to choosing what to show and how to show it—not like Olga Nethersole in *The Last Scene of the Play*.

\* \* \*

Before the war, it would have been hard for American men to see suffering among the groups most invested in suffrage, leaving aside the working poor, with many women among them who didn't have time to agitate. One suffragette, fresh from an English prison, painted a blooming picture of the lives American women led from their having "free access to the State and Federal legislatures" and being welcomed "with courtesy and open arms." "They hold street meetings unmolested," which was a marvel, "and sell their papers as they like."[78] Sarah Bernhardt, on tour across America in the early

1890s, had been surprised at seeing that "Woman reigns and reigns . . . absolutely." Even the most ordinary American woman, she thought, "orders, wills, exacts, instructs, spends money recklessly, and gives no thanks."[79] Shopping had become one of the ultimate American exercises in self-expression, and was more likely to be so among citizens who couldn't vote.

Materialism was near to the heart of the independence Bernhardt couldn't help but admire. For Americans, who you were and what you could become were marked, with little apology, by how you spent your money. Having more money was a good thing, of course, and acquisitiveness gripped women and men alike. Typically, however, suffragists stateside aimed to be as "attractive, stylish, charming, dignified, and . . . personable, likable, and modern" as they could be.[80] There was plenty of money to go around, or so it seemed. The prospect of a material heaven lifted some of the resentment the Pankhursts had tapped in London.

In variety, Irene Vanbrugh's plain-jane costume in *The Twelve-Pound Look*, and Lillie Langtry's prison dress to end *Helping the Cause*, had been exceptions to the rule. The Lily, with Mrs. Patrick Campbell, stood foremost among British stars in using "modishness as a necessary weapon . . . to fight caricatures of the hammer-wielding suffragette."[81] But there was the same class division in Britain's suffrage movement as there was across the society as a whole. Variety moderated class-differences somewhat. There, star turns didn't allow the actresses time to change from one dazzling outfit into the next. On the other hand, British stars didn't need to struggle to find gowns to push the hammer-wielders into the shade.

Nor was it simply that more American suffrage supporters were fixed on worldly goods. Many women's enthusiasm for the material world blurred lines that were more clearly marked in Britain, "between political and consumer-oriented means of self-realization."[82] Softer definitions of "self-made" made it easier for American women to believe, or hope, that any of their gender could be as stylish, or nearly so, as the most stylish among them. Self-realization, it was understood, made its own statement, political *and* material, not necessarily in that order. In America, Kate Sims's simple frock would look less like a fall in class and more like an expression of rugged individualism.

By the time Ethel Barrymore (1879–1959) came to *The Twelve-Pound Look*, she'd been a fashion-plate for a decade. At her first stardom, she'd epitomized the "Gibson Girl," corseted but athletic, with thick golden hair piled high in the glossy images abundant in American advertising at the beginning of the last century. Ethel was her father's daughter, too, with a refined diction to go with her boarding-school graces. Raised in a family of rabid Anglophiles, she was one of the few Americans to have reached the London stage, and an even fewer invited to the most fashionable gatherings there, and the only one courted by Laurence Irving—pioneer in variety with as great a name in his country as she would help make "Barrymore" in hers—and by the budding politician and, even as a young man, tireless guardian of empire, Winston Churchill.

By 1910, according to one of her contemporary activists, Ethel had moved into the American suffrage movement's front ranks. She "made the theatre work for us," as Harriot Stanton Blatch wrote in recalling Barrymore's acting in three plays by the British actress and suffragist Beatrice Forbes-Robertson.[83] A year later, in the theatre, Barrymore played Kate Sims for Charles Frohman, who had the nearest thing to an artistic conscience among his famously crass partners in the Theatrical Syndicate. For American suffragist actresses, it was true, there was no organization like the Actresses' Franchise League. But Barrymore commanded respect for being one of suffrage's most estimable and glamorous spokeswomen.

She entered vaudeville in the fall of 1912 as someone who, by anyone's standard, had been a staunch suffragist. However, as was well known, her youth in a stage-family had been turbulent. Perhaps in consequence, she held stardom at least as close to her heart as she did suffrage itself. Her towering fame demanded that she play only sympathetic roles, *pace* Lena Ashwell.

By summer of 1912, several lackluster engagements for the Syndicate had shrunk her fee. Marriage and motherhood, both fairly recent, were straining her finances. It couldn't hurt, she knew, to show Frohman, his partners, and her fans that she could remain the star while being a model mother and wife. She was looking to vaudeville to restore her fortunes as it had restored her father's, for a time.[84]

To navigate the storm her entering vaudeville was certain to cause, and the controversy that suffrage had raised already, Barrymore honed in on domesticity. Just as she joined vaudeville, facing a long stretch on the road playing the solitary Kate, she spoke of the difficulty of leaving her home and the first two of her children. Still, she'd decided, "when a manager [read 'Charles Frohman'] tells me I must play in something that is palpably a weak play I can refuse."[85]

Not that she refused often. She'd built her stardom by declining, demurely, to marry young. She had her chances, of course, with squads of bachelors beating a path to her door during and after her gadabout stay in London. But evenings when beaus could take her out on the town were scarce from her doing the work that she did. She stayed one of America's highest-earning and most marriageable young women through her twenties.

In 1909, at last, she chose Russell Griswold Colt to be her husband, who was heir-apparent to a fortune in rubber. The marriage was troubled from the start, and she later claimed that he had never supported her or the children. Eventually, at her divorce trial, she testified that Colt was beating her within weeks after the wedding, as she remembered her father doing in the weeks, at the least, before he'd been institutionalized.[86] Vaudeville promised to give Barrymore not only freedom of sorts from Frohman, but relief from Colt so long as she stayed away from New York. Whatever demands that giving turns imposed on her, they may have seemed more manageable than her husband was, waiting at home.

She'd done well enough in *Look* onstage to have no hesitation in choosing it for her maiden turn. Like Irene Vanbrugh, she'd had success in several Barrie plays, and for that reason she might have expected free choice to any of his works. But instead of appealing to the avuncular playwright as Vanbrugh had done in London, Barrymore, in New York, had to petition Frohman himself, who owned the rights to *Look*. She remembered that he'd had "no suitable play for me" at the time, "and I, as usual, had no suitable income."[87] Frohman, as chance would have it, wasn't only her producer and Barrie's in America, but the one who had footed the bills for opening *Look* in London two years since.

Barrymore remembered Frohman's throwing up "his hands in horror" at her request to take *Look* into vaudeville.[88] Once over the shock, he insisted that she take *Look* only onto western circuits, far from his stronghold in New York City and Keith and Albee's evermore worrisome dominion there.[89] Whatever independence she found was granted under conditions laid down by Frohman, and in the necessity she found from her husband's inability or refusal to support the children. This scarcely founded her first turns in the generosity of the three courtly men who'd squired Irene Vanbrugh into variety.

When Barrymore had played *The Twelve-Pound Look* in the theatre, one New York critic saw her letting go the "pretty personality" roles in favor of striving onward and upward to the "drama of importance[90] (see figure 7). In vaudeville, she wanted to convey importance to the widest audiences to be had in the years just before feature films took hold. To be practical, she always had printed programs specify that £12 was equivalent to $60. Doing this served less worldly viewers well, especially the women flocking to Barrymore's daily matinees. They may have taken little interest in rates of exchange, but a keen one in whether their work could be rewarded, and if not, whether it was valued, and if so, how. The warmth she felt prompted Barrymore to conclude that *Look* settled better on vaudeville crowds than it had in the theatre.[91]

It wasn't only warmth the star was craving. Her first venture into vaudeville paid her $3,000 a week, equivalent to what now would be about $59,000. This made a salary to tie the record for stage stars set several years before by an aging matinee idol named James K. Hackett. Barrymore's weekly fee was four times what her father had made from vaudeville at his peak. It was fifty times more than the money it took Kate months to earn before leaving the future Sir Harry with the one curt note.

It was fitting when other hardworking women joined Barrymore on the bills. At the Chicago Majestic, where she gave her very first turn, she watched among the other acts, the dancer Ida Fuller's showing "poetic illusions and [living] pictures most resplendently illuminated."[92] Fuller's exertions may have left her perspiring more than Barrymore did with temperatures in Chicago hovering in the nineties during daylight hours. To meet vaudeville's demand for dispatch, and its customers' need for beverage and relief, Barrymore

**Figure 7** Ethel Barrymore in James M. Barrie's *The Twelve-Pound Look*. Barrymore, in her expression and her squaring herself toward the camera, shows the transparency she used to make her roles seem as one with herself. (Special Collections Library, University of Michigan; *Theatre Magazine* [New York], April 1911.)

trimmed six minutes, or nearly one-fifth from what had been *Look*'s running time in the theatre.[93]

Just as she opened in Chicago, the Woman Suffrage Party of Greater New York was giving a collective turn at Hammerstein's Victoria near Times Square. *Variety* met the event with sneers. "It's some stunt," its writer judged, "getting nice women who think they are brainy because they are nervy, to exhibit themselves before people who pay for the privilege of looking at them. 'The Suffrage Week' is some 'freak act,' without a shadow of a doubt."[94]

Barrymore wasn't going to stand for anyone calling hers a freak act. In vaudeville, she was planning to work her way back to New York, building demand into Manhattan, where lay the promised land for stars in every venue. It was also the chief proving ground for suffragists such as herself.

She'd tested Manhattan vaudeville briefly, when she'd made a stop in *Look* in January 1913 at the Colonial. Whatever responses she'd gotten then, or lacked, hadn't put enough distance between herself and standard turns like Reine Davies' as "The American Girl," and the corpulent Maggie Cline's as "The Irish Queen of Song."[95] And even the hearty support hadn't let Barrymore's bill draw as well as the headliner Eva Tanguay's had the week before. Tanguay was a Canadian-born star with a hyperactive style that left vaudeville audiences aquiver. Known as the "The I-Don't-Care Girl," she did songs like her most feverish one, "I Want Someone to Go Wild with Me." Wild or not, she nursed a grudge against Barrymore and carried it on in public to the stars' mutual gain. Only the next year, Tanguay would play the Palace to prove that she could outdraw Barrymore there as she'd done at the Colonial.[96]

On Barrymore's Colonial bill, it was Reine Davies who wowed crowds with insistently wholesome tunes like "Everybody Loves Somebody in Some Place, Some Time," "Shush," and "Let's Razoo on Our Kazoo," throwing kazoos to the audience so they could join in on the choruses. Davies finished strong, singing in stage-rain wearing wet-weather gear to reiterate the "Reine" in her name.[97] Still, generally speaking, personalities like Tanguay and the all-American Reine Davies learned to shift for themselves for lacking written characters like the ones in which the drama queens flourished.

By the time Barrymore reached the newly opened Palace in New York in late April 1913, she'd been touring *Look* for more than seven months. For the sake of novelty, perhaps, she dropped Barrie's play in favor of American writer Richard Harding Davis's *Miss Civilization*. She may have gotten tired of the merely polite reception *Look* had gotten often in the hinterlands even before she'd brought it to the Colonial. In *Miss Civilization*, in a classic melodramatic way, a wealthy socialite protects her invalid mother from thieves on the rampage.

The negligée Barrymore wore let her hide a pregnancy still in its early stages when she reached the Palace. What then was known as her delicate condition would have given her another reason to set *Look* aside, with its costume that showed a more revealing line. Pregnancy then, for women of means, called for confinement. The star would have been judged harshly for not acceding to custom, then measured in months.

Barrymore may have had another reason for replacing *Look*. She would have known that Langtry and Nethersole had tested turns that referred to women's rights and incensed their viewerships in so doing. Whether Frohman shared the antagonism suffrage had raised, or suspected that its novelty was dwindling, he reversed himself to let Barrymore show *Look* at the Colonial.

At the Palace, to the good, *Miss Civilization* had suspense to recommend it. It gave Barrymore another paragon to play, who was easier to read than Kate was with her ironies and shades of gray. Accordingly, for the first of her many visits to the Palace, on a mission to restore her quotient of sympathy, *Miss Civilization* brimmed with a rectitude that allowed laughs at nothing except the robbers' ineptitude.

There was more of the feeling of crusade in *Miss Civilization* than in *Look*. Before taking *Look* into vaudeville, Barrymore showed something other than humility when she said that showing it outside New York would provide a "lesson" that "should be seen in that part of the country."[98] *Miss Civilization* showed a clearer lesson with its family-first outcome, and a more stylish and less fully clad heroine as the instructor. *Miss Civilization* gave the star another character who found strength that surprised herself. Even so, after guarding home, hearth, and mother, the heroine was shown fainting as the curtain fell.

For all its good points, the turn put off one critic who accused Barrymore of "deserting" *The Twelve-Pound Look*. He (or, in fairness, though far less likely, she) faulted the playwright Davis for writing "down to the level of his variety audiences." "The result" the reviewer continued, was "a crook playlet of absurd action, trite dialogue and time-worn comedy incidents."[99] The derivative qualities of *Miss Civilization* didn't serve it well against more splashy attractions such as the warp-speed "Pavement Patter" between J. Francis Dooley and Corinne Sales, and a singing trapeze act from Mademoiselle Mars,[100] assisted by two sisters while she wore what *Variety* called, in fractured hyperbole, "a pair of tights that could have been heard a block away."[101]

In late summer, after delivering her third child, Barrymore had an unusually short convalescence. She acted in one play and then another one in short order, and made little impact. She rejoined vaudeville in *Look*, showing it only briefly on a pass through the Palace in August 1914 before taking to the road with a turn called *Drifted Apart*.[102]

Written by Sir Charles Young in the 1880s, the star's latest offering was stodgier than *The Twelve-Pound Look* or *Miss Civilization*. Barrymore played a middle-aged society woman who reconciles with her estranged husband by sharing memories of their baby who'd died long ago. Perhaps it was the same critic who'd trashed *Miss Civilization* the previous spring who noted that the words "little angel feet" had been lofted across the footlights more than once.[103]

Such weepiness left *Drifted Apart* ripe for Jack Wilson's blackfaced turn that travestied other acts on the bill.[104] It's not recorded whether Wilson made fun of Barrymore. If he did, he was relying on his blackface, backing and shuffling as he went, to make his barbs inoffensive by claiming the license that ignorance allowed.

The star had her reputation to buffer her against the Jack Wilsons of the world. More important over the long term were her skill and tact. In vaudeville, having hoisted the flag for motherhood and building the nest-egg for her last childbirth, Barrymore followed the happily divorced Kate with a mother-loving crime fighter in

*Miss Civilization* and the still grieving mother and marriage-saving wife of *Drifted Apart*. As American suffragists joined British ones on the defensive, Barrymore joined Irene Vanbrugh, Lillie Langtry, and even the fractious Lena Ashwell in gravitating toward reassuring prototypes. The stars' rear-guard action blunted some of the resentment against the suffrage movement on both sides of the Atlantic.

Barrymore stayed true to the Cause, in her fashion. She deflected criticism of herself and of suffrage, and she exercised quiet influence away from the molten center of controversy. As suffrage's most vigorous proponents came under attack, the star found characters of growing vulnerability. Such were the demands of a kind of stardom like Langtry's, only more sterling. The ideal goodness that Ethel Barrymore aimed to project elevated her beyond any single character or set of characters she could have played.

\* \* \*

The war pushed votes for women into the background. Ethel Barrymore continued to do well enough in films and the theatre. In 1915, a German U-boat took Charles Frohman and the *Lusitania* down off the Irish coast, though not before he'd stopped casting Barrymore regularly. In March 1921, the month Warren G. Harding was inaugurated the first American president elected by women with men, Barrymore's last separation from Russell Colt made the news. Three months later, she went straight from a theatrical engagement with her brother John into *The Twelve-Pound Look*, first at the Palace and then along the eastern seaboard. The play had lost almost all of its topical bite by this time, and reports of her failed marriage left *Look* seeming like a tidier version of her life.

Two years later, within days after her divorce was granted, one reporter caught her "nervous and upset and not nearly herself" in her latest *Look* at the Palace. She'd "jerked the lines out with an acceleration of tempo," and had rushed through the dialogue "in a manner foreign to her usual delivery." Hawthorne and Cooke, billed as "old wheezer and hokum," followed her and dared to kid "some of the lines she had previously spoken." "Respect for Miss Barrymore," the reporter stated gallantly, "should have been reason enough to have desisted."[105]

Even the finest performer can have an off night or a miserable matinee. Whatever was bothering Barrymore didn't affect her long, or not in such a way as to be noticed. *Variety* reported her Kate making "a seasonal appearance at the Palace . . .[that] will serve for seasons to come."[106] This prediction, made in 1923, was borne out.

Barrymore toured *Look* for another eleven years, usually during the summer when only a few theatres stayed open or after she'd finished a film. In 1927, with her nearing fifty, the painter Nicholas de Vadasz saw a quality in her that he found "wonderfully beautiful." "Love and suffering," he wrote, "have etched their beauty on her face."[107] What became her annual pilgrimage in *Look* had her play a divorcée more humble than any star could ever be. The character drew sympathy more evenly along the demographic than it had at the bitter height of the suffrage campaign.

Through the rest of the 1920s, Barrymore used *Look* to show audiences her own scrimping in times of plenty. In her dressing room at the Palace in 1923, she was seen reading a book called *Writing for Vaudeville*, in hopes of hammering out a turn for herself, royalty-free.[108] She never took the step but knew others who had, including her aunt, Mrs. Sidney (Gladys Rankin) Drew, who'd written and staged turns featuring other family members and herself. Also in 1923, Barrymore joined Albee's house union, the National Vaudeville Artists. She'd stayed in Albee's good graces even after helping found the bumptious union for stage actors, called Actors' Equity Association (AEA). The AEA quickly took to denouncing vaudeville for monopolizing in ways that hampered the livelihoods not only of its membership but of the regular vaudevillians, too, whom it was hoping to recruit.[109]

In 1924, Barrymore campaigned for the rock-ribbed Republican Calvin Coolidge for president. He was more likely, she said, to foster an economy that would build audiences of every kind.[110] Coolidge won the election, but the boom-times didn't last. His successor, Herbert Hoover, during his campaign for a second term, couldn't deny the stark look America had taken on. In the early 1930s, with the nation in the depths of the Depression, *Look* showed Barrymore playing a character whose thrift seemed more steadying than ever.

It's curious that an actress who never shed her upper-crust mannerisms, nor ever wanted to, should have seemed so salt-of-the-earth in vaudeville. She toured *The Twelve-Pound Look* as a vaudeville turn until 1933, and followed this with her single variety engagement, likewise in *Look*, in London in 1934. Writing twenty years later as an old woman, she called Barrie's play "a lifesaver."[111]

Eventually films took vaudeville's place as her lifesaver. Reunited with her brothers in Hollywood, Ethel, with Lionel and their younger brother John, made a second generation of Barrymores whose careers took some of the same careening turns their father's had. Among Maurice Barrymore's children, Ethel was most like him in using vaudeville and *The Twelve-Pound Look*, as he'd used vaudeville and *A Man of the World*, as a hedge against the future.

In Britain before the war, *Look* was seen in both the theatre and variety.[112] During the war, Lena Ashwell played Kate as a woman serving the national good by replacing a man gone to fight. The Actresses' Franchise League stayed active, but lowered its profile in respect to the war to end all wars. Still, *Look* was the only play AFL members showed both to men in uniform and to suffrage groups.[113] In the early 1920s, amateur companies used *Look* to help organize the British Labour Party as successor to Asquith's vanquished Liberals.[114] Through it all, the former Kate Sims was brought to life by a string of actresses, not all of them stars, who played her to the moment.

In America, *Look* helped Ethel Barrymore through some of the rougher seasons in her life. The typewriter her Kate lugged suited Americans' passion for efficiency. The character's hopefulness stood against whatever was blighting the land.

In the August of 1914, just as Barry's daughter was shooting twelve-pound looks at her latest Sir Harry, a war was breaking out in Europe. The destruction would reach a scale previously unknown and undreamed of which beggared whatever violence women's suffrage had wrought. During the war, stars—more women than men, for different reasons this time—would shine as patriots, arbiters, memory artists, death specialists, and peacemakers. The same services gave stars the best way, sometimes the only one, of keeping themselves in a light that could grow too bright to be borne.

# 5. War and Peace, 1914–1918 ❧

*War and bloodshed will find no place in the twentieth-century drama, as
before long they will find none on the stage of the civilized world.*

H. Potter, "The Drama of the Twentieth Century" (1900)[1]

Not fond hopes or dire prophecies could keep the Great War
from being declared in solemn, leaden increments in the
late summer of 1914. The warring parties didn't begin to
feel the consequences until fall. The lag-time was longer in the
'States, which stayed neutral for the next two-and-a-half years and
partly protected thereafter from the slaughter in Europe, and on a
lesser scale in the Near- and Middle East, and in Africa.

After caucusing during the war's early months, British suffragettes
joined suffragists to stand behind the fighting men. By spring of
1915, Emmeline Pankhurst, the sternest suffragette of them all, was
urging every countrywoman to support the troops and sailors. In
what for her was a departure, she made her

> debut as a star turn at the London Pavilion on Monday night [March 8,
> 1915], where she was heartily welcomed by a large audience, among
> which were many of her supporters. At the back of the stage from which
> she had so often preached lawlessness was hung a large Union Jack, and
> never have Union Jack and sentiments been pressed home with such
> charm and eloquence.

Lest anyone mistake her intentions,

> the Suffragist leader paid a kindly tribute to the "courteous management
> of this hall," and praised the Government. She enlarged on the part that
> women were playing in this war, sending forth their sons and brothers

and husbands and sweethearts. We had no use, she said, for the peace-at-any-price party, who talked about internationalism, when nationalism was the only thing possible in such a crisis as we were passing through. The inspiring address was punctuated with applause, and the lecturer was several times recalled.[2]

Calling Pankhurst "suffragist" was *Era's* way of commending a forcefulness that finally spoke to the nation. She'd never been a peace-at-any-price kind of girl.

Like Mrs. Pankhurst, star actresses took several months to find their footing. Once they did, they stepped into war- and peace turns far more often than male stars did. Wartime offerings from leading British actresses treated more topics related to war, and more subjects besides. The actresses' nearest male counterparts were past fighting age, in part because it took longer to make a star then, before film stardom came along. The men's distance from combat didn't keep their turns from offering a taste of battle now and again.

America's neutrality allowed for reflection, with some of it done in public where more entertainments than ever were lining the thoroughfares. Whether diversions brought clarity to public debate was another matter. However, no sooner did American films hunker down in Hollywood, as they did in virtual lockstep with the war, than it was as if the cinema had dragged the standard for celebrity across the continent with it. British stars turned up in Hollywood then as now. But during the war and owing no small part to it, Hollywood rose largely unchallenged by any film industry abroad. More and more American actors of stature who could choose, chose films.

British stars, lacking a Hollywood of their own and caught up in the war as American actors never were, joined variety in record numbers. Sir Herbert Beerbohm Tree was one of them, though for a single time only when he toured a turn in *Trilby.* It had the virtue of nearly twenty years' aging and so was decked in nostalgia and escape.[3] Not long after Tree's tabloid *Trilby,* he repaired to Hollywood to pose for the camera. He waited out most of the rest of the war not there, though on American soil.

Before and after Tree crossed the Atlantic, stars on the home front gave turns to show the flag. It was the rare star, generally a younger, second-rank one, who would actually wear a uniform in battle, even when he wanted to, or said he did. The crop of young men culled from stages across Britain left older actors, men and more and more women the longer the war lasted, to carry on.

Vaudeville's boom times were to end during the war. This mirrored variety's flattening trajectory, though that was easier to blame on the war. But while vaudeville saw the nearly complete absence of substantial dramatic actors to respond to the war, even after the United States ended its neutrality, variety paraded top-of-the-line dramatic actors together with the usual light fare—to uphold God, country, and empire. Actors, along with every other British subject not to enlist, had no choice other than to join the war effort if they wanted to be spared the shame of not going to fight.

*   *   *

Lewis Waller (1860–1915) still had an electrifying voice and bedroom eyes when he arrived at the Empire on Leicester Square. He'd always liked playing the hero, and his relish stood him in good stead early on. He recited as powerfully as he'd been known to do for the week that began on Monday, August 17, 1914, less than a fortnight after Britain had declared war on the Germans. Waller was making his first appearance in his homeland in three years. Audiences were glad to see him at this juncture.

Each of his first three selections was by Rudyard Kipling: "Snarleyow," which was gory, "If," which was contemplative, and the "Ballad of the *Clampherdown*" about a British naval triumph. Waller then finished big with his patriotic warhorse, the St. Crispin's Day speech from Shakespeare's *Henry V*. The piece has King Harry sending his men into battle with these ringing words: ". . . [A]nd gentlemen in England now abed / Shall think themselves accursed they were not here, / And hold their manhoods cheap whiles any speaks / That fought with us upon Saint Crispin's day."[4] Holding manhoods cheap called up a disquiet that only bold shows could dispel. Waller was manliness personified, even if he was too old to fight.

He joined others on a bill to exalt armed might on the side of right. A rendition of the "National Anthem of the Allies" brought patrons to their feet, while the newsreel included a

> fine series of pictures of "Fighting Ships of all Nations," and "Boys of the
> Bulldog Breed." Some excellent films of the French fleet in the
> Mediterranean have now been added; and, as regards War news, it is
> worth recording that the important telegram announcing the safe land-
> ing of British troops upon French soil was thrown upon the screen on
> Monday evening with a rapidity which would have done credit to
> [London's] Fleet Street [hub of British journalism].[5]

The war effort was turning the nation into more of a garrison than
maintaining an empire had ever done.

With Waller's fellow Britons mired in the present, he showed how
ensconced he was in the past. His cutting from *Henry V* called France
the enemy, instead of the ally it was about to become. His robustious
style was as quaint as it was inspirational. Nearly twenty years before,
George Bernard Shaw had been aghast at Waller's shameless acting of
Hotspur, a volatile character as written by Shakespeare in *Henry IV,
Part One* that Waller kicked up another notch, or three. "Some of the
things he did," Shaw wrote,

> were astonishing in an actor of his rank. At the end of each of his first
> vehement speeches, he strode right down the stage and across to the
> prompt[-er's box] side of the proscenium on the frankest barnstorming
> principles, repeating this absurd "cross"—a well-known convention . . .
> for catching applause—three times, step for step, without a pretense of
> any dramatic motive.[6]

Subtlety had never been Waller's virtue. War did nothing to tease it
out of him.

The thrills that were his gift to supply were as endearing as ever.
He would have kept thrilling crowds if he'd lived beyond the next
year. Sad to say, he died from a chill he caught while playing golf
along the windy shores of the sceptered isle. In early wartime,
though, his town-crier style struck a chord. Kipling was only in his
forties at the time and had been a Nobel laureate since 1907. But
with Lewis Waller's unwitting assistance, the Bard of Empire was
replaced quickly and for the duration by the Elizabethan Bard.
Shakespeare emerged, again, as the poet of heroism, and what proved
evermore important as time went on, of escape.

The week after Waller departed the Empire came good news: the British cruiser *Highflyer* had sunk the *Kaiser Wilhelm der Grosse* off the western coast of Africa. The reaction in variety made it seem as if the *Clampherdown* had been refitted as a ship of the line. Godfrey Tearle, later a film actor of note, recited C. E. Burton's "Mother of Nations" at the head of a "picturesque grouping of representatives of the Allies" for a turn at the Alhambra.[7] Just around the corner, the Empire featured a panoramic ballet called *Europe* to take Lewis Waller's place on the bill.

Variety, facing being blacked out as an early measure of austerity, leaped to sponsor war-related charities. Oswald Stoll offered to make his spacious Coliseum available

to the Lord Mayor [of London] . . . free of charge on an occasion suitable for the Prime Minister's address to London and the country. Accommodations would be increased to 5,000 and if an admission fee of 10s. [shillings; about $47 in the early twenty-first century] or more per head were made in aid of the Prince of Wales's Fund a handsome contribution would be realised.[8]

The Lord Mayor and the prime minister, on behalf of the Prince of Wales, chose not to accept Stoll's offer. Godfrey Tearle and other young actors soon enlisted. Even so, in late November there were still enough men on hand to fill out turns like *The Enemy* and *Saved By the British*. Another piece called *The Slacker* may have hit home for young men not yet in uniform. All three plays opened on the same day, Monday, November 30, 1914, at second-tier variety houses around London.[9]

A month before, in late October, H. B. Irving (1870–1919) had begun a variety tour in Manchester at that city's Palace. Brother of Laurence Irving, variety pioneer, this Harry was elder son of Sir Henry Irving, who had not only been the first actor to be knighted but was also among the most eminent of Victorians. The first audiences to catch H. B.'s turn would have been sobered by news of the sinkings of British dreadnought *Audacious* off Ireland, and of His Majesty's cruiser, *Hermes*, more alarmingly, in the Straits of Dover.

Irving stepped in with a turn that dramatized a story by Sir Arthur Conan Doyle, creator of Sherlock Holmes. *A Story of Waterloo* gave

Irving no hawkeyed detective to play, or some fearless hero, but the failing, senescent Corporal Brewster. Recalling his exploits during the Napoleonic Wars, the character hearkens back to his

> heroic dash through the enemy lines to bring the powder for the Guards [which] comes as an inspiration with force and appeal to every British young man whose ambition is to serve his King and Country. The story is too well known to repeat here, but the realistic manner in which Mr. H. B. Irving plays his father's famous role of the old man is a triumph of the actor's art.

Irving showed a quavering study in pathos, who,

> as he shuffles across the room to the window to watch the regiment pass, with the band playing tunefully . . . draws himself up with soldierly dignity, and shoulders his walking-stick as though he were again handling his rifle, only the next moment to totter and be supported by his grand-niece. . . . Then comes the final call as he sits almost helpless, and with a supreme effort he rallies and calls out "The Guards want powder. Then damn me they shall have it," falling back into the chair dead.[10]

The enemies at Waterloo were again, of course, the French. Old wars were dying harder than Irving's Corporal Brewster did.

For more than a decade, essentially since Sir Henry's death, Harry Irving had been taking roles his father had played. This gave him a kind of rickety authority to appeal to audiences built-in among the older set. Comparing the son with the father, one critic thought H. B. sacrificed the humor that had marked Sir Henry's Brewster.[11] But the elder Irving would have found it easier to harvest laughs with the Empire holding steady, more or less. Harry Irving knew how to call up laughter, too, using the stiffness he shared with his stork-like father. But the war seems to have leached laughter from an event so sanctified as a poor man's valor at Waterloo.

In November 1916, between Irving's two wartime variety tours as Brewster, he gave a formal lecture in London. Morale in Britain was hitting bottom with the Battle of the Somme just halted. The scholarly H. B. barely referred to the catastrophe. Instead, he amended his father's famously low opinion of popular culture. In his talk on "The

Amusement of the People," Irving praised America and its commercial diversions. "Among our young people to-day," he said,

> one cannot help noticing . . . a distaste in entertainment for anything that can be described as "high-browed." This last is an American word, and, like so many American words, very expressive. It implies in its general attitude a dislike and suspicion of the intellectual. It represents the antithesis to the German spirit of culture and high philosophy, which we have seen devoted to the propagation of sinister and aggressive purposes.[12]

If American culture had seemed crude before the war, it was looking better by the week against the ponderous *Kultur* Germany was rolling out. More American turns were crowding onto variety- and music-hall bills with so many native performers gone to fight and the Atlantic still relatively safe to be crossed. The need for escape served not only native vaudevillians but also traditionalists like Harry Irving, who felt as much stake in the past as in the future.

At the Coliseum, for his first turns in *Waterloo*, Irving shared his week's billing Evelyn Millard in *My Friend, Thomas Atkins*, named to honor the "tommies" or foot soldiers at the front. Millard played a Red Cross nurse pleading "with a Prussian Captain of Patrol for the life of a Belgian boy."[13] In exchange for his mercy, the German makes her promise to let him ravish her. She's saved from her unholy bargain by a Scottish highlander who, armed and ready, happens onto the scene in the nick of time, Tommie on the spot.

*My Friend, Thomas Atkins* was among the earliest dramatizations of rape or its threat to surface during wartime.[14] "The fate worse than death" provided a womanly analogue, of sorts, for battle. Images of women's vulnerability were invoked continually, onstage and elsewhere, in ways that wouldn't contest or belittle the sanctioned slaughter that was men's work. As a wartime scenario, the rape of women and children fed what a recent scholar calls "traditional notions of separate spheres for men and women" that often take hold during wartime. This is not to suggest that rape was pure fabrication, as more recent wars have shown, again.

The week after Millard performed her womanly heroics, Irene Vanbrugh shared Christmas week at the Coliseum with H. B. Irving in *Waterloo*, held over. Her turn was called *Der Tag* (The Day), and it was her latest vehicle courtesy of James M. Barrie. She embodied a character called, loftily, "The Spirit of Culture," dressed ancient-Greek-like in "flimsy drapery and laurel wreath."[15] However stately the star looked in classical gear, it couldn't keep a patch or two of modern British womanhood from showing through.

The star's lanky body folded fair Britannia into ancient Greece. Figuring the nation as Irene Vanbrugh had Barrie drawing on her high profile and she sustaining his dreamy allegory. The simple sight of her subordinated audiences' sense of aggression or squelched it, in the moment.[16] The star's shining example showed Greece and Great Britain aligned across the ages in a desperate attempt to save civilization itself. That wasn't going to be easy, with *Der Tag*'s barbarized Chancellor urging his Emperor (read "Kaiser") to attack a Britain "at issue with herself, her wild women let loose, her colonies ready to turn against her, Ireland aflame, [and] her paltry British army sulking with the civic powers."[17] Worst-case scenarios weren't far from anyone's mind.

Vanbrugh's Spirit of Culture blunted supremacist claims coming from Berlin and Vienna. In *Der Tag*'s final moments, Culture is left alone with the Emperor, assuring him in tones of sweet reason that "If God is with the Allies, Germany will not be destroyed."[18] Blessed were the peacemakers, and Vanbrugh was among them, again, with Barrie's able assistance. The store of goodwill she'd gathered during the suffrage years kept her Spirit of Culture from seeming shrill or vengeful, much less the victim of rape.

The *Times* praised the star for stating "the case of the world against Prussian ideals,"[19] and another eyewitness remembered *Der Tag* for offering "an opinion far removed from mere vindictiveness."[20] Nor was vindictiveness evident in the two Russian acts joining Vanbrugh and Irving on the bill. Straight from the nation that had been, like France, an enemy but was presently an ally, Lydia Yavorska and company showed a revue called *For Russia* for the week beginning January 4, 1915. A troupe of dancers on desperate loan from the Imperial Russian Ballet gave a turn, too. Borscht-soaked acts and others joined hearty native fare like the high-decibel Arthur Spissi singing in front of the British Patriotic Chorus, Fred Ginnett in a sketch called *The Boy Army*, and film clips of the "War in Pictures."[21] Stoll was determined to keep his bills upbeat by what he left out as much as by what he kept in.

No bill at the Coliseum, not even with Irene Vanbrugh guiding it, could have eased the hatred toward Germany. Felix Barker, at Stoll's right hand, later wondered whether in spite of *Der Tag*'s

> programme note insist[ing], "There will be no attempt on the part of the actors to suggest artificially, the appearance of the characters they represent," was a clean-shaven Norman McKinnel really to be taken for the Kaiser? Barrie had treated him far more sympathetically than public taste at the time permitted.[22]

The un-star-like McKinnel was left to preen and agonize as the Kaiser, while Vanbrugh had renown to bless her efforts.

*Der Tag* had one of the longest runs of any wartime turn, lasting a full eleven weeks at the Coliseum. But when Vanbrugh came to write her autobiography, she didn't mention the play among all the others she'd done for Barrie. *Der Tag* didn't hold fond memories for Sir James, either, who in 1928 had it removed from future editions of his works.[23] The war and its outcome would leave personal triumphs less satisfying and Pyrrhic victories less admirable.

\*   \*   \*

E. M. Sansom wasn't thinking only of *Der Tag* only when he wrote early in 1915 that audiences "were out of patience with war sketches as a whole." "There is in England," so far as he could see, "none of that spirit termed 'jingoism.' "[24] Sansom admired his countrymen for staying level-headed as it dawned on them that the war wasn't going to end without radical concessions from their side or intervention by the United States, which then was a far from foregone conclusion.

In early 1915, hopes for peace were running high, still, among women beyond the warring nations. The fight for suffrage had convinced plenty of women that even without the vote, they could shape events. Among peace-loving Americans was the expatriate painter

Mary Cassatt, who wrote to a countrywoman that "If the world is to be saved, it will be the women who save it."[25] Women in the arts, especially, anointed themselves. Their work, they thought, was balm for every ill.

In America, it wasn't only women artists, their patrons, and suffragists at large who hoped to save the day. The Women's Peace Party was an umbrella organization that included a healthy membership stateside and a larger one elsewhere. It held a conference dedicated to peacemaking in April 1915 at the Hague in the Netherlands. Jane Addams, America's leading settlement-house worker, was called on to preside. Her place on the rostrum showed European women looking to American ones to help broker a cease-fire.[26]

It was the prospect of peacemaking that drew Alla Nazimova (1878–1945) into vaudeville. A Russian *émigrée*, she had by 1915 spent a decade in the United States. She laid out a bold vision of internationalism within weeks after her native Russia had entered the war. "I have long wished to be an international actress," she said, adding that

> I have wished to play parts, characteristic of each country, in each of the great countries. I wanted to play in English in England—in France in French—in the German Empire in German and in Russia in Russian. . . . It may be that the new art which is to arise out of a new and regenerated world may be so broad as to include all values.[27]

She believed that her art allowed for all values and that stage plays could serve the cause of peace. Hers was an extreme version of the optimism afoot among the women's wing of the American peace movement.

Nazimova was even more the optimist in reckoning that vaudevillians were to be enlisted in her peace brigade. As variety had done, vaudeville allowed turns that raised controversy, but never for long, as the suffrage debate had shown. Nazimova was still a foreigner in many ways, who may not have known of vaudeville's reputation for avoiding unpleasantness unless it was to raise laughs.

She had begun her American career dyed in the image of the high-strung, politically engaged Russian artist.[28] During her early years in the 'States, she'd plowed her way through a series of Henrik Ibsen's searing social critiques. She'd delighted in being provocative once she found the level of provocation that was tolerated in the 'States. Whatever she knew of vaudeville wouldn't have predicted her choosing it to promote internationalism, much less to save the world.

On the other hand, her latest ventures in the theatre had left her disenchanted. After exhausting Ibsen's commercial appeal, she'd played a series of what even she later called "vamps" who were, in her own words, "creepy, pantherish, sinuous, eerie women of a hypnotic type."[29] Her most recent outing had come in Basil MacDonald Hastings's *That Sort* in which she played a woman separated from her children by divorce. Even the luridness of her character's post-traumatic drug addiction hadn't helped the play run into a fourth week. Neither had the star recouped the money she'd spent to get *That Sort* onstage. She joined vaudeville under duress. But she had decided not to offer a turn that didn't meet her generally high standard. Her eagerness to serve humankind was as soaring as ever.

She found a short play called *War Brides*. The author, Marion Craig Wentworth, had enjoyed only a single modest success before the war with a suffrage play called *The Flower Shop* that had been too refined even for refined vaudeville.[30] Wentworth had based her latest work on a recent edict from the German government requiring that all soldiers marry before leaving for the front. German women were to breed with the fighting men they'd "chosen" for standing at stud, in effect, to guarantee fresh conscripts against whatever the future might hold. *War Brides* denounced the war machine at its most dehumanizing.

Nazimova's character—"Hedwig" in the published version but "Joan" for sounding less Teutonic and more in the heroic mold for vaudeville—protests the enforced marriages taking place all around her. When she learns that her husband has been killed in action, and herself stands accused of sedition and treason, neither her life nor her pregnancy can loosen her finger from the gun she uses to end it all (see figure 8). If Barrie had based *The Twelve-Pound Look* on Ibsen's *A Doll House*, Wentworth had distilled *War Brides* from the murkier spirits of Ibsen's pregnant, suicidal, by this time iconic Hedda Gabler. Nazimova, as it happened, had played both Nora and Hedda.

178

**Figure 8**  Alla Nazimova in Marion Craig Wentworth's *War Brides*. The star's wringing her body expresses the emotional extremity that was her trademark. (University Library, University of Michigan; from Wentworth's *War Brides* [New York: The Century Co., 1915].)

The Russian star was not alone in agitating on behalf of women and against the war. In 1913, with the war only brewing, British expatriate Maurice Browne toured his Chicago Little Theatre company in a production of Euripides' *The Trojan Women*, about survivors treated as spoils for the Greeks who'd won the Trojan War. In 1914, with the fighting in Europe underway, the American chapter of the Women's Peace Party sponsored a play called *War and Women's Awakening*. It showed, among other things, a boy decapitate a girl's doll to illustrate, as one historian has put it, that "belligerent habits developed in grown men who then groveled at the feet of 'Commerce,' for whom government rulers were mere puppets."[31]

Works like *War and Women's Awakening* could come off as shrill and preachy. With opinion dividing across the land, turns touching on war in any serious way needed a light touch to correct heavy-handedness on the part of the most respected newspapers. In the war's early weeks, the *New York Times*, for instance, shed its editorial equipoise by accusing Europeans on both sides of sinking to the "conditions of savage tribes" whose claims to being civilized were "half a sham."[32]

Like-minded views ushered a few pacifistic plays into vaudeville, such as Beulah Marie Dix's *Across the Border* and Maurice Campbell's *Thou Shalt Not Kill*. The first turn, after modest success in the theatre, vanished quickly. *Thou Shalt Not Kill* stirred some interest as a vehicle for Henrietta Crosman, a fading star visible during the suffrage movement who happened to be married to the playwright Campbell. The couple joined forces to show a mother terrified at giving up her only son to the draft. But whatever the sympathy *Thou Shalt Not Kill* curried, it wasn't enough to keep the play from coming and going quickly at the Palace, even as Nazimova was readying *War Brides* for its grand opening there.

Nazimova might have taken warning from *Variety's* editor-in-chief, Sime Silverman, who gave *Thou Shalt Not Kill* the back of his hand. The playwright's use of "Too much open face talk," grumped Silverman, was typical of the turns stage stars favored. He thought the play bent over backward to be fair, but he faulted the Campbells for letting go of the chance to make "a strong peace appeal."[33] For some time, Silverman had been standing self-appointed gatekeeper to vaudeville. His response to *Thou Shalt Not Kill* suggested that any play treating war, or peace, needed a more inspiring plot or a bigger star, or both. The prospect of Nazimova in war-weighted drama recommended itself on grounds that if such material could succeed as a turn, this was it.

However, the purism that had carried the star into vaudeville didn't cut her much slack with the rank-and-file. They nicknamed her "No Mazuma," or vaudeville-speak for "no money."[34] The journeymen and -women would have known about her recent flop in *That Sort*, and that she was recovering herself, partly at their expense, to the tune of $2,500 a week or what now would be about $49,000.

Nazimova refused to dignify the meanness. "I have suffered from high brow artificiality for a long time," she told an interviewer. "At last I am happy," she said, at finding "a great new public that want simple, honest, universal things." Furthermore, she said, *War Brides* passed "all frontiers," and

> a woman of China and a widow of Galicia [at various times counted as part of Austria, Poland, and the Ukraine] understand it equally. The only great art is universal art. . . . I hate war. I loathe and abominate the system that makes women its helpless victims.

She sounded a call to her fellow peace-lovers everywhere by proclaiming thus:

> When I go out on the stage I am a Jeanne d'Arc of Peace, as sincere in my mission as Jeanne was in hers. I am glad that *War Brides* is big drama, for it makes the message carry. Vaudeville is wonderful. There is no place for windy rhetoric or sophistication—one must display gold from the mint with the stamp of truth and honesty and human values.[35]

Wentworth's play had restored Nazimova to her more radiant self. Still while rehearsing *War Brides* and spoiling to show it, Nazimova wrote to her fellow actress and dauntless suffragist Fola La Follette to tell her that, "I breathe again. I have a right to look . . . into my own eyes and not blush. I am doing honest work, work that gives me a reason to be on the stage, work that makes me better."[36] La Follette would have imagined hearing Nazimova's accent winding its way through the English.

The star's sense of mission, by itself, couldn't have carried a turn for long. But she gained a certain authority, at least, by refuting civic reformers who condemned vaudeville for offering fluff, or worse, temptation. Ruth S. True's book, *The Neglected Girl* (1914), for instance, had even the brand of vaudeville claiming itself "high class," "refined," or "big-time," more popular and insidious than the first generation of feature films was proving to be.[37] Jane Addams, whose settlement work in Chicago took her to the head of the international Women's Peace Party, promoted her Hull House Players in her entire certainty that "The streets, the vaudeville shows, the five-cent theaters [nickelodeons showing bits of film] are full of the most blatant and vulgar songs."[38] These were harsh criticisms to be leveled at gatherings in which there were so many women and girls, especially at matinees.

Vaudeville, in some of its pre-war outposts, had answered attacks by cultivating women, sometimes shamelessly, through the worst wrangling over voting rights. Hammerstein's Victoria near Times Square was known for featuring "freak" acts, into which category were folded suffrage events. Willie Hammerstein, perhaps the purest showman in the family, found freak acts four years running in rallies the Women's Suffrage Party of Greater New York held each fall from 1909 through 1912.[39] Fola La Follette, Nazimova's confidante and the daughter of a U.S. senator, took a prominent part in the gatherings.[40]

Suffrage-supporting actresses knew that delivering patently political messages was risky. Some issues got too hot to handle, even with humor. Hammerstein stopped booking "Suffrage Weeks" when he saw his clientele shrink and not enough suffrage sympathizers, or the merely curious, to replace them.

None of this boded well for *War Brides*. In the first place, it hadn't been conceived as a turn as some of the failed suffrage plays had been, and with British stars to front them. Neither did Wentworth's play, not even with Nazimova in it, fit the almost invariably upbeat or at least inspirational headliner's slot next to last on the bill. *War Brides'* grimness forced it into the spot just before intermission. Audiences would need time to recover. So would any act to follow it on the bill.

*War Brides* was so somber that it had vaudeville bookers and managers scouring for ways to lift the gloom. Frank Fogarty came in handy at the Palace. He was an Irish-American comic known for his trademark line, "Am I right, boys?," and not, perhaps, the first act Nazimova would have chosen to follow her on the bill. But follow her Fogarty did, on the occasion of *War Brides'* unveiling at the Palace's Monday matinee on January 25, 1915. One reviewer credited him and his "pesky playmates" for raising "tears of joy in the place of the real tears that *War Brides* had collected but a few moments before."[41] Performances later in the week saw Fogarty relocated to the slot just *before* Nazimova's "to provide some comedy for the [bill's] early half," as *Variety* thought was needed.[42] Merrymakers like Fogarty were more than willing to run roughshod over art.

For all the doom-saying in *War Brides*, and around it, the play and its star toured for nearly a year. It added interest wherever newspapers that didn't ordinarily report on vaudeville covered it. The *New York Times*, for instance, pronounced the play "a powerful sermon against war."[43] Other papers of record, and journals less respectable, dwelt on Nazimova to the virtual exclusion of the other acts. Walter J. Kingsley, writing in the *New York Dramatic Mirror*, praised *War Brides* for transcending vaudeville. "No one sees the play without sobbing," he wrote,

> and the house employees have found it impossible to resist its pathos, so they give themselves up to a good cry twice a day. Women leave the theater ready to become crusaders for suffrage and against war. How far *Bella Donna* [one of Nazimova's recent "vamps" under Charles Frohman] seems when one sees Nazimova as Joan, the peasant wife.[44]

The sight of women against war and *for* suffrage, sobbing all the way, raised as much concern as it allayed. The *Times* supposed that *War Brides* was "hardly likely to hold the interest of vaudeville audiences in general for the length of time it takes in the preaching."[45] The *Times* proved wrong this time, but that owed mostly to Nazimova's tenacity.

She can hardly have ignored the bulletins coming out of Europe. The day after *War Brides* opened, the Kaiser's government was reported expropriating the nation's food supply. On February 4, 1915, with Nazimova still at the Palace, and Vanbrugh in *Der Tag* in London, Germany declared that it would regard the seas around Britain and Ireland, including the English Channel, as a war zone effective in two weeks. The Germans didn't need to remind their enemies that they had a fleet of submarines ready to enforce the interdiction. The news struck many American immigrants hard, Nazimova among them, who'd sailed for the new land from a European port. The danger of ocean travel was more sobering with the *Titanic* still on people's minds three years after it had sunk on its first Britain-to-United States leg, in preternaturally peaceful if chill waters.

Germany's stern measures frightened Americans, native and foreign-born, who were hoping to get to Europe or to return from there to the United States. Businessmen who felt they needed to get to Europe, or back from there, were outraged. Some Americans risked the trip. More than a few paid with their lives. So did American seamen on merchant ships.

Against the rising anxiety, Nazimova remembered audiences turning against *War Brides* suddenly, while she'd toured it through San Francisco in late June of 1915. The shift of opinion had coincided, she recalled, vaguely, with America's entering the war.[46] Her memory in the matter of timing was faulty; America didn't join in until nearly two years later. The star was correct altogether in recalling a downward spiral.

In May 1915, her audiences in Pittsburgh heard one of their senators plead "for Belgian relief at the conclusion of the bill."[47] The same month, two more ships carrying Americans were sunk by German torpedoes. An American tanker passing Sicily took the next hit. The week after, a single torpedo sank the passenger liner *Lusitania* off Ireland's southern coast. The ship was carrying one of the filthy rich Vanderbilts along with Charles Frohman, who'd produced plays starring Nazimova, Irene Vanbrugh, and Ethel Barrymore. On the sinking ship, Frohman's *sang-froid* and silken urbanity couldn't save him, or Alfred Gwynne Vanderbilt, or any of the more than one hundred Americans, a fair number of them of privilege, among the nearly 1,200 souls who perished at sea.

Discussions between the German and U.S. governments on the rights of American shipping slipped into stalemate through the rest of May and into June. Secretary of State William Jennings Bryan resigned to protest what he saw as President Wilson's indefensibly punitive attitude toward Germany. By July, in Los Angeles, the *Examiner* reported that the "usually irresistible Elizabeth Murray," in blackface, was "as funny as a jester at a deathbed" as she'd mugged her way through the turn after *War Brides*.[48]

When Nazimova resumed her tour in the fall, she met with other reactions like the *Memphis Commercial Appeal's* from the heartland. "While most impressive," it judged, "*War Brides* is a hysterical offering and . . . the least effective part the Russian actress has appeared in in this city."[49] There had been only one other American ship sunk in recent weeks, but debate was growing more shrill across the nation as fighting extended farther into the Balkans.

J. P. Morgan & Company loaned one-half billion dollars (~$9.8 billion now) to Britain and France. In October, men in the State of New Jersey rejected women's suffrage handily. In December 1915, in Pittsburgh, Nazimova had to share billing with performers who made fun of her. At the city's New Davis, J. Francis Dooley and his partner Corinne Sales commented "on their act and Nazimova's" with what the reporter called "refreshing candor."[50] Dooley and Sales dared to speak what others were thinking,

To the sound of scattered applause, occasional sobs, and unfailing uneasiness, Nazimova finished the year in *War Brides*. She'd already started planning the filmed version. In fall of 1916, the cinematic *War Brides* was released as her first motion picture. It wasn't made without incident.

The American government had objected, as later she recalled, to shooting the play as written.[51] But the authorities had given way, it seems, when Selznick Pictures agreed to set *War Brides* unquestionably in Germany instead of in the generic "War-Ridden Country" specified in Wentworth's studiedly neutral stage direction.[52] The film showed Germany strictly accountable for the troubles, and it lightened Wentworth's dirge-like opening with "unrelated events and an overabundance of routine movie comedy."[53] The film circulated in the United States but was never shown in any country that became America's ally, much less in one that became its enemy, the following year.[54]

Wentworth had written *War Brides* to denounce war for putting women's lives, their spouses', or their families', in jeopardy. Nazimova pressed the case on film in one of the ways she'd done it in vaudeville: by casting her husband, Charles Bryant, as the soldier who bullies Joan's sister-in-law into marrying him before he leaves for the front. The star's using Bryant to play the agent of a flagrant injustice implied that war exposed *all* women to the same heartlessness his character showed Nazimova's Joan. Disturbing as Bryant's presence was, the star's was more so in a character whose suicide took a fetus and future soldier with it. Such an outcome twisted customary reverence for motherly self-sacrifice into shock and horror.

The star may have had other motives. She was what now would be called bisexual. In the way of the day, she didn't want the public to know it, but neither was she very attentive to preserving the illusion of her wedded bliss. As a young woman in Russia, she'd entered into one or two of what were, by any of the few reports, conventional marriages. In her thirties, she took another husband in Bryant, or so the two of them made it seem. Some time after *War Brides*—which among its other demands kept her on the road off and on with Bryant for a year—she fell in with the self-proclaimed Russian expatriate-*cum*-designer/performer, Natasha Rambova (*née* Winifred Shaughnessy; a.k.a. Winifred Hudnut). When Rambova, in the full flower of her alias, married Rudolph Valentino, Nazimova claimed to have been the only witness. Valentino's first wife, the actress Jean Acker, had been Nazimova's lover, too. This sequence showed, if nothing else, that the Russian vamp and the Italian sheikh had similar tastes when it came to the ladies.

But whether Nazimova was married or unmarried, bisexual or lesbian, star or has-been, she never lost her inclination for showing men unworthy when present, and women dangerous when wronged. In the early 1920s, for her last two starring ventures in Hollywood, she played title roles in *Camille* and *Salomé*, the first abandoned by the man she loves, and the second one who in a fit of necrophilic passion beheads a saint. In 1931, long freed from Charles Bryant, Nazimova played Christine Mannon in *Mourning Becomes Electra*,

Eugene O'Neill's Civil-War recasting of Aeschylus's ancient Greek *Oresteia*, with its husband-murdering antiheroine Clytemnestra. Four years later, she played another willing widow in Ibsen's *Ghosts*. Toward the end of her career, before returning to Hollywood as bit-player with a heavy accent, she acted the famously destructive Hedda Gabler some thirty years after first taking the role. If Hedda spoke to her, Nazimova seems to have spoken as candidly as she cared to through Hedda Gabler.

The hopes Nazimova pinned on *War Brides* may have seemed as naive to her contemporaries as they do now. But vaudeville let her uphold Americans' newfound passion for remedying injustice from a distance, and at closer range if need be. Nor was she the only foreign visionary to show up in a turn, sharing bills as she did with the English-born, music-hall-bred Charlie Chaplin onscreen in *The Tramp*.

Before Chaplin had gone into movies, he'd given turns, too, not only in his homeland but in vaudeville in what he made his first adopted country. In wartime, as a creature of the cinema, Chaplin's larger-than-life visage lighted Nazimova's way into silent films. In the longer term, Chaplin helped endow Hollywood with its own universalism, conceived in silence and heedless of language except in subtitles translated easily from one language to another, and from one nation to the next, with America producing and purveying.

While Chaplin was taking films to new heights, Nazimova saw films complement her in vaudeville and then entice her away from live performance. By the time America entered the war, she'd trans-ferred her loyalty to Hollywood. She would have hung on longer there if she could have, and she ended there anyway during her fitful retirement. It must have galled her to have failed to become more the internationalist than Bernhardt had been. Both women were pio-neers in their ways, as Chaplin was for pushing his celebrity as far as it would go.

Both Bernhardt and Langtry would follow Nazimova into vaudeville during the war. Unlike her sister stars, however, the Russian one headed straight for Hollywood after her year on the road in vaudeville. It's hard to imagine Irene Vanbrugh or any native-born

American actor holding out so long against such adversity as Nazimova faced in the dark night of the soul that was *War Brides*.

\* \* \*

In March 1915, Gabrielle Réjane (1857–1920), who was, after Bernhardt, France's leading touring star, returned to London. More than three decades had passed since she'd begun her first foreign tour there, and nearly five years since she'd first tried variety. She'd come this time to show *The Bet* at the Coliseum. She did this just as Irene Vanbrugh was bequeathing *Der Tag* to her understudy at the same house, Emmeline Pankhurst was reviling Germany at the London Pavilion, and Nazimova was taking to the road in *War Brides* across the waters.

*The Bet* had been written by Regina Regis, one of a number of women whose work the war was bringing to wider view. The play mixed French and English dialogue to bring a spot of cheer to what one reviewer called

> the lighter side of the war . . . The scene is the hall of a chateau near La Bassée, and the action commences with a young lieutenant, just created a Chevalier of the Legion of Honour, whose wounds have been dressed by Réjane . . . returning to the firing-line. He makes a bet with his comrades that the famous actress will keep her promise to have supper with them at the chateau on Christmas Eve. The day arrives, the supper is set, the guests are waiting, but no Réjane.

The uncertainty didn't last long, once

> orderlies enter[ed] bearing an immense bunch of mistletoe, and a message is delivered that Réjane, unable to come herself, has sent the mistletoe for decoration. As sprigs are being broken from the branches, merry laughter is heard, and the idol of the brave Frenchmen steps forth, and gaily explains that her ruse seemed to her the only way to get through the lines. We may easily guess that the brave lieutenant falls in love with the actress, who outwits a German officer in command of forces in the neighbourhood.[55]

With the charm that was her hallmark, Réjane played herself. Famous people had been doing it for ages, and Bernhardt had become a kind of whipping girl for it. George Bernard Shaw wrote it of Bernhardt that "She does not enter into the leading character: she substitutes herself for it."[56]

Réjane had spent a career sidestepping Bernhardt's shadow. In *The Bet* she exploited her comedic gift when she registered surprise on hearing a German officer mutter "Réjane" without recognizing the name. She "evidently found it the most unkindest cut of all," one reviewer wrote, that even after he "picks up a portfolio, and spells out and mispronounces her name, he is quite ignorant of . . . who has been receiving him."[57] The joke was on the German. Audiences knew Réjane, or if they didn't, thought they should. The star's good nature exposed a humorless foe in his foreignness. Réjane's single name made the password to laughter. Communing with the star let her audiences huddle closer as she nudged them toward the frontlines of the imaginary.

The month after Réjane packed the Coliseum, Lena Ashwell led a second wave of British stars in turning out for the war. The first play she chose had a title as unvarnished as Ashwell's acting could be. Written by Wilfred Coleby among the kindred of lesser-known writers in wartime, *The Debt* had Ashwell play an intrepid Canadian named Sarah Mann, whose contribution to the war unfolded as far from the battleground as Réjane's turn had crept, figuratively, near it. As the devoted sister of a soldier, Sarah steels herself on learning that her

> brother, wounded at Mons, has been shot by a brutal Prussian officer. On the track of her revenge, she enters the flat of a German spy, who has taken the name of Geddington, and after searching for papers she comes across a mysterious long box, in which she discovers a large gun, which, if fired, would easily blow the Admiralty and Whitehall into the Thames.

The heroine saves the day first by recovering the key that would have let the gun be fired at His Majesty's government.

> She's forced into bolder action, then, when Geddington follows her and makes love to her, and she, pleading that she is hard up, borrows a hundred [pounds; ~$8,900] from him, payment being by cheque, which she immediately tears up. When Geddington's wife arrives, in a state of furious jealousy, Sarah exposes the husband for the German spy that he

is, and, giving a signal by Morse code to detectives from Scotland Yard, they arrive just at the crucial moment and prevent the gun going off.[58]

Sarah's resourcefulness pitted the Commonwealth against any German spy who dared to pass himself off as British. Ashwell's effort was more bracing coming from someone who'd been brought up, as she'd been, in Canada. The star wasn't playing herself, exactly. But she was depending on audiences to hear traces of the Canadian in her speech. With the war on, the same diphthongs that had held her back during her early years in London called out to patrons there who were feeling under the gun. Her turn, gripping as it was, confirmed the general fear.

Five months before, a real German spy named Carl Hans Lody had been executed in the Tower of London. Londoners would fear for their safety again when less than two weeks after Ashwell left the Coliseum, Germans in zeppelins dropped bombs on the city and killed four people. And though *The Debt* did not leave much comfort behind it, patrons may have taken some solace from knowing that Ashwell was using her earnings to staff her theatre with women working as what one reporter waggishly called the "the call 'boy,' the limelight 'men,' and most of the scene shifters."[59]

The September following, with the war a year old, Ashwell revived Barrie's *The Twelve-Pound Look* at the Coliseum. The turn was applauded for showing a woman in the workplace bearing up under strain. It's not surprising that other productions of *Look* cropped up during the war to put the piece in front of women's groups and gatherings of soldiers, sometimes the both of them together.[60]

The war kept calling, and Ashwell answered. She managed the Kingsway until she began organizing shows for troops that took her near the frontlines. She left variety for good, but not before giving one last turn in *The Maharani of Arakan*.

Based on a story by Sir Rabindranath Tagore, the first Nobel laureate from India, the dramatization was done up in style at the Coliseum during the hard weeks of June 1916. The turn featured "wonderful scenery by Mr. Arthur Weigall, weird music . . . played by the Indian musicians of Inayat Khan, [and] Edith Craig's Eastern costumes . . . daintily designed." The music and exoticism created a "langourous Oriental atmosphere," in the middle of which stood

> the Fisherman-King, Dazia . . .[who] puts off his royal state and woos and wins the Mogul princess Amina [played by Ashwell], who is living in secret in the fisherman's hut. Later comes the lover-king's message to Amina to tell her that he has been enslaved by her beauty and will come to fetch her to take her place at court as his wife.

The course of true love doesn't run smooth when Amina's sister demands that she take

> cherished revenge by assassinating Dazia because his father had killed theirs. But when the curtains of Dazia's palanquin are drawn aside, and Amina recognises the beloved wooer of the hut, the dagger falls from her grasp, and the vendetta is ended. Human hatred is killed by the power of divine love.[61]

The fairy-tale quality of Ashwell's turn fell in line with another cartoon-like offering that showed a "naval song scaena . . . on the deck of *H.M.S. Patriot*" with "a realistic picture of formidable guns and the grimness of a man-of-war. The chorus sing 'Three cheers for the Red, White and Blue' and 'The Day.' "[62]

The forcefulness of such patriotic display may have left Ashwell's Amina looking as wishful as the star was for having done "all that is possible with the role."[63] She left variety with the same distaste for it as when she'd started there. But in her last turn, in the rarefied air of Arakan, violence did not beget violence. This made quite a leap from the snide turns she'd given to support suffrage. She could easily have done worse during wartime than giving her dense little turns to needy crowds desperate for hope.

\*    \*    \*

Like Ashwell, Mrs. Patrick Campbell gave three turns while the war was on. In fall of 1916, Robert Hichens's *The Law of the Sands* had her playing an "Orientalised Englishwoman"—picture of the dutiful wife until she finds her "love betrayed and trust abused."[64] Campbell's overheated effort was easily the least frivolous among three star turns Stoll had lined up at the Coliseum, including *Elegant Edward* with Charles Hawtrey, and Lillian Braithwaite in Barrie's *Rosalind*. There was no ignoring the carnage from the Somme. Stoll sent stars onto the Coliseum stage as variety's version of shock troops.

Campbell's next turn came in February 1917, and it was set closer to home. George Cornwallis-West, her second and last husband, had been mustered out of the army in bad health—an outcome many an enlisted man was praying for. While Cornwallis-West convalesced, he wrote a spy-turn called *Pro Patria* (Latin, For the Home Country). Campbell's character curses her too-trusting nature when the man she believes is her long-lost son turns out to be a German spy. Cornwallis-West acted the German, full of guile.

If the playwright's effort smacked of the gentleman amateur's, it gave Campbell a *tour de force* as an Alsatian widow who discovers that her house is

> being used during October, 1914, as a rendezvous for German spies. Chief among these was her supposed son, Jean Bonnet. How she thwarted his machinations is depicted in a stirring, if somewhat melo-dramatic, manner. Incidentally, it also turns out that Jean is not her son at all, and the author has had recourse to nothing more novel than that good old piece of stage artifice—the interchange of bonnie babies [stan-dard in melodrama]. . . . Mrs. Patrick Campbell makes the most of the opportunities afforded by the part of Therese, and stirs all hearts with her emotional appeal.[65]

An account of Therese's rape at the hands of a German officer fore-shadowed the treachery of Cornwallis-West's spy.[66] The call to vigi-lance let audiences overlook the oedipal component in the Cornwallis-Wests' curious collaboration, which was not so different from Mrs. Campbell's playing lover to her son Beo's character in his own clumsily written *The Ambassador's Wife* in vaudeville.[67]

Mrs. Campbell's long-suffering had been more compelling when she'd been more beautiful. With the war on, she fed a grosser version of the hysteria in which she specialized. Her ability to inflame viewers was served by *Pro Patria's* setting in Alsace, a region caught up in endless tugs-of-war between French- and German-speaking territories. The star was left to play the rape survivor with her usual full-bodied if neurotic authority.

Campbell gave a last wartime turn in August 1917 at the Coliseum, in the suffrage-writer W. L. Courtney's *Simaetha*. The title character made a witchier version of Shakespeare's Juliet for loving a man against her family's wishes, and the state's. Courtney had written a parable on blood feuds, and Campbell cut a striking figure by wearing "semi-barbaric attire." When the heroine saw that her people were about to kill her man, she took his life and her own "in an uprush of flames 'called up' by the magic craft of the sorceress," realized courtesy of the Coliseum's special effects.[68]

Campbell ended the war in sacrifice herself, though not by choice or sorcery. Beo Campbell, whom she'd brought into vaudeville in a flourish of nepotism, was killed in action only weeks before the Armistice was signed. She wasn't the only star to suffer such a loss.

\*   \*   \*

In the summer of 1916, Oswald Stoll was keeping things lively at the Coliseum by printing programs with encouragements such as Lord Derby's "Let us be cheerful," and the new Prime Minister David Lloyd George's jaunty challenge, "Why should not England sing?" The need for fortitude had never been greater than when Sir George Alexander (1858–1918) made his second knightly entrance into variety in August 1916. With the Somme's sickening casualties for his silent partners, Alexander appeared, decked in *gravitas* and his usual beautiful tailoring, in J. D. Beresford and Kenneth Richmond's *Howard and Son*. The play was Ibsenesque for taking on corruption in the British arms industry.

Far from the battlefield as it was set, *Howard and Son* bore on the war by bringing two men together, one good, the other not. Alexander played the good one,

> Sir Anthony Howard, the head of an old business house, on the verge of bankruptcy [who meets] . . . a rascally financial agent, George Biggins [who] . . . proposes to save the firm from ruin by advancing £25,000

[~$2.2 million] to Sir Anthony on the condition that he ship to Sweden some steel castings containing copper. Sir Anthony is just about to put his name to the contract note when he opens a telegram—hitherto unnoticed—that announces the death at the base hospital of his only son, Basil, from wounds received in action.

Alexander's Sir Anthony can't sign a contract written in the blood of British boys. As the character says,

> There is a greater firm than his—England! His brave boy died fighting for her honour. If the firm of Howard and Son must die, it will do so with its reputation untarnished.... In spite of its occasional conventionality—or perhaps because of it—the playlet should have a long career of popularity.[69]

The star's "most effective passages" brought a "rousing cheer" at the end of a speech denouncing the profiteer.

Even the heartiest cheers only confirmed Alexander's feeling that he was out of step with current demand for "musical plays, revues or spy plays that ended in serious defeat for the Germans."[70] Nor can the star have felt easy about sharing his Coliseum debut with Cliff Berzac, "whose bucking jackass gives a couple of niggers a good many falls," and the contortionist Chester Kingston stowing "his body in the space of a lady's hat-case."[71] Berzac's breezy racism and Kingston's remarkable speciality were more up-to-date than Sir Anthony Howard's code set in Sir George Alexander's mouth.

The next January, in 1917, Sir Frank Benson (1858–1939) joined Alexander and Tree among the knighted actors to give wartime turns. Benson had gotten his title the year before, and driven ambulances in France in the meantime. His son, Erik, had joined the army prior to the war. He'd risen to the rank of lieutenant colonel in the King's Royal Rifles before being killed in action.

Sir Frank was nearing sixty, and three months into mourning, when he gave his first turn. It came at the Brighton Hippodrome on England's south coast. He played a week there before coming to the London Palladium in "Shakespeare's War Cry." He'd culled it from scraps of Shakespeare that, in *Stage*'s words, had "special application to the present international crisis."[72]

In view of wartime privations and the star's stoic grace, *Era* commended Benson for reciting

without the aid of either scenery or costume . . . the story of what is going on now in Europe told in the language of the Bard and in the words of our forefathers.

The first selection was designed to exhibit the crafty and cruel foe, as we have found him, and was from *Richard III*, the speech in which the hunchback tyrant said: "I can smile and murder while I smile."[73] Delivered with great point, as well as power, the application was made obvious at once.

Proceeding with what he named "the plot of the pitiless," Sir Frank next dealt with "the venal murder of men, ravishment of women and the destruction of cathedrals and all that made life sweet," and with the pent-up cry from Belgium, from Poland, Servia [*sic*] and Rumania, in the passage from *Macbeth* commencing:

"Oh, horror, horror, horror!
Tongue nor heart
Cannot conceive nor name thee!"[74]

Next to exhibit what "stood in the way of the lust of blood," namely the men who came from Canada, Australia and other of our British possessions, a passage from *Henry V* was passionately declaimed, styled "The Challenge of the Free Men."

The doom of the pitiless, the cries of the fathers and mothers, the sacrifices of the war, were set forth in another selection from *Richard III*: "My lord, my lord,—your son is dead" [lines interpolated into Shakespeare's play].

Finally, as an example of the courage described in the day's paper of a captain falling whilst leading his men, crying: "I'm hit boys, but carry on," King Henry's famous speech at Agincourt was delivered with all sense of its serious import and also with stirring fervour.[75]

Sir Frank had been a barnstormer like Lewis Waller. He closed his turn with the same call to heroism that Waller had rung out in *Henry V* with the war just underway.

But Waller was nearly two years dead, and Britain far deeper in loss. More than one reviewer praised Benson by patronizing him, for getting special leave from his ambulance-driving to appear in variety. The news didn't impress enough of the viewers who were little familiar with Shakespeare and less so with Benson. George Bernard Shaw described one such gathering he'd joined at a variety hall when he'd sat "beside a young officer, not at all a rough specimen." Shaw noticed that even "when the curtain rose and enlightened him as to where he had to look for his entertainment, [he] found the dramatic part of it utterly incomprehensible."[76]

For patrons so dumbstruck, Benson made it through a week only at the Palladium. One reviewer mentioned him near the end of a notice as an afterthought or mere courtesy. Benson had aimed "Shakespeare's War Cry" at "too lofty a standard."[77] He wasn't Waller nor would ever be. His lingering Quakerism may have muffled his war cry at a time when pacifism would have been hard for anyone to defend.

Later in 1917 Benson surfaced in an abridged version of Shakespeare's tough-love comedy *The Taming of the Shrew* with Lady Benson playing Kate, the testy bride. Things went better for the Bensons together. But he still had to listen to advice from a local variety manager that he "pinch his tabs," or speed up his act on a warm summer's night in Glasgow.[78] Lady Benson remembered him reciting selections from "Shakespeare's War Cry" as an encore at some of the smaller towns, and one ventriloquist complaining that "Sir Frank will go and recite that blinkin' Shakespeare to 'em, and of course 'e drops it all, and I've got to pick it up again, and all in ten minutes!"[79] Benson's turn, as the most broken-down music-hall veteran could have told him, forced his bill-mates to pinch their tabs, too.

Not every older star taking to variety was a man beyond fighting years. Two renowned actresses joined Benson and Waller in showing Shakespeare, and the women kept things much lighter. Mary Anderson (1859–1940) was nearing sixty herself when she gave her first turn at the Coliseum on the very day that Benson first played "Shakespeare's War Cry" to restless boredom at the Palladium. Anderson was an American-born beauty who had begun her career in Kentucky and come to fame in London by matching Lillie Langtry in the statuesque and acting in better style. At the height of Anderson's career, she'd married an English country squire and retired from the stage as noted actresses often did on being taken to wife by wealthy men.

Anderson was still, like Benson, young at heart. But apart from the occasional charity event, she hadn't faced a paying crowd in nearly thirty years. She showed little hesitation, though, in choosing the balcony scene from *Romeo and Juliet* for her turn.[80]

Juliet had been her breakthrough role, and the star revived it opposite a much younger Basil Gill as her Romeo. Audiences seem not to have minded the difference in age. One viewer recalled later that "the entire house rose and cheered standing" at her last performance.[81]

Her long absence from the stage couldn't keep Anderson from looking enough like her younger self, with the aid of some artful lighting, to be admired on that score. Audience members who actually remembered her can't have been many. But something was there to raise phantom memories even in the Coliseum's upper reaches. One reviewer admired how gently "time seems to have dealt" with the star,

> who approximates, at any rate, rather more closely to the Juliet of one's youthful ideals than a good many exponents of the part, and whose diction is as musical as ever. A Veronese heroine fully grown rather than girlish, of utterance deliberate and dwelling with some emphasis upon all of the familiar phrases, and with a tendency to lay stress both upon the lighter traits required by the scene and upon the attempt "to lure this tassel-gentle [Romeo] back again."

The selfsame critic found Anderson's Juliet "still full of beauty and dignified grace as she, in robe of apparently light blue hue, leans over the rose-adorned balcony, from which at the close she flings down flowers kissed with some semblance of passion."[82]

This actress's value didn't lie in passion. To make this clear, the reviewer added that

> With regard to Mary Anderson's welcome, if only temporary, return to the boards, it should be noted that she is devoting "the proceeds of this engagement to War and other Charities in which she is interested."[83]

The star's philanthropy spoke even to patrons who found a little of the Bard more than enough. Joining her turn, which included none of *Romeo and Juliet's* sharp, sudden violence, were Russian classical pianist Mark Hambourg and the American wiseacres Dooley and Sales. These comics made light of matters differently, or of different matters, than they'd done at Nazimova's expense in *War Brides*.[84]

Even against the spirited competition, Anderson did well. Three months later, in April 1917, she was back at the Coliseum in another of her former roles, as the mythical Galatea in W. S. Gilbert's *Pygmalion and Galatea*, which saw her character changed from a statue into a woman. Many who caught the turn were hoping for quick magic with Anderson's native country moving, at last, to join the Allies. To dress the occasion, Lady Tree, with just "the right touch of alternate fire and tenderness," took a supporting role to aid war charities.[85]

Toward the end of 1917, Ellen Terry (1847–1928) followed the several of her distinguished colleagues in using Shakespeare to meet the war. For her first turn of any kind, she had cuttings from *The Merry Wives of Windsor* that had the lusty Falstaff, at the wives' mischievous advice, cramming his bulk into a basket of stinking laundry and later into women's clothes to escape detection by the not-so-merry husbands. Terry played the leading prankster to the hilt. She followed that, early in 1918, with a more deliberate turn as the justice-dealing Portia in *The Merchant of Venice*. The role had been the star's most shining one in Shakespeare, and had commemorative value.

Portia, posing as a man, pronounces on life and death before using legal niceties to keep Shylock from exacting his pound of flesh. The extreme situation—tilted easily toward anti-Semitism when the actress playing Portia lacks an actor of similar weight to play Shylock—skirted war more closely than *Merry Wives* had. This didn't keep *Merchant* from carrying the seventy-year-old through a second tour of provincial variety. Terry was in fine form, still, impressive, even, given her age.

In London, audiences at the Coliseum welcomed her as warmly as the critics did who found her merry wife "full of fragrant reminiscence" and "bright and winsome as ever."[86] Her Portia pleased, too,

**Figure 9** Ellen Terry, in her jubilee portrait, 1906. Grandmotherly as she looks, Terry would continue her career for nearly twenty years after this photograph was taken. (Special Collections Library, University of Michigan; *Theatre Magazine* [New York], April 1907.)

particularly with the speech that begins, "The quality of mercy is not strained, / It droppeth as the gentle rain of heaven . . ."[87] The fervency in Portia's words made a bold touch for Terry at a time when few viewers can have been feeling merciful. It's hard to imagine a male star calling on the better side of human nature in quite the same way.

Terry held up her end as Mary Anderson did by turning back the clock (see figure 9). When Waller, Alexander, H. B. Irving, and Tree all died during the war or soon after, it marked the end to an era that measured its ambitions against ones struck first in Shakespeare's time, as later in his name. For as long as the war lasted, stars, men and women, avoided his most searching plays, or the parts of them that considered violence as anything other than the necessary working of good against evil.

*    *    *

Lillah McCarthy was young enough to be a child of the older stars. She'd made her name in premieres of Shaw's plays, and had joined Irene Vanbrugh, Lena Ashwell, Lillie Langtry, and others in founding the Actresses' Franchise League. After giving only a single turn in pre-war variety, she gave four more from July 1916, with the Battle of the Somme at its height, until the summer two years later when the war entered what turned out to be its final months.

Each of McCarthy's turns came at the Coliseum, which early in 1917 became the only one of London's leading variety houses still to host stage stars. Her marriage to Harley Granville Barker was in shambles, and her career with it. While he partied in America with the heiress he made his second wife, his first wife labored in wartime variety.

Even in McCarthy's darkest hours, she attracted care and counsel from wise if not wholly disinterested men of the theatre, as elsewhere. Charles Hawtrey, veteran of vaudeville and variety, was the first to come to her aid when he staged her turn in Basil MacDonald Hastings' *The Fourth Act*. She played "a pushing young widow who has written a play . . . and calls upon a wealthy patron of the drama for his support."[88] The plot owed its premise to the suffrage years, but that didn't make it timely or escapist enough to meet despair on the scale the Somme was bringing.

One reviewer called McCarthy's turn "a trifle dull," which to a seasoned professional could sound more ominous than disapproval did.[89] Another reviewer faulted McCarthy for choosing so "frivolous and unsatisfactory a piece" instead of something worthy of "leading people of the legitimate stage."[90] She still gave off a certain glow, but not enough of one, it seems, to cut through the pall.

McCarthy tried deeper drama for her second wartime turn, in James M. Barrie's pre-war Vanbrugh vehicle, *Half an Hour*. The playwright's admiration for McCarthy moved him to stage the piece himself. It opened at the Coliseum in April 1917, whereupon he wrote to tell her how pleased he was at her "splendid performance" and for looking "adorable" despite her character's misery.[91] McCarthy's turn spoke to her recent marital troubles by touching on women's rights to equitable separation and divorce, much as when Irene Vanbrugh had used the play to defuse hostility the suffragettes had raised before the war.

McCarthy, like Vanbrugh, played the adulterous Lady Lillian Garson, who ends the play by skulking back to a vicious husband after her lover's sudden death, which outcome must have rung truer with casualties on everyone's mind. McCarthy showed the abused wife hysterical in ways that mimicked the shell shock seen in soldiers coming home from battle. They were feeling less manly for showing terror in what one historian has called the "language of the body" that had long been associated with women.[92]

The last thing McCarthy wanted to do was to pass judgment on men shattered by war. Showing trauma as she did it acknowledged the soldiers' plight without shaming them. *Stage's* reviewer applauded the "power exercised by the later dramatic episodes" that had been lacking when *Half an Hour* had been shown "some time ago at the London Hippodrome." Using the war as his measure, the critic cited the play's fresh impact as proof "of the widely differentiated psychology of audiences" during wartime.[93]

McCarthy wasn't alone in tracking the national state of mind. Stoll did it, too, billing *Half an Hour* with lighter attractions like the elegant dancer Adeline Genée, and Ellaline Terriss, daughter of the sainted William Terriss,[94] in a bouncy rendition of "Aren't You Awfully Glad that You Are British?," the Irish Players' knockabout in *Doctor*

*O'Toole.*[95] However glad Britons were for being British, Stoll joined others in high places to urge his compatriots to pay lip service at least to the possibility of Irish home rule. There was a fear across Britain that someone Irish might offer aid and comfort to German spies or provide the staging area for a German invasion.

In this atmosphere, McCarthy showed sterner stuff in her next turn. Shaw had written *Annajanska, the Wild Grand Duchess* expressly for her to unveil in variety. Partly he was being kind, concerned, as Barrie was, for McCarthy's state of mind. Using her as his mouthpiece—she'd done well by him that way repeatedly—he wanted to expose the warmongers as buffoons. These were ambitious goals given the moment.

Shaw wrote a character for her who couldn't have been more different from the cowed Lady Garson. Unfortunately for him, by this time his rants against war had been published widely enough to have left him *persona non grata*. Before the war, he'd written plays for variety that hadn't seen the stage there, except for the suffrage-inspired *How He Lied to Her Husband* that he'd turned out more than a decade earlier. He feared that his unpopularity would scuttle any play he was known to have written, star turn or no star turn. Accordingly, he tried to pass *Annajanska* off as a translation of a play by "Gregory Biessipoff" in what was another childish packaging of his initials from the earlier, even more transparent "G. B. Sippoff."

McCarthy's title character was, by turns, glamorous, impulsive, charming, and decisive. *Annajanska* let its star enlarge on her support for women's suffrage while the author hammered away at the cult of manly heroism. McCarthy's messy split from Granville Barker, whose absence in America was seen by some as shirking, was common knowledge. His having left her added sympathy to her efforts. Shaw hoped that any goodwill she raised would redound to his credit so that he could show his name on his work again.

In writing *Annajanska*, Shaw had drawn on news reports coming out of Russia.[96] Civil war and revolution had overtaken large stretches along the Eastern Front, and Russians were dying at the hands of more than one fighting force, and of sickness and famine besides. Even Russians who managed to stay out of harm's way, many of them, were facing desperate conditions.

Given the apocalyptic moment, Shaw took the step—he could scarcely help himself—of making *Annajanska* funny. The play showed befuddled Russian officers dither while Annajanska took command as she'd been bred to do. McCarthy embraced the character with the same enthusiasm she'd shown Shaw in happier times. She put her faith in him again as the latest man to show her to advantage.

Shaw obliged her by arranging a star-entrance to suit what McCarthy later recalled, with almost crystalline clarity, as

> the vast space of the Coliseum stage and auditorium which demands breadth and grandeur. I wore a gorgeous white uniform half covered by an enormous green overcoat trimmed with black fur. . . . At the opening of the play, I am led on in the hands of soldiers. My first gesture is to bite their wrists and free myself, so that I may approach the general. I have to fire a fusillade at the soldiers to enforce my demand to see the general alone.[97]

Annajanska's overcoat, worn with McCarthy's sense of style, inspired fashion-maven Margot Asquith, wife of the by-this-time former prime minister, to copy the garment for herself.[98]

To please the uninitiated including foreign- and native soldiers in the Coliseum balconies, Shaw loaded *Annajanska* with sight gags. Then he made himself the drillmaster to realize his vision. He peppered McCarthy with directives. Only hours after her first performance, he was writing to ask her why,

> after I took the trouble to get [the hapless General] Strammfest out of your way by the window trick, leaving you the entire centre all to yourself, and prolonging the anticipation sufficiently to enable the audience to take it fully in, have you undone it all? At the first performance it was the only point that missed fire; and it took the end of the play from you and handed it to Ayrton [playing Strammfest].

Nor was Shaw content to offer the single rebuke. He launched into a list of complaints despite the fact that, as he admitted, he'd seen the turn go

> very well to-day until the end; but every time you dropped a bit of our arranged business you missed the effect it was meant to produce. Unless you say "all the king's horses" in profile, upstanding, and with the

playfulness over the sadness, you will not get the full effect of the contrast when you sink over him immediately after.

Do kick the dynasty *out* with your left foot, and not *in* with your right. It makes all the difference in the intelligibility of the gesture.

I could not see the lighting from my stage-box; but it seemed to me that the dazzling whiteness of the uniform has gone. Has *that* been altered?

In great haste, G. B. S.[99]

If the letter expressed Shaw's solicitude, McCarthy felt as though his "truncheon [had] landed on my head."[100] If distress had made her tentative, Shaw wasn't going to let it show. His own troubles only made him more the martinet.

Taxing as she found Shaw, McCarthy seems to have served his play well. *Era* was intrigued at seeing such a

a comic picture of the sad condition of the Russian Army and of Russian higher affairs, which are to be settled by a General who, although he has lost thirteen battles has been a faithful servitor of the Royal House, and the Wild Duchess who looks positively lovely in a gorgeous white uniform as the woman who will save the revolution.

Comparisons to other battle-tested heroines left the critic extolling

a kind of modern Jeanne d'Arc, who has escaped from prison and fought (and bitten literally, as her guard could testify) her way through untold obstacles to the scene of the play, which is a General's office in a military station on the East Front of "Beotia" [a name coined by Shaw, but resembling "Boeotia," a region dominated in ancient times by the city of Thebes]. General Strammfest, whose family has served Annajanska's for seven hundred years (and no less), is, of course, not so much concerned to win battles as he is to know how to treat Annajanska, who is at one and the same time his prisoner and his Queen.[101]

Even when praising McCarthy and bits of Shaw's staging, the critic attacked the play for raising "laughs at the expense of anything unfortunately Russian." Another review criticized *Annajanska* for its "unwise attitude towards a nation in the tragic pangs of a new birth." Proceeding on the assumption that Shaw had written the play rather than merely adapted it, as he claimed so lamely to have done, the critic taunted him for his "milk and water Shavianism."[102] For once, Shaw didn't take the bait.

A few years later, after waiting out the war, he wrote the hugely successful *Saint Joan* with its warrior-maiden following her calling to a terrible end at the hands of pitiless Englishmen. Shaw's peasant Joan, like McCarthy's Bolshevized Annajanska, offered a womanly version of the scold their Irish author took pleasure in being. Because Annajanska spoke for the playwright, he let her dominate every man in the play. He also kept the star who played her on a very short leash.

*Annajanska* put McCarthy far from her pre-war turn as a blithely promiscuous showgirl opposite Granville Barker's anxiety-ridden ladies' man. Yet the Wild Grand Duchess was very like *Anatol's* Arimi in masking McCarthy's dependence on a man she'd let choose her role and shape her in it, whether it was Granville Barker, Hawtrey, Barrie, or Shaw. Shaw pushed her hardest, and she didn't push back, or not much. Instead, she used him as her own Pygmalion, to bring her into form and favor again, three years after he'd written *Pygmalion* for the difficult Mrs. Patrick Campbell, whom he'd tried to love, for a time, before the war.

*Annajanska* didn't give Shaw the triumph that *Pygmalion* had or *Saint Joan* would. But it ran for a while. Stoll helped prop up its third week at the Coliseum when he billed it with Lillie Langtry in *Blame the Cinema*, which was slight even by the Lily's standard. According to *Stage*, her turn was

scarcely worthy of the excellent treatment to which it is subjected at the London Coliseum. It is of the flimsiest description, with a rather weak and unsatisfactory finish, and gives the well-known actress an opportunity to appear as a smart jewel thief. Beyond that there is really little to be said.[103]

The frivolity didn't owe to the star's faint heart. She'd shown toughness in her suffrage turns. The war brought it out again.

Langtry's moment of truth came, perhaps in the trifling *Blame the Cinema*, perhaps in another turn she'd given for Stoll three months before. At any rate, a bomb exploded nearby while she was standing onstage. The Coliseum had a glass roof hanging over its stage, installed when the bombing of London by air had been unthinkable.

To the best of her recollection, and consistent with what others knew of her, Langtry barely flinched. In safety years later, she remembered that

> the crowded audience felt [the explosion] was uncomfortably close, and the gallery made such a din that not a word of the play could be heard. We went on steadily with our lines, and I was surprised to receive an ovation from the audience at the close. Subsequently, the stage manager, waiting in the wings, seized my hands and thanked me for my *sang-froid*, which he said had averted a panic. But as the stage of the theatre, with its glass roof, was the real danger-spot, the auditorium being protected with sandbags, I do not know why the packed gallery made such a fuss.[104]

Soldiers in the crowd may have been more skittish than the civilians were.

While she'd been in America touring turns of slender merit, Langtry moonlighted at benefits to aid the British war-wounded along a vaudeville tour that took her through what she remembered as "most of the big cities."[105] She was proud of having raised funds for Britain there, before America entered the war.

As for Lillah McCarthy, she gave just one more turn after *Annajanska*. It came at the Coliseum in July and August of 1918, in Barrie's *Seven Women*. The piece had her play a chameleon like Barrie's Rosalind, but who changed, successively into what were, in the playwright's description, "coquette, murderess, [a woman with] no sense of humour, too much sense of humour, politician [i.e., suffragette] . . . [a woman] of the good old-fashioned, obedient cling-ing kind that our fathers knew," and a more conventional mother.[106]

Barrie had written the play at full-length as a kind of upscale pro-tean exercise for Mrs. Patrick Campbell before the war. Wartime audiences, seeing McCarthy grapple with Barrie's Cubist fragments, could have come away from it unsettled. But whatever concerns *Seven Women* had raised with suffragettes on the loose were put to rest by Barrie's addition of patriotic touches. No longer did *Seven Women* show a suffragette as it had been written to do. In her place was "the organiser of a Government Department."[107] Captain

Rattray, the young man McCarthy's character sets her cap for, has "just returned from hunting submarines." The strenuous demands on the star showed McCarthy as more the workingwoman even than Shaw had shown her to be in *Annajanska*.

For all of Shaw's later triumphs, and McCarthy's more provisional ones, women of the obedient, clinging kind came back into fashion once the war was over—though not then or ever in the plays of G. B. S. That didn't keep McCarthy's wartime turns, especially the one that had her play seven women in one, from lending credence to Sarah Bernhardt's opinion that acting was a "feminine art."[108]

In 1918 with the war in its final months, British women finally won the vote, or at least the ones did who'd reached their thirties. This owed more than a little to feminine art as it was displayed during a war that turned more awful than anyone could have imagined. Even the mayhem Shakespeare showed in his plays—what little of it was to be seen in the war years—seemed beneficent next to the destruction in what would ever afterward be harder to call the civilized world.

\* \* \*

France alone among Britain's allies, and later America's, had fought Germany before. The Franco-Prussian War in 1870–1871 had caught Bernhardt in her mid-twenties, early on her road to stardom. She suffered through her nation's rout and tasted the deficit, demoralization, and recrimination that followed. When the newest war began, she was three months shy of seventy. Her patriotism was intact. In the fullness of her age, she stood for France more than ever. Her stamina wasn't what it had been, and shorter performances were *de rigeur*. She traveled in style, still, as much as the times would allow.

In 1915, after years of chronic pain and fruitless treatment, she had her right leg amputated at the knee. Her anesthetist, with a bird's eye view of the surgery, recorded that Bernhardt called first for

her son Maurice who came to embrace her. During the tender scene she was heard to say *"Au revoir*, my beloved, my Maurice, *au revoir*. There, there, I'll be back soon." It was the same voice I had heard in *La Tosca*,

*La Dame aux Camélias, L'Aiglon.* Turning to [the surgeon] Denucé she said: "My darling, give me a kiss." Then to me, "Mademoiselle, I'm in your hands. Promise you'll really put me to sleep. Let's go, quickly, quickly."

Even in her professional capacity, the young anesthetist couldn't help feeling that

I was at the theatre except that I myself had a role in the painful drama. . . . The wound is dressed and the great tragedienne, crowned by her peignoir and satin-lined sheepskin, is wheeled back to her room. When she is in bed she screams: "I want my beloved son, my Maurice, my darling child." He kisses her, saying: "*Maman*, you look just fine, you're all right, all right." "Where is Denucé and the young woman who put me to sleep?". . . I tell her to be calm and not to talk. "I'm talking because I must speak a little. Oh, I'm suffering, suffering." The drama continues. One feels she is always acting, playing the role of someone who has just undergone a grave operation.[109]

The star faced her own demise by playing a stricken lady of the camellias. She made her surgeon and son into Armands-of-the-hospital, standing fast in love and devotion. And she survived the ordeal, as she did another surgery two years later.

Bernhardt had shown a righteous streak after the Franco-Prussian War by refusing to act in the Kaisers' domain. With the next German invasion underway, French war-leader Georges Clemenceau persuaded her to leave Paris by assuring her that the *boches*, if they took the city and found her, would ship her to Berlin and a splendid captivity not unlike Napoleon's son's in *L'Aiglon*.[110] Clemenceau wanted to save her for performances like ones she gave not long after the amputation, reciting patriotic and sentimental verse to small groups of soldiers in barns, hospital wards, mess tents, deserted chateaux, and villages near the battlefields at Verdun and the Argonne.[111] Some who watched her were missing limbs too, in what were telltale signs of modern warfare and nearly modern surgery.

As soon as she was able, off she went to Britain. She gave turns there to underscore France's suffering and its allies' obligation. In January 1916, she spent her first two weeks at the Coliseum showing

Eugène Morand's *Les Cathèdrales*. It called for six actresses and her, each to personify one of France's most glorious gothic churches.

French acting companies were short of men, and *Les Cathèdrales* called for only one of them to begin the play. He's a soldier dreaming of cathedrals coming to life as he lies in

> a wood behind the trenches in Northern France. . . . To him appear six [*sic*] figures, dressed in grey and white, and seated in stone-coloured chairs, who allegorically represent the cathedrals of the Notre Dame de Paris, Rheims, Bourges, Arles, Saint Pol-de-Léon, Amiens and Strasbourg.

The star played Strasbourg, the seventh and last cathedral, and the only one of them that had stood under German control since its annexation during the Franco-Prussian War.

Giving voice and body to Strasbourg Cathedral let Bernhardt speak lovingly of it, and of France,

> and her magnificent declamation of beautiful verse electrified the house. At the close the great audience stood and sang "The Marseillaise" with a fervour, [and] the popular Frenchwoman was seen to rise and to interpret the noble hymn by gesture. It was the most inspiring moment in a memorable afternoon.[112]

She'd had to be carried into place and would be through the rest of the war and, indeed, whenever she acted until she died. Her supporting actors supported her literally onstage, tracking her every move, providing leaning-posts where she stopped, and breaking her falls in the big moments.

After ringing out Strasbourg's defiance, the star needed only the slightest pause before leading "The Marseillaise." One reviewer noted that *Les Cathèdrales* wasn't really "a play at all," but "a piece of theatrical literature inspired by the war."[113] Britain's Queen Mother Alexandra, long past Bernhardt's dalliance with the departed Edward, sat with Queen Amelie of allied Portugal to grace Bernhardt's first Monday matinee at the Coliseum. If ever there was a set-piece for a stately occasion, it was Bernhardt's lapidary turn in *Les Cathèdrales*.

Her second wartime outing in variety came in *Du Théâtre au champs d'honneur* (From the Theatre to the Field of Honor). She attributed the piece to an anonymous French soldier at the front, but probably had devised it herself so that she could stand in for the embattled France. Like *Les Cathèdrales*, the turn was more a recitation than a play. It was also more unequivocal in its call for retribution.

*Du Théâtre* gave Bernhardt two poems to speak: in order, Louis Payen's "Prayer for Our Enemies" and Paul Deroulède's "*Au Porte-Drapeau*" (To the Flag-Bearer).[114] The curtain rose on the star lying onstage, in uniform, playing a dying soldier who wishes that

> the God of justice deal out justice untempered by mercy to the crucifiers of Belgium, the murderers of infants, the violators of women, that they may be forced to suffer to the last torment, in their turn, the woes they have inflicted on others; and the burden of each verse is *"Ne leur pardonnez pas. Ils savent ce qu'ils font"* ["Father, forgive them not; for they know what they do"].

The reviewer felt compelled to add that what he'd heard was "Not a Christian sentiment, perhaps,"

> but very passionately, grimly human, put as it is into the mouth of the young French colour-bearer . . . Spoken as only the greatest tragedienne of her time can speak them, a medium for the quenchless ardour of her lofty spirit, the lines gain the tragic force and dignity of a cry for vengeance from the outraged soul of a people.

The second poem substituted raw patriotism for outrage, once

> The aid of the Red Cross comes too late to save Marc Bertrand, the actor-soldier; and he dies clutching at the flag he had defended with his life, the words of Deroulède's, *"Au porte drapeau; mon camarade, tu tiens la France dans tes mains,"* [Oh flag-bearer, my comrade, you carry France in your hands] on his lips.[115]

To shore up *Du Théâtre*'s gravity, Bernhardt ended it by wrapping the tricolor around herself to make her character's shroud. The gesture was virtually identical to the one her countrywoman Gabrielle

Dorziat had performed on the same stage the year before in a recruiting sketch that likewise folded the women waiting into the men at arms.[116]

While Bernhardt railed against Germans, a turn called "The Song of Hate against England" threaded its way through German cabarets and music halls.[117] Fury wasn't in short ration on either side. Britons' taste for laying blame kept Bernhardt on tour in *Les Cathèdrales* and *Du Théâtre* for two-and-a-half months through provincial halls. Then she returned to the Coliseum in *Les Cathèdrales* for another week before giving her last variety turn there in *Une d'elles* (One of the Women), written by her granddaughter.

Lysiane Bernhardt showed a title character in the grip of mortality, and France with her. As *Era's* account had it,

> the "elles" of the title are the mothers who have given sons to feed the Moloch of war. The play is a study of the tortures arising out of suspense and fears suffered on account of her soldier son by the Comtesse de Mérisande, whose malady of the heart has reached a critical point. There is an unpardonable blunderer of a stage doctor, who blurts out to a family friend, loudly enough to be overheard by the invalid, that a shock will be fatal to her in her present state.

Her failing heart makes the Countess

> afraid to open a telegram when it arrives for fear that the hypothetical bad news in it may kill her before she bids farewell to her second son, also about to depart for the front. But the dread has already done its work upon her, and the Comtesse dies . . . in the high-backed chair, the large eyes wide open, the mouth half-smiling. It is great acting.

Even in the presence of such greatness, the critic couldn't help but wonder whether

> the grief of a bereaved mother [was] ever as wordy as this? Somehow one suspects that the Comtesse not only realises how pathetic and interesting a figure she makes, but that she wants her entourage to realise it, too.[118]

*Era* wasn't alone in finding the turn excessive.

May Agate, who'd joined the star's birthday tour of variety in 1912,[119] felt that the war had Bernhardt plumbing emotions that the more staid British did not care to sample. "There is a point with us," Agate wrote, "where the exhibition of feeling becomes bad taste and beyond which it is even suspected of insincerity."[120] Still, Agate had to admire the star for the moment when Bernhardt had stood up suddenly, clutching the table in front of her:

> For one horrible moment I thought she had forgotten [that she had only one leg] and was going to step out into the void. So did the whole house, for there was a gasp and someone gave a little scream—I think it was Miss [Ellen] Terry, who told me afterwards that she had called out. But we all failed to realize with whom we were reckoning. Once up from her chair all she actually did was to lean across the table, her weight supported on one hand; but the effect was of a big move.[121]

Whatever morbidness drove the action, *Une d'elles* avoided the funereal quality of *Les Cathèdrales* and the bitterness of *Du Théâtre au champ d'honneur*.

Bernhardt's still formidable power left audiences feeling drained enough that Stoll put acts around hers to touch only lightly on the war. Florence Smithson sang pleasantly in "a low-cut 1830 crinoline frock, all white satin and pink rosebuds." "The juvenile Mex" from Australia sang and danced while looking like "the angelic choir's boy who died young." Billy Gould and Belle Ashlyn kept things light in "cross-talk duets of the now familiar American type."[122]

American types were gaining interest in countries where people prayed that the United States would intercede on their behalf. The newest great power had inherited the prerogatives of great powers before it. Bernhardt crossed the Atlantic again, at risk to herself and her company, in hopes to incite Americans to exercise the godlike discretion the war had bestowed on them.

\*   \*   \*

As her steamer bore southward past Nantucket, German submarines were seen lurking in the area. They never fired on the ship that landed Bernhardt, her company, and the grips to fetch and carry for her, in Manhattan for her latest and, as must have seemed likely even to her, her last American tour.[123]

She spent most of the next two years appearing in the theatre in short plays and plying vaudeville in two installments. Her first stint there took up the early months of 1917. Then, after a second deep surgery, this time on her kidneys, followed by a few months on theatrical tour, she traveled in turns that took her from December 1917 until November 1918, within days of the Armistice. On the first of her last vaudeville tours, she chose turns to draw the United States to France's side. That done, she charged Americans to be steadfast in war or something other than insular in peace.

Vaudeville had sponsored only a few dramatic turns treating war after *War Brides*. Whether or not Bernhardt knew this, she stayed in theatre for several months, mixing short pieces on war with her standard pre-war repertory. Her first stops in North America, through early 1917, saw her travel the northeastern United States and eastern Canada.[124] She gave turns or turn-like portions of longer plays in theatres much as she'd done along the vaudeville- and variety circuits.

In February 1917 her theatrical tour ended. Lacking a conventional vaudeville engagement, she produced her own "Road Show," featuring herself and company with a handful of other acts. This troupe played theatres not ordinarily used for vaudeville in Brooklyn, Boston, and smaller towns across New England and eastern Canada. As she'd done in the theatres, she alternated between or among short plays over a week's time in vaudeville. She aimed always to show strength in her characters, even when it was fleeting. Such fearlessness played bolder against the gathering signs of her own frailty. The other turns dedicated themselves to setting hers up.

Before the war, vaudeville had promised the future. By 1917, with all but a few European filmmakers off line, American movies had been outdrawing vaudeville and the theatre together for a few years. Hollywood stars had quickly joined Bernhardt among the most celebrated people in the world. Charlie Chaplin, Douglas Fairbanks, and Mary Pickford—English, American, and Canadian, respectively—appeared together at rallies selling Liberty Bonds to help pay for the war that Americans joined at last. The film stars' celebrity may have helped to sell the conflict, but it didn't generate many films touching on war, with Chaplin's comical *Shoulder Arms* a lonely exception. More if anything once America joined the fight, audiences wanted good cheer. Liberty Bonds sold briskly. Newsreels gave pause. Stars' prices skyrocketed in Hollywood. Films about Napoleon flourished.[125] The war went on. And business got better.

Vaudeville went on sponsoring patriotic turns and ones to raise money for charities. But the bigger the star, the more likely it was that the actor would turn up onscreen. When famous actors appeared at live events, they performed as one of a group. It was more dignified, more seemly, more military-like.

If Bernhardt had wanted to work her way into Hollywood, she probably could have. In the name of propaganda, she might have made more films like *Mothers of France*, which she'd shot on a shoestring budget next to the Cathedral at Rheims. Her character was shown pleading for mercy from an unusually prepossessing statue of Joan of Arc. The film wasn't meant to be droll or sacrilegious. Nonetheless, it showed the star praying if not to herself then to the icon whose double she'd become.

Hollywood didn't suffer in her absence. It cranked out films and distributed them as widely, domestically and internationally, as the times would allow. With newsreels and Hollywood movies draining revenues from live entertainments, Bernhardt earned "only" $5,000 or $5,500 a week for her vaudeville tours in 1917 and 1918 (around $65,000 on the low end to $85,000 on the high).[126] This was a lot of money, to be sure, for anyone but the very rich. But her fee was down by about half, allowing for inflation, from what she'd made five years before.

Cutting back on some of her amenities while traveling—or at least on coverage of them—comported with the modest approach she took to her turns. The times called for self-abnegation. She met those demands while keeping herself the mainstay of the enterprise.

\*    \*    \*

Sir Herbert Beerbohm Tree was eager likewise to raise money and sympathy for his homeland beyond its shores—when he wasn't raising money and sympathy for himself. He canceled what would have been his second variety tour in 1915 to spend most of the next two years in America.[127] The variety turn he'd just given, as the serpentine mesmerist in *Trilby*, had added to the store of nostalgia spawned by the war.

In North America, Tree stayed away from vaudeville. He did yield, however, to what had brought him across the Atlantic, which was "a tempting request to pose in picture plays . . . to be prepared by an all important firm in Los Angeles. Shakespeare [i.e., *Macbeth*] will again supply Sir Herbert's principal material."[128] After finishing the film, Tree tried theatre on the East Coast, playing other doomed characters in Shakespeare's *Henry VIII* and *The Merchant of Venice*.

Unlike Bernhardt, Tree had crossed the Atlantic in retreat. His ties to Germany had been so unmistakable. His father had been educated there and run a business serving the Prussian court. The star had gotten some of his education in Germany, spoke the language, and cultivated people of learning and rank there. He'd brought his company to Berlin in 1907 to perform at the behest of Kaiser Wilhelm II, who conferred the German Order of the Crown on him. Four years later, he gave a command performance in London for the new George V and the Kaiser, the King's cousin.

Americans saw Tree play the brooding, self-pitying souls he'd come to embrace. The Yanks and his choice of roles allowed him his ambivalence, though it wasn't something for crowds to flock to see. Liberated, in a way, he showed greater complexity in his perform-ances than his compatriots might have allowed him, or American stars allowed themselves.

His silent *Macbeth*, even for lopping off huge chunks of the play, showed a more mixed picture of deliberate killing than any other star would try in wartime variety, including Sir Frank Benson in "Shakespeare's War Cry." Benson had spoken only an excerpt from the Scottish play to apply it to German atrocities. Tree, having failed as Macbeth on the stage, hoped to meet a different standard from the one he'd faced in London. In America, he never ceased working for the Crown, giving his gracious little speeches to raise money for Britain and the Allies.

Owing to the efforts of Tree, Bernhardt, Langtry, and others, by the beginning of 1917 when the United States was still technically neutral, loans from its citizens to the Allies had exceeded $2.5 billion (~$45.5 billion). Germany and Austria-Hungary, for lacking spokespersons so persuasive, collected only $127 million (~$2.3 billion) from Americans, or about 5 percent of the sums sent Britain and France's way.[129] America was declaring its sympathies by donation. It wouldn't be for the last time.

\*   \*   \*

Bernhardt was always rededicating herself to France, whether in vaudeville, American theatre, variety, or the battlefields in her home-land. She played brave women in America—and victims again—in Cleopatra taking her life after falling captive to Romans, and Joan of Arc facing torture and fire at the hands of an occupying force. The star added turns from *Camille, Madame X*, and *L'Aiglon* that didn't refer directly to the present war, either. But each character showed the suffering that the star had made her signature and the war had refreshed.

She suggested France even in turns that didn't treat the war. Her Camille and Madame X lived in France and may have struck French Canadians harder on that account, and for speaking the same language they did, who had fathers, sons, and brothers dying on land and at sea.

After her second experience under the knife in April 1917, to improve her kidneys' function, Bernhardt was back touring theatres by August, performing short pieces, rotating them over a week's time, and appearing with other live acts to make up a full afternoon's or evening's worth of entertainment. The last of her only nominally the-atrical tours of North America ended at Montreal in December 1917.

In the meantime, wartime regulation had classified her as a "for-eign act" in vaudeville.[130] If she took this amiss, she didn't say so, and was welcomed at the Palace for the 1917 Christmas season at what was ordinarily a slack time of the year. A brisk holiday traffic stopped *Variety* from its usual complaining at Bernhardt's getting more atten-tion than native stars and true vaudevillians did:

> Tuesday evening there wasn't an available seat left—and that was just six days before Christmas. It's certain no vaudeville house in the country is playing to such big business during this week and very few, if any,

legitimate houses are doing as much either. Which is the answer to the only Bernhardt.[131]

Halfway through her first week, she shifted from *Du Théâtre au champs d'honneur* into *Camille*, which showed no partisanship, at least overtly. The star's expiring tubercular diluted some of the bile that Bernhardt was hawking up in *Du Théâtre*.

On leaving New York, she added *Le Procès de Jeanne d'Arc* (The Trial of Joan of Arc) as a third element of her touring repertoire, with *Camille* and *Du Théâtre*. The first and last of these showed the human costs of war. She often played Joan early in the week when she knew more critics would be on hand to catch the newest of her turns and help build audiences toward the weekend. At midweek, when she wasn't traveling on a split-week engagement, she shifted into one of the two older pieces, usually *Camille* as she'd done at the Palace. That play, though it wasn't war-related, ended similarly to *Du Théâtre* with a tableau of exalted death.

Bernhardt was shrewd in other ways. She changed the uniforms of the surgeon and stretcher-bearers from French ones to "the khaki of America" in *Du Théâtre* at the Palace. She wanted to acknowledge, it was reported, Americans' presence "in the hospital corps [in Europe] even before our entrance into the fray."[132] Her tour was billed as "Her Last Visit," as if she'd been invited to join the folks for a sit-down in the parlor.

Bookers and local managers kept the turns around hers light but respectful. Jack Benny and Al Woods performed in "violined syncopation," Woods on the piano, in April 1918 for the bill they shared with Bernhardt at the Chicago Majestic.[133] Benny, at twenty-four, was fiddling as nicely as he did before turning his violin into the comic prop he used for the rest of his long career. As a performer, he would finally surpass Bernhardt in age while keeping his years frozen, in fun, at thirty-nine. Benny, in middle- and old age, claimed to be younger than he was, showing a fey vanity associated ordinarily with women. Bernhardt, in wartime, played women who looked their age.

In mid-October 1918, with the war in its last weeks, she unveiled what turned out to be her final turn. This came at the Cleveland

Hippodrome in *Arrière les Huns* (Stopping the Huns). It was a new piece, written not by a relative or a soldier this time, but by René Gervais of her touring company. Bernhardt played "a French countess who refused to leave her chateau during the German invasion and gave shelter to wounded French and American soldiers."[134] Her character didn't die, but kept to the sanctuary where she made others welcome.

After more than two years away from her beleaguered France, the star chose a farewell turn that dispensed with death. She'd spent much of the war bringing the conflict to people who could experience it only at a distance. She'd shown turns ranging from the vengeful to the peace-loving, and from the peace-loving to the resigned. She'd avoided spy-plays for not upholding the dignity she aimed to project. *Arrière les Huns* had a harsh title, but it was steeped in the spirit of peace. The war didn't end in peace, unfortunately, but in a hard truce. The Huns, it seemed, had been stopped.

\*   \*   \*

For all the rage Bernhardt expressed early in the war, her last turn joined Vanbrugh's and Nazimova's only ones during the war years, and Ashwell's and Campbell's last ones then, to prepare the way for peace. For American men, including stars, the war had offered "scant opportunity for . . . individual heroism, freedom, and prowess," as John F. Kasson puts it. "On the contrary," he writes, the Great War "represented the powers of modern depersonalization and mechanization at their most ghastly."[135]

The mechanization required in making, distributing, and showing films helps explain how Hollywood was able to publicize the war so quickly once American servicemen began to join the other combatants. Films were easier to duplicate and transport than live shows were, and could be shown far more widely. They supplied commercial entertainment's answer to the machinery that fed the Great War. More than a few Americans in the business of leisure profited nearly as much as the leading industrialists did.

An early, widespread, and what turned out to be shallow pacifism generated American antiwar films such as Thomas Ince's *Civilization* and D. W. Griffith's *Intolerance*. Each venture turned larger profits than *War Brides* did with Nazimova to promote it. But once America entered the war, the biggest stage stars, women and men, kept their distance from vaudeville. Film stars, many of whom had found their first stardom on the stage, recruited men into the armed forces and raised money for war on the largest scale ever. Lesser performers led audiences in sing-alongs and in competitions to choose the best war ditty.[136]

In Britain, the war set actresses on firmer footing than suffrage had. In America, it was true, momentum for suffrage had been lost, largely, before the country entered the struggle. Not until American boys were shipped off to Europe did suffrage picketers, their instinct for public relations as poor as British suffragettes' before the war, staked out the Wilson White House and suffered violence against their persons for their trouble.[137] These events can't have seemed promising to stars hoping to advance suffrage, or to lob war turns at the patriarchy as Nazimova did.

After *War Brides* and more markedly following the United States' declaring war, star actresses avoided pro- and antiwar turns alike. They left it to Bernhardt to show some of the very few exceptions to Nellie Revell's dictum that "There is no place in Vaudeville's sun for war sketches."[138] Bernhardt's willingness to show turns related to war made her the only star to sponsor such fare on both sides of the Atlantic.

In variety, a handful of British leading men had fixed on turns of pathos and knee-jerk patriotism. Star actresses, meanwhile, had played more on the notion of a war to end all wars. Leading players of both sexes found, with all but a handful of their viewers, that full-scale war brought utter exhaustion. With that, at the last, the warriors and the women gained a sense of proportion better judged than any entertainment could nurture or any battle could allow. They knew of nothing that could represent the war as it was. Nothing can now.

# 6. Parting, 1921–1934 ✧

*It is a tremendous thing to live—dying is next to nothing. Beasts and birds die—living is everything. The universe is sensitive to the merest touch and therefore it is possible to set wheels in motion that shall outrun the world.*

John Wanamaker, American department
store magnate (1911)[1]

Celebrity weighs heavier on those who hold it than on those who hold them in awe. "A punishing last act in the career drama of the celebrated restores our sense that good luck is not lasting," in Richard Schickel's words.[2] Jib Fowles sees stars as victims of a "brutally simple, ineluctable process of aging."[3] Decay and dying in public satisfy curiosities of crowds that in former times would have had public executions to watch, or seen loved ones dying at closer range than many of us do now.

Perishable as some of the most celebrated actors had proven to be during and after the war, the institution of celebrity showed resilience. The Great War demonstrated that celebrity could survive even the most cataclysmic events, much less the passing of any single celebrated person or group of them. Not only did celebrity survive the war, but it thrived through the 1920s, with America amassing a growing stock of celebrities, native and foreign, and the resources for making more of both. Britain, having lost scores of young men who might have made a difference in its postwar film- and theatre industries, lost more actors to the land of milk and honey.

The young Laurence Olivier was one of a cadre of British stars whose plummy accents were heard across America after the advent of the talkies. Smaller fees than Olivier's had even his journeymen compatriots basking in pool- and seaside luxury in Southern California.

While the Depression was cannibalizing the global economy, Hollywood carried on in fine style. Foreign actors, British ones in particular, grew in demand where demand was growing as few things were doing.

One side-effect of Hollywood's rise was that any vaudeville- or variety turn a stage star gave after the Armistice showed an actor between films, or who'd failed to catch on in films, or whose screen career had gone belly-up. Stars in crisis were easy to stalk along the road to oblivion. Film close-ups, no matter how artful, documented aging and magnified it. Some stars adapted well. Many of them didn't. The faster the world moved, the harder people found it to grow old gracefully.

With films offering celebrity's lushest garden, postwar vaudeville and variety became more arid, not just for stage stars. The longer and later noted actors were giving turns, the farther behind they were falling in the celebrity derby.

\* \* \*

The most renowned British star to give a turn after the war was Ellen Terry. She'd reached her mid-seventies by the summer of 1921. Her eyes were failing, and so was her memory. She'd been forced to sell the house in London where she'd lived for years. Age had left her feeling, she wrote, as though she were caught in a state of perpetual "puzzledom."[4] Her longtime partner Henry Irving was sixteen years dead. Both his sons were gone, too.

Her turns during wartime had left her bemused, as when she'd written to a friend that "the audience each day tells me it loves me!! Wot Rot."[5] Four years later, she was showing less pluck, and less still on learning that her daughter, Edith Craig, wouldn't be traveling with her to the variety engagement that the star had arranged for Manchester. That city's once-proud Gaiety, which had a distinguished history as a legitimate theatre, had been turned into a cinema after the war. Terry agreed to appear with other live acts during intermissions between films. This was, as it turned out, a bad idea.

En route not far from Manchester, she "was met by a large number of admirers, who accompanied her by decorated motor-cars and motor-cycles as escort into the city."[6] In Edith Craig's place to fend for Terry was Marguerite Steen, a sometime actress and an old family friend. It's not clear what Steen was expecting. At any rate, she found the Gaiety's patrons disappointing and

> little capable of appreciating what that combination of Shakespeare and Ellen Terry amounted to. The programme in which she appeared was of an unbelievable vulgarity—"The Orchestra with a Soul," Gaumont's "Round the Town," a Vitagraph Comedy, a Pathé Gazette [newreel]. Ellen Terry's contributions to this symposium were the Mercy speech [from Shakespeare's *The Merchant of Venice*,][7] the Sleep speech from [Shakespeare's] *Henry IV*[8] [*Part 2*] and a Christina Rossetti poem, "[In] The Round Tower at Jhansi."[9]

Steen's misgivings had begun well before she ushered the star to Manchester.

Terry's planning had been so out of touch that Steen had to convince her not to recite the hackneyed English school-poem, beginning with "When daisies pied." Steen also flatly refused Terry's request to act opposite her in the shortened version of *The Merry Wives of Windsor* that the star had capered through during the war.[10] Terry's shrinking memory had reduced her repertoire to pieces she'd learned as a girl or had kept in mind during what had become a lengthening diminuendo to her career.

Terry knew she needed several pieces to fill out a solo turn. She settled on the "sleep" speech spoken by the haunted king in Shakespeare's *Henry IV, Part 2*, ending with the insomniac lament that "Uneasy lies the head that wears a crown."[11] To this she added Rossetti's "Jhansi," one of many colorful accounts of the Sepoy Mutiny in India. She probably didn't know that she was harrowing the same ground that Amy Roselle had walked in 1890 at the Empire Varieties, when the British Empire had been resplendent.

Terry was afraid of standing alone onstage. She stood solitary nonetheless when she opened her first turn at the Gaiety. She'd created a comfort zone, of sorts, by choosing the most familiar bit of Shakespeare she could have chosen for the occasion: namely Portia's speech praising "the quality of mercy" from *The Merchant of Venice*. The star's greatest success had come when she'd played Portia to

Henry Irving's Shylock. In the years since, she'd kept the speech fresh by using it for the lecture demonstrations she'd given to make ends meet, and during the war as the crowning moment in the turn she'd extracted from *Merchant*. In Manchester, Terry must have been hoping that the Mercy speech would win her some mercy in advance of any faults she might show.

At her opening, she seems to have risen to the occasion and spoken "The quality of mercy" with some of her old authority. The *Manchester Guardian* explained what happened next by blaming the Gaiety's management for making Terry give three turns a day when she'd reached "an age well over seventy."[12] The reviewer took some of the blame on himself when he wrote that "Hard things have been said of our disregard of artists, and one felt last night that we deserve them all." He found the Gaiety's recent renovation tacky, with its "Lanterns of a 'jazz' design" clashing with "vases of a pseudo-Egyptian convention." Merciful as the account was to Terry, it couldn't hide the reporter's alarm that the star had needed Steen to prompt her so often. Even the star's oversized eyeglasses, it seems, couldn't help her read letters printed "an inch high" for her benefit on the script she could be seen referring to often, and dodderingly, whenever she faltered.

At the end of her first turn in front of a Gaiety audience, Terry had her wits about her to know that she hadn't done well. She made excuses as rambling as her readings were, to judge by the *Guardian's* ellipsis in quoting her: "She was not well. . . . She had difficulty in learning new lines." The *Manchester Evening News* chimed in, noting that "the performance was not without its pathetic side, for Miss Terry, as she herself admitted, was feeling the strain of indifferent health."[13] The *Manchester City News* called up Terry in her prime, whereas

> Now, alas! as we saw her halting figure, heard her voice, still wonderful and beautiful but distressed, and noted the groping for a word which, in the old days, came unhesitatingly, saw her read through big tortoise-shell spectacles, pain penetrated those memories we fain would have held fresh and fragrant as was the great actress herself in by-gone days. To-day her spirit is brave as of yore, but the flesh is weak.[14]

A late July heat wave had onlookers worrying more about the grand-motherly star than they might have done otherwise. The stifling weather, with her three turns a day, put her in bed for two weeks on her return from Manchester.[15]

She ended by making £100 (~$5,300). At least one person close to her profited more than she did. According to Steen, Edy Craig spent her mother's money, without a question, on herself.[16] Even the upstanding Steen was not above accepting a check from the Gaiety's proprietor, and with it "a cigarette-case, warmly inscribed." He was grateful, he said, because "We'd never have got Miss Terry on to the stage unless you'd been here." Steen had taken the money only because, she recalled, it had come in handy "for tips in the theatre and the hotel."[17]

Terry took pride in simply having survived the engagement. She scrawled a note that read, "Granny at the Gaiety, Manchester, July 16–24th" on the printed program that listed her on the bill. She added, for what she meant to be a keepsake for her granddaughter, " 'Baby' from 'Granny' bless her little heart" and listed the pieces she'd recited.[18]

Reciting while she'd been alone onstage had left her more out of her element than a full-length play might have done with others onstage to cover for her or to prompt her on the sly. She might have fared better on a straight variety bill, with other acts to flatter hers and pick up the slack. But the Gaiety was showing more films and longer ones, and relieving the films with fewer and fewer live acts, as small-time vaudeville had been doing in the United States since 1910 or so. By the 1920s, films were signaling the future more than ever, though they never figured much in Ellen Terry's future.

It wasn't until four years later, in the year she was dubbed Dame Ellen, that she did her last acting. The engagement came, as was fit-ting, in a theatre in London in Walter de la Mare's *Crossings*.[19] She played the ghost of a character who'd recently died. She had no lines to speak. Her audiences would have been grateful for small mercies.

She lent her ethereal presence to the proceedings by crossing the stage at crucial points in the action. Even a task so simple probably called for someone in the wings to push her on. Like her last turns in variety, *Crossings* had her playing a ghostly version of herself.

Her incandescent visage, white hair crowning in the light, figured as the British Empire did: partly present, partly vestigial, and partly gone.

*   *   *

The Great War introduced Alla Nazimova, in order, to *War Brides*, vaudeville, and Hollywood.[20] Her film stardom lasted until the early 1920s, when movies with her playing the pure-hearted courtesan in *Camille*, the womanchild in Ibsen's *A Doll House*, and the biblical temptress in *Salomé* all failed.[21] She tried vaudeville again.

The fall of 1923 found her touring George Middleton's *Collusion* along the Orpheum circuit. The turn showed a prostitute degraded by one customer's need to establish his adultery, or its appearance, to secure a divorce from the unfaithful wife to whom it fell, by law, to initiate legal proceedings. Edward F. Albee monitored the reception Nazimova got in parts westward. Middleton, at someone's advice, probably Albee's, changed the title to *The Unknown Lady*, which sounded more aboveboard. The playwright's concession left Albee more convinced of the turn's appeal. The producer hyped it as "dramatic dynamite" and brought it to the Palace's stage, several floors below his cushy office.[22]

Any critique of divorce laws for being virtual subsidizers of prostitution would have been inflammatory. Middleton, with Nazimova's collusion, had taken dead aim at statutes making marriage difficult to dissolve even with mutual consent. *The Unknown Lady* proved inflammatory all right, though not in ways Albee could have foreseen or Nazimova controlled.

Sime Silverman, *Variety's* founder, was known for being straitlaced, but he was far from the only moralizer to take offense at Nazimova's latest. Summoning up his most righteous indignation—it was easier for him to do this than to engage Middleton's argument—Silverman took *The Unknown Lady* to task for its bad language:

> The two extremes of the show business are meeting at the Palace this week, or they did Monday evening—Art and Dirt. And Art won, muchly and as represented in the Russian Art Co. [in music and dance], while Dirt was *The Unknown Lady*, the Nazimova sketch . . . [which] had not changed one word or one oath at the [Monday] night performance.

Silverman added rough language and sacrilege to *The Unknown Lady's* offenses against propriety:

> There are three "damns," two "hells" and "God" is mentioned four times in the sketch, while highballs are ordered, delivered and drunk [with Prohibition in force]. If that doesn't bust every rule ever issued by the Keith office for profanity on the stage, there are some rules unknown.

Silverman threw graver doubt on Albee's judgment —the two men were never the best of friends—when he predicted,

> There will be many a person leaving Keith's Palace this week surprised at having found a sketch like *The Unknown Lady* in a Keith theatre. In a house dedicated to cleanliness in material it's an affront to those not expecting anything else. This is one time where the "play or pay" contract has a dangerous back-fire for the house.[23]

The Russian dancers, at least, conveyed the refinement Silverman wanted from Nazimova's turn.

There were others to help torpedo the play. The playwright Middleton complained that greatest pressure had been applied "by an individual who asserted that he spoke on behalf of a religious organization." The Catholic Church had sent a delegate to Albee directly, Middleton learned, whereupon the producer had cancelled *The Unknown Lady* after only its first two showings at the Palace and despite its quite favorable reception. Nazimova was upset enough to write an apology to Middleton, in which she claimed that the Palace was prepared to book her in "anything but" *The Unknown Lady*.[24] Albee, with lightning speed, replaced the play with a featherweight sketch called *The Cherry Tree* that gave no offense.[25]

Albee even took Sime Silverman's advice, in a roundabout way. He conceded the "play or pay" clause in Nazimova's contract and laid out $3,000 a week to cover the star's fee for what would have been the remainder of her five-week tour. The payments made an outlay of what now would be about $174,000.[26] Whatever credit Albee earned in the eyes of the moralizers came at a cost to him of $7,500 (~$87,000), in effect, for each of the two performances Nazimova actually gave.

This made her, if only technically, the single stage star to earn more per outing than the $7,000 Sarah Bernhardt had gotten by the *week* in 1912 and 1913 for giving at least twelve turns and sometimes as many as fourteen. Nazimova was glad for the money, though not for the way she'd come by it. She went on to success in the theatre and in vaudeville. Through it all, in turns or in full-length plays, she never wavered in her support for women's rights, though in vehicles less strident than *The Unknown Lady* was, not to mention *War Brides*.

In 1926 she played a turn in Basil MacDonald Hastings's *That Sort*, the failure of which at full-length had landed her in vaudeville some eleven years before. Nazimova's stripped-down *Sort* actually met a better reception in vaudeville than it had in the theatre. Divorce, which furnished the precipitating context in *That Sort*, was becoming more common owing to the same shift in attitude the Catholic Church was trying to stem when it shut down *The Unknown Lady*.

In *That Sort*, Nazimova played a divorced woman driven to drugs by her former husband's cruelty in keeping the children from her. The turn ended with the star's ravaged character picking up the vile narcotics and throwing "them away after a heavy display of will power," as *Variety's* "Skig" put it.[27] The character's self-control seems to have laid every objection to rest. The play placated Catholic elders by showing what harm divorce could do.

Bolstered by the high drama of what Skig called Nazimova's "mother" role, she toured *That Sort* for two months. She'd just seen her marriage to Charles Bryant exposed as one in common law only. She was concerned that this, together with nagging rumors about her choice of bedmates, might keep her from getting American citizenship.[28] To make herself as respectable as she could, she took to the heartland playing a mother-love stouter than the most savage addiction.

Nazimova's next turn came less than a year later in *A Woman of the Earth*. Edgar Allen Woolf's play recast the Bible's Mary Magdalen as a gypsy girl in Romania who kills the man who's seduced and abandoned her. Woolf, wanting to avoid the stink *The Unknown Lady* had raised, resolved his play by leaving a village priest to draw the girl's story out of her, and "evidence that the murder was justifiable."[29] The playwright's choice in putting the most sage character in churchly garments helped Nazimova tour vaudeville twice in *A Woman of the Earth*, first beginning in January and again in September 1927.

Between the two vaudeville tours, she took *A Woman of the Earth* to the Coliseum in London for her first engagement in Britain in twenty-two years. *Variety* had trumpeted her "walloping dramatic playlet" at New York's Palace several months before *Era's* review of her Coliseum appearance praised Nazimova for being "nothing if not magnetic," so much that "one almost senses the vibration of the thrill in every breast."[30] She took eleven curtain calls after opening the turn in London. Ellen Terry, near the end of her life, sent her secretary with regrets for not being able to attend what became one of the little gems of the London season.[31]

Noël Coward, a *bon vivant* and star on the make, was among the fashionable crowd to catch her turn. He gave Nazimova his bubbly if equivocal praise, telling her, "You were obvious enough to please anybody in the world, but your performance was crammed with subtleties."[32] The American film director D. W. Griffith had shown similar enthusiasm at the Palace, where after seeing *A Woman of the Earth*, he'd stood and shouted "Bravo" and wasn't alone as the star took curtain call after curtain call.

Knowing this left Nazimova only more inconsolable when Griffith failed to offer her the film contract to restore her place in Hollywood. In fact, what she saw as the screenmaster's two-facedness had her write in her diary that God, working his will through Griffith, had taken "a knife to find my heart."[33] Even with that, *A Woman of the Earth* took Nazimova farther on the road for a longer time than other stars were managing to spend there. By the late 1920s, it was the rare actor who ran for longer than a week at any of the shrinking number of big-time houses concentrated in London and New York. Radio was peeling patrons away from vaudeville as films had been doing since the 1910s, in lockstep with the rise of small-time vaudeville in which films were more integral than live performances were.

In 1928, Nazimova gave her last vaudeville turn. Edgar Allen Woolf had written another piece for her, called *India*, in which she played the upper-caste wife of a well-to-do Indian husband. When she sees her baby "trampled during a parade in honor of an English prince," she "exhorts the women of India to unshackle their bonds of ancient traditions."[34] This outcome didn't promise a happy reception from the many Britons still enraptured by the Raj; and such dim prospects on the far side of the Atlantic kept Nazimova from trying variety again. She still needed work, though, and so agreed to try *India* out at a small-time house in Bayonne, New Jersey. From there, she hoped, she could take the turn to the Palace to raise money to buy the hotel she was counting on to ease her into retirement.

But her strenuous efforts brought on a nervous collapse.[35] Nearing fifty, she may not have relished the prospect of playing a twelve-year-old bride twice a day for several weeks—if she was lucky enough to have the turn catch on. And Nazimova wanted the turn to catch on, so she wore a costume *Variety* called "scant." This might have gotten less notice had the Palace not taken to using its newly appointed master-of-ceremonies, the lip-smacking Taylor Holmes, who followed Nazimova's turn by reading "girl-undressing press clippings."[36] Holmes, and probably Nazimova, were tapping tastes for the striptease the 1920s had quickened. Even the sight of her flesh and the raunch that followed it couldn't fill the Palace. *Variety* sounded almost resigned to the fact that "vaudeville houses can have attractions of quality and still do not get business."[37]

As Nazimova played out the string in vaudeville, vaudeville faced its demise. In 1927, Joseph P. Kennedy, father of the future American president, bought the Keith chain. He fired Albee summarily and removed him from his sanctum in the upper reaches of the Palace building. Kennedy renamed the Keith circuit "Radio-Keith-Orpheum," or RKO for short.[38] The acronym made vaudeville an afterthought.

Vaudeville *was* an afterthought as far as Kennedy was concerned. He'd set his sights on Hollywood. In short order, he moved on to film production and took film actresses for mistresses as his sons would do after him. Kennedy's West Coast connections kept him clear of vaudeville in steep decline. He'd found a better place to house his investment.

\*    \*    \*

Other gimlet-eyed speculators wanted no part of vaudeville, any more than rising actors saw it to their advantage to show up there.

Certain stars of longer standing had less choice. The advent of sound drove some familiar faces from silent films into variety. Betty Blythe and Jackie Coogan among Americans, and Ramon Novarro, Sessue Hayakawa, and Pola Negri at the head of an international contingent, appeared in sketches at the London Coliseum and sometimes on provincial tours of the dwindling number of variety houses. Stars in exile from Hollywood needed to establish credentials as speaking- or singing performers to launch comebacks into film. Even when they succeeded, their films didn't often fare well.

Pola Negri was an Eastern European like Nazimova, though not from as far easterly, from Poland. She had the same dark beauty that had served Nazimova and Theda Bara well, if briefly, on the silent screen. For Negri's engagement at the Coliseum in 1931, she tried to pry an original script from Maurice Rostand,[39] son of the more famous father who'd given the world Bernhardt in *L'Aiglon*. But when Negri failed to persuade Rostand of her abilities, she settled for what even she called later a "flimsy" piece. *Farewell to Love* had her playing a cabaret singer who

> incidentally sings a song in Russian . . . A vivid night club setting is used, and coloured lights, wax models of club visitors, and music off stage by an electric reproducer. . . . But not even a stage setting that resembles one of the ultra modern arrangements of an Oxford Street dress shop window can compensate for the lack of appeal of a poor sketch.[40]

Negri never trusted the turn.

She masked her reservations in an interview she gave under the headline "The World at Climax." She claimed that the crisis in her career had brought her to a place

> where the road stops. You have come to Climax. But still you must go on down—down—or up. The talking pictures have come to Climax. Oh, but they are bad now, terrible, just talk that is endless. And silent pictures are dead for ever and ever. So there must be a new technique; more than that, a new medium, a new form, a new art. From where?[41]

Even in the act of heating up her readers, she must have supposed that the new art, orgasmic or not, wasn't going to come from silent films or from variety, either. Her two-week run in *Farewell to Love* came just a month before Sir Oswald Stoll—for so he was by this time—stopped producing variety in his twenty-seventh year at the Coliseum. He replaced it with a saucy revue from Berlin in its heavy-breathing, pre-Hitler phase.

Not long after that, Negri made a pass through vaudeville giving three turns a day in a piece so inconsequential that she couldn't remember the title or was too embarrassed to cite it in her memoirs. She went into vaudeville owing a lot of money, and she recycled the setting she'd used for *Farewell to Love* and then stored as a hard asset.[42] Things went even less well for her in vaudeville than they had in variety. She and her turn, whatever it was, disappeared.

Several years before, Stoll had hired another former film star, this one a veteran vaudevillian who sang, danced, acted, and told stories. The American jack-of-all-trades was Fannie Ward, who'd been circulating through light entertainments in the 'States and in Britain since the 1890s. She'd been a variety headliner since 1909. The summer of 1927 saw her at the Coliseum billed as "The Wonder Woman—The Sensation of the United States," and she returned the next summer, promoted as "The Miracle Woman."[43] She appeared as herself in both turns, preaching what one reviewer called "the comforting gospel of how to circumvent that convention which we shall call age."[44] She claimed to be sixty in 1927, and by calculating her age on the high side, as it seems she did, she took an unusual step, especially for a woman.

However old Ward was, she left *Stage* as breathless in 1928 as when she'd touched down in variety the year before. "To be sixty-one years of age," the reviewer marveled, "and to appear about twenty in looks and actions is a considerable achievement even in these flapper days."[45] *Era*, London's other major trade paper, was also impressed:

> The return of Fannie Ward is regarded in the spirit in which we contemplate the appearance of a comet. "The most remarkable looking woman for her age of our age," is how the programme at the Coliseum describes her and we can find no exaggeration in the statement. She seems to symbolise a hankering that has beset the world . . . which is stronger than ever to-day when we have lost the art of growing old gracefully without learning how to remain young.

Whatever fatalism lingered after the war, the writer was gratified to behold its walking contradiction in

> a woman who has passed three score years without losing the look of girlishness in face or figure. What cause for wonder can be added to that? . . . she dances; and she allows us to see her change her frocks behind a transparency. But we are very inattentive concerning what her songs are about and what steps she executes. Merely to look at Fannie Ward is enough. "Oh," we sigh, "that we could emulate her."[46]

Ward's changing costumes behind the see-through screen offered the lure of striptease something in the way Nazimova had done while suffering her way through *India* in her scanties.

Ward, far from Nazimova's high art and racing metabolism, was promoting dieting as the new religion. To ballyhoo her appearance in variety in 1927, she wrote under her own byline: "One experience is enough for any woman where fat is concerned. Even a few pounds age her. I do not say be too thin, but I do say you *must* keep your weight down." "I am never going to grow plump again," she assured readers, "just as I am never going to grow old."[47]

Ward never achieved perpetual youth. But she seems to have held her own pretty well. She lived on after dying, in a manner of speaking, by appearing posthumously in 1965, in archival footage inserted into a film called *The Love Goddesses*. To believe in Fannie Ward meant living in hope that will power could stymie death itself.

By the late 1920s, though, she was preaching to middling crowds in an entertainment that had lost its way. Her speaking to the future was compromised by the place she'd chosen to sound the message. Since then, other performers have scorned aging as she did, sustaining youthfulness for short periods in a medium of their choosing. Sometimes they do it for years. Eventually they learn, with the many others who learn it likewise, that youth everlasting requires tight control to be translated from a state of being into a state of the art.

\* \* \*

Ethel Barrymore gave her last turn in vaudeville in 1933, at New York's gargantuan Capitol Theatre. She made $2,500 a week (~$38,000) for doing five shows a day in her standby, *The Twelve-Pound Look*. Her pay was down from her pre-war, two-show-a-day fee of $3,000, and down even more allowing for inflation and the amount of work she had to do. The Depression had big-time vaudeville in a tailspin. Anyone who could find work there, falling stars and all, knew they would be facing less than ideal conditions.

As Ellen Terry had done with her last turn, Barrymore made one of the live acts between short films and a feature-length movie called *Storm at Daybreak*. On seeing her in *Look*, again, *Variety* thought she'd been "a little slow in warming up, not being used to such large theatres as the Cap."[48] Her small company tended toward the geriatric, with the mid-fiftyish star supported by her cousin Georgie Drew Mendum, identified by one reviewer as "an elderly member of the house of Barrymore."[49] Letting Mendum play the dim-witted Lady Sims made Barrymore's Kate look younger and smarter, and it favored a member of the extended family as the Depression bottomed out.

Barrymore gave her only variety turn the next year in London at the Palladium, as Kate again in *Look*. The star was bringing the play home to Britain, though not, she thought, to lay it to rest. By 1934, with women having voted since 1918 in Britain and 1920 in the 'States, *Look* didn't call up suffrage or any other issue then current. In the United States, Barrymore had turned the play into a neater version of her own life which, once the Depression hit, inspired fresh interest as a lesson in thrift. But in Depression-era England, she lacked fans who knew enough about her broken marriage and single parenthood to appreciate why she'd kept playing Kate for so long.

One critic who saw Barrymore's *Look* in London granted that

> Her reception on Monday was cordial enough, but, to be frank, the big Palladium audience is not the most suitable place for the intimate, literary quality of Sir James Barrie's sketch, nor, with all due respect to an acknowledged artist, can the present generation of London variety goers be expected to know much of Miss Barrymore's fine record in the American theatre. Nor does her performance, good as it is, of the typist ex-wife give audiences any adequate idea of her quality.[50]

Another reviewer waxed nostalgic, describing the star

> dressed neatly in a blue costume, carrying a typewriter, her hair cut short
> and flowing free . . . [which made it] difficult to believe that this youth-
> ful person could have played with the [Henry] Irving of phantom
> memory—in those incredibly distant 'nineties. These Americans wear
> their years as a child wears a crown of daisies.[51]

Barrymore joined "these Americans" of a certain age, like Fannie
Ward, in carrying an energy that looked childlike and not altogether
wishful. She couldn't draw out the illusion of youthfulness for as long
as Ward did, but who could?

Barrymore's reception at the Palladium deteriorated within days
of her opening, when she was booed for inaudibility and had the curtain rung down on her. She'd become an alcoholic like her brother
John, and the drinking was affecting her work.[52] Aileen Stanley, a
seasoned vaudevillian who joined her on the Palladium bill, had
known her for years. When Barrymore asked for advice, Stanley
remembered telling her, simply, "Quit."[53] The star ended by cutting
her losses at the Palladium, or having them cut for her. But she
couldn't afford, nor did she want, to quit acting with her career in a
slump and her long attachment to vaudeville at an end.

In her memoirs, she gave a different account than Stanley's, and
showed the steeliness—and denial—that had kept her star aloft.
Years later, she was blaming Depression-era Palladium audiences for
not liking *Look*. They'd "hated it," in fact, and

> said it was "old-fashioned"—I don't know what they didn't say about it.
> I had banked on it for so many years, had thought it was practically a
> classic, and it was a shock to discover that as far as England was con-
> cerned its day was past.[54]

One of the benefits she found in calling her autobiography *Memories*
lay in remembering what she wanted to.

Shocking as she found her rude welcome in London, it didn't keep
her from using *Look* again for one last time in America. In the
autumnal glow of her career, she played the indomitable Kate in
1950, for a benefit held at the Ziegfeld Theatre in New York City.[55]

In her last years, vaudeville called up only fond memories for her. It had raised her spirits and her fortunes. She praised it at greater length than any other actor of her standing would do. "It was demanding," she conceded,

> but very rewarding. I learned so much watching other artists. I found out that you have to be awfully good in vaudeville. It is a real taskmaster because there are so many acts in it, like slack-wire artists, for instance, that require absolute perfection.

She appreciated the amenities vaudeville had provided her and other performers, in buildings that had been "beautiful, not only in the front . . . but in the back [-stage areas] as well." "The performers," she wrote,

> seemed to have been remembered by the architect; the dressing-rooms were nearly always superior to those in any other class of theatre. Things ran as systematically and efficiently as in a large business concern. I loved everybody I met—all the people on the bill with me—and I was never tired of standing in the wings watching the different "turns."

She paid tribute to "the vaudeville public" as "an exacting one." For them, nothing could be "slurred." It had to be "perfect in the afternoon and perfect at night, over and over again for weeks and weeks."[56]

Her words rang with the same spirit she'd shown during the first week of her maiden vaudeville tour in 1912. She'd told an interviewer then, on opening in Chicago, that "the question isn't so much what a player does as how well he does it, whether to dance, or give a monologue, or do a roller skating trick."[57] It was a lesson that might have embittered her. But Barry's daughter remembered enough to feel grateful for the lifeline that vaudeville had thrown her when she was drowning in cares. Having stared serendipity and disaster in the face, she didn't want to be remembered only for the golden *ingénues* she'd played in her Gibson-girl youth.

By the time she died, she'd become the rare performer to have carried celebrity for almost sixty years, sometimes for richer, sometimes for poorer, from the turn of the century through most of the 1950s. The legacy she left came in the portion of renown she passed on to the Barrymores who have followed her maternal grandmother and grandfather, the Drews, her mother Georgie and her father Barry, her brother Lionel and her little brother John with *his* children and grandchildren, into a spotlight that can scorch.

\*   \*   \*

In March 1920, a year-and-a-half after Sarah Bernhardt gave her last turn, *Variety* had her set to appear in vaudeville for what would have been the fourth time.[58] Her prospective price had fallen to $2,500 a week,[59] which while it would amount to about $25,000 today—no small peanuts—was down, given inflation, by nearly two-thirds from what she'd made in vaudeville during the war, and by more than 80 percent from her 1912–1913 salary. She didn't tour vaudeville again, or try variety. She probably knew that she'd grown too frail to carry even the briefest turn, let alone one that required dying onstage in the dynamic ways she did it.

The Great War had made her shed some of the high-mindedness she'd shown on her first pass through vaudeville, when she'd refused to share bills with blackfaced acts. In the final months before the Armistice, she played opposite a number of minstrels, the last of them Walter Weems, listed as the "merry blackface performer" on a bill that included the very last turns she gave and her final appearances in North America, at Keith's Hippodrome in Cleveland.[60] Her eagerness to stop the Hun must have subdued whatever objections she had to burnt cork applied to faces black or white.

She lived another four-and-a-half years after sharing the bill with Walter Weems. In her dressing-room following her last appearance in London, by royal command in the year before she died, she answered Queen Mary's question about her health by saying, full of spunk, "Your Majesty, I shall die on the stage; 'tis my battlefield."[61] She'd been dying onstage, of course, her whole adult life. But her prophecy proved accurate, or nearly so, when she played a clairvoyant in a film shot in her Paris apartment within days of her death in 1923.[62]

ADIEU

**Figure 10** Sarah Bernhardt bidding adieu, 1912. This image decorated the final page of the souvenir program the Palace Theatre published on the occasion of her first engagement there. She would say her goodbyes many more times, several of them in vaudeville and variety. (Special Collections Library, University of Michigan; from *The Palace Theatre Presents Madame Sarah Bernhardt in Vaudeville* [New York: Martin Beck, 1912].)

The camera caught her character gazing into the future while letting the star leave something of herself behind. So did vaudeville's Orpheum circuit, in a different way.

George Middleton was the unfortunate playwright who'd seen the turn he'd written for Nazimova shot down at the Palace. Just months after Bernhardt died, Middleton found himself standing next to Douglas Fairbanks and Mary Pickford at the onetime greatest star's graveside in Paris. There "on an upright support to the covering slab," he saw "a bronze plaque . . . riveted." On looking closer, he was startled to see that the plaque had been "put there to commemorate the fact that the Orpheum Circuit had first invited Sarah to play in vaudeville."[63] If Middleton saw other decoration, he didn't mention it.

Himself having profited when his play had toured the Orpheum Circuit, and having lost royalties when *The Unknown Lady* left the Orpheums for Gotham, Middleton was dumbfounded to see vaudeville using Bernhardt's resting place to promote itself. Then again, the sight he found incongruous was only a variation on the self-promotion the young Sarah had done by lying in a coffin to have her picture taken. But even she might have had a hard time imagining her memorial stone turned into the front half of a sandwich-board. Or, she might have winked (see figure 10).

Pickford and Fairbanks, in still-blissful union at the crest of their own towering celebrity, seem to have taken the scene in stride. On the way back to their hotel, Middleton recalled crowds screaming, "Dou-glass! Mary! Dou-glass! Mary!" as the limousine he'd shared with them wound its way through the streets of Paris. There, once upon a time, he wrote, "Sarah had been queen." She'd built a celebrity which, like the pyramid around a pharaoh, entombed her.

# Afterthoughts ❧

> *It is an enormous paradox that democracy . . . which claimed moral superiority on the basis of extending quality and freedom to all, cannot proceed without creating celebrities who stand above the common citizen and achieve veneration and god-like worship.*
>
> Chris Rojek, *Celebrity* (2001)[1]

Democracies in Britain, France, and America have produced some strange constellations of celebrity. Sarah Bernhardt's renown far outshined Sir Herbert Beerbohm Tree's in his homeland, and Ethel Barrymore's in hers. Lillie Langtry followed Bernhardt in being a citizen of the world, traveling in luxury, dressing with style, and using her life to enliven her acting. There was less of Langtry's acting to be enlivened, to be sure, but enough to sustain the glow.

Many celebrated actors have followed Bernhardt and Langtry in using scandal, or hints of it, to stoke their fame. There lies risk in doing it, and even Bernhardt's results were uneven. It was known that some of her sexual partners in her younger days had paid for her services, and it was whispered about that some of her lovers were women. Nazimova's partners surely included women and men, whereas Tree's, Langtry's, and Bernhardt's heterosexual, extramarital liaisons became the stuff of legend.

Adultery, bisexuality, homoerotic appeal, and hypersexuality, sometimes all of them together, electrify the celebrity entertainers command. Someone who's attractive and attracted, even hypothetically, to girls and men with boys and women, or to many members of any single group, seems more expressive and daring for it. Erotic ambiguity, multiplicity, or obsession suggest superhuman energies that the celebrated possess, or that seem to possess *them*. Stars, whether flouting convention or floating rumors, attract those who would be familiars of someone they've never met. The apparently simple current phrase "virtual reality" signals confusion as to categories that apply to celebrity.

Bernhardt's eroticism, and her morbidity, fed her renown, though never moved her celebrity into the realm of power beyond what she exercised over her employees. But she certainly exercised influence in her choice and playing of roles, and she slept with men who had power, as Langtry did. Highly sexualized self-promotion, in Langtry's case, left her acting all but moot. With these two notorious women in the lead, star actresses gained visibility in celebrity's front ranks that they've never yielded. Every diva owes something to Bernhardt's example, as Lillie Langtry did nearer the source.

Even now, the celebrity women gain in the performing arts, the fine arts, and literary life, complements the predominance men enjoy still in politics, in statecraft, in warfare, in jurisprudence, in medicine, in commerce and the corporate world, in science and technology, and largely, still, in the academy. The tendency of some learned people to belittle celebrity owes no small part to the fact that so many of the most celebrated people have been, and remain, the women who've followed Sarah Bernhardt.

As for her chief predecessors and contemporaries: the violinist Niccolo Paganini and the pianist Franz Liszt, with the opera- and concert singer Jenny Lind, P. T. Barnum's "Swedish nightingale," were all of them international performers on something like the scale Bernhardt achieved. Charles Dickens and Mark Twain parleyed careers as authors into lucrative tours reading from their own works to large, mixed audiences.

The kind of celebrity that had been defined and enlarged by these people was mostly in place by 1900. By that time, show-business could be seen encroaching on electoral politics in the United States, particularly when it came to the presidency. Theodore Roosevelt combined writing, adventuring, and soldiering with the drive that carried him to America's highest office. Woodrow Wilson was a distinguished scholar before he went into university administration, the governorship of New Jersey, and the presidency of the United States for two terms. Performing, or writing, or both, gave the chief executives a path to celebrity, and, for the future presidents, to power. At present, there is every sign that celebrity and politics are converging more than ever.

For the last century, it's been commonplace to say that celebrity intrudes on sound judgment, true faith, and pure heroism. And yet, however much celebrity brings on misguided enthusiasm and mindless euphoria, it's been a marker of entertainments' ability, in a mediated culture, to reflect, reject, or on rarer occasions, sponsor change.

*   *   *

Drawing from examples in this book, I would advance five propositions.

First: That America has proven more eager than other nations to fête foreign celebrities. This has been taken as a sign either of fawning by the nation's critics, and celebrity's, or of inclusiveness by its partisans. In 1914, for instance, within months after Sarah Bernhardt had gotten wider coverage in vaudeville than America's own Ethel Barrymore, Charlie Chaplin, English *émigré* and veteran of music halls and vaudeville, was drawing as many people or more to his films than Mary Pickford could, or a little later, Douglas Fairbanks.

Chaplin and the celebrated couple who joined him to form United Artists knew that their popularity rested in their ability to draw millions from across the lines of class and gender. Over time, Chaplin fulfilled this requirement even better than Pickford and Fairbanks did. Whatever else can be said about him, Chaplin lent a new massiveness to mass culture, and to American popular culture in particular.

Chaplin's celebrity was launched out of Hollywood and redeemed there after his dalliances with leftist causes and young girls. Even after he'd come into disfavor, Hollywood cited his foreignness, and, indeed, his universal appeal, to exempt him from conventional standards of accountability. In return, he used articulacy, among his other talents, to uphold Hollywood's claims that films could be artful and profitable at the same time.

Chaplin, by helping make Hollywood, performed a function for films that was analogous to Bernhardt's in taking stage stardom into global markets. More recently, other members from Britain's laboring classes have borrowed from American popular culture to find celebrity on a global scale in pop music and musical theatre. The more widely American pop culture is adapted and exported—and the more foreign celebrities it enlists—the less purely American it can be said to be. In this sense, the celebrity America has sponsored has proven to be as multicultural as the nation itself.

Second: That Britain has been more protective of native celebrities than the United States has been. In this respect, Britain has come to resemble France as in the late nineteenth century, conserving native culture as solace for losing an empire. It may be that countries just on the downside of their power enjoy an advantage in launching celebrities into international markets, where they don't threaten in the same way as personalities do from more domineering nations.

On the other hand, it was British chauvinism, in part at least, that undercut the expatriate Chaplin's standing in his homeland, where he couldn't help looking as though he'd been minted in the United States. The United States, meanwhile, extended its commercial empire by selling products of its popular culture. This may help explain why the nation defers so often, still, to Europe as the site for true art and high culture. America continues to mark its deference to the British stage by giving British stars plum roles and lofty awards as regularly as clockwork.

Third: That celebrity-making on the largest scale has remained the province of the United States. With satellite technology and around-the-clock programming, a celebrated performer working in America can appear in sitcoms, serial dramas, or films, or be heard and seen in commercials, or sit as a guest on talk shows, or be exposed in more than one of these formats or in several at once. These days, there are many millions of images of the celebrated peering out from websites. Televised news coverage, documentaries, and political advocacy have all been joined by analogues on the Internet. Under these conditions, politicians are exposed to public gaze nearly as fully as celebrated performers have been.

On films, on television, and now on computer screens, commercials and sound bites have become the speeded-up, latter-day versions of vaudeville- and variety turns. In the economy of celebrity, short, multiple viewings balance constant repetition against coy brevity much in the way turns did. Many brief exposures make renown last longer and worth more. Short multiple viewings under highly controlled conditions have come into vogue in political life, and as in other pursuits, again with America leading the way.

Fourth: That when political life relies heavily on images and brief messages, it's little wonder that celebrated performers should seek and win elections. To give Ronald Reagan his due, he performed what is surely the most peerless celebrity turn yet by moving from film acting to the governorship of California and two terms as president of the United States. He stands as the epitome, though hardly, I think, as of the culmination of the celebrification of the presidency.

This tendency gathered strength at the same time performers' celebrity was being advanced by variety and vaudeville. In 1901, Theodore Roosevelt, author turned urban reformer, military hero, governor of New York, and vice-president of the United States, succeeded to the presidency when William McKinley died from an assassin's bullet. Roosevelt became the first man holding highest office to use yellow journalism, supplemented by some of the earliest newsreel footage, to sway public opinion.

Woodrow Wilson's inaugural parade in 1913 was the largest yet seen. He addressed Congress more often than any president has before or since, and he spoke in public more than any of his predecessors had.[2] Franklin Roosevelt used his fireside chats to take the measure of the huge listening public that commercial radio created. Jack Kennedy ramped up presidential affiliations with Hollywood, where his father had been a producer and his brother-in-law a star of the second order. Kennedy used television to get himself elected, and it used his body and image to frame the mourning at his loss. Kennedy was telegenic in a way that can only have encouraged Reagan. He was sexy in a way unmatched until Bill Clinton came along.

Events toward the end of Clinton's presidency showed how deeply the trappings of show-business celebrity, and of tabloid journalism, have infiltrated American politics and governance. In Clinton's case, accounts of his sexual escapades were reported, in official prosecutorial documents no less, to resemble coverage of the love lives of the stars.

The same cameras the candidate used in virtuosic ways were turned against him by those who saw his sexual conduct as arrogant, ungovernable, and unforgivable. Clinton's public life overlaid a private life that was traced even into the Oval Office, recast as a cockpit where lay a luridness that, for every detail brought to light, would never be fully exposed.

Voyeurism figured among Clinton's adversaries and his allies in ways that kept his transgressions on view long after his conviction on the articles of impeachment had become impossible. The president's friends, together with his enemies, saw him behaving like the movie stars whose haircuts his imitated and whose fetishes his aped. He reflected a certain celebrity on his main accusers, unglamorous lot that most of them were. A few of those accusers have carried their impeachment-won profiles into the administration of Clinton's successor.

The second Bush ran on a name that showed lineality and a platform that promised change. The uses he's found for his cowboy-like image have far outstripped his more drab and courtly father's, himself transmitter of the star-struck slogan, "a thousand points of light." George W. Bush's influence stands to grow in proportion to his ability to play the president in difficult times. The extent to which he does this will have become clearer by the time you read this. His administration has shown every sign of trying to control the news more tightly than ever. Control the image, control the power. It's simple to understand, harder to do.

Fifth and finally: That the political right are not the only ones complicit in celebrifying the American presidency and, increasingly, other offices in other lands. Celebrity's imperatives have, by increments, turned the United States' highest office into a masterly performance doled out in sound bites and camera ops. The primacy that the presidency has assumed in the nation's political life mimics stardom. So do the lavish publicity and more lavish rewards given lately to chief executive officers in the corporate world.

I do not mean to imply that a presidency vested in celebrity is less effective or less legitimate than the models that preceded it. The presidency-celebrified certainly reaches a larger electorate and may be more transparent, in its way, than the backroom politicking, glad-handing, and stump- and front-porch orating of the nineteenth century, or the earnest exclusivity of America's founding fathers.

Even now, as celebrity points to the future, it refers to the past by trading on qualities that once were exclusive to the royalty it now shores up in Great Britain and substitutes for in the United States. Celebrity recapitulates monarchy not only with display, but in the lineal way it can extend from one generation to the next. Michael Quinn has written, with more than slight exaggeration, that "every star seems to have not only a performing spouse and children, but brothers and sisters, nephews and cousins."[3] In politics, the same pattern applies to the Bushes as it did to the Kennedys, and before them the Roosevelts, and from a more bygone era, the Adamses.

In this book, the list of heirs who gave star turns or supported them shows lineality, too: in the three children of Maurice Barrymore, the two sons of Henry Irving, and the lone offspring of Sarah Bernhardt, and her only grandchild. Other relatives showed up in turns, too, among them Maurice Barrymore's in-laws, Mrs. Patrick Campbell's son and second husband, Maud and Herbert Tree's daughter, Irene Vanbrugh's husband, sister, and brother-in-law, and the spouses of Jessie Millward, Lillah McCarthy, and Frank Benson, with Alla Nazimova supported by domestic partners of both sexes, though not so far as is known, at the same time.

It's not surprising that so many stage stars should have chosen turns, and full-length plays, that treated family matters. Such short pieces gave star actors a way to reiterate themes they'd developed already in the theatre and that women stars have needed to vindicate their place in the public eye. The more celebrated a person becomes, the more interest there is in seeing her or him coupled, or not, and procreating, or failing that, taking on otherwise parental obligations.

It's noteworthy that star actresses in vaudeville and variety, in the rough sampling this book contains, outnumber star actors by a ratio of three to one. Since then, the face of celebrity among entertainers has supported the notion that celebrity is, to borrow Bernhardt's caption for acting, a feminine art.[4] Biased or antiquated as her opinion may sound, the perennially high numbers of women celebrated as performers call into question Tyler Cowen's recent assertion that "The use of fame and renown to support a male-dominated vision of society runs consistently through the history of ideas."[5] Even when women performers owe their prominence to being objectified, they've turned sexism on its head, some of them, by speaking to and for women and girls who admire and would emulate them.

If Sarah Bernhardt gave form to celebrity as we know it, the late Diana, Princess of Wales, showed how pliant it can be in the hands of someone who is not a professional entertainer. Although much of Diana's renown owed to the British monarchy, she used her standing before, during, and after her marriage, to rival and contest the royal family that had extended some of its prerogatives to her. She used celebrity, more than ever after her marriage failed, to champion causes she believed in, including herself. She carried an aura of royalty even as she increased the distance between herself and the royals-of-the-blood. She challenged the Windsors in ways they were powerless to check. Like the greatest celebrities who've died young, she went out in a blaze.

The new millennium shows celebrity more varied than ever. Osama bin Laden and Saddam Hussein figure in videotapes made in parts of the world little enamored of Western culture. Intellectual and academic life have joined politics in being overtaken by what Barbara Stafford has called, in irony, the "tainted society of spectacle."[6] Arnold Schwarzenegger, body builder, action hero, and in-law to the Kennedys, has been elected governor of the Golden State. A film called "The Passion of the Christ" has celebrated the torturing of a messiah as the latest in a series of crucifixions Hollywood has spun out in the spirit of righteousness for righteous times.

But whether spectacle is tainted, or righteous, or not, the celebrity it serves has never appealed only to the disempowered and unsophisticated. In a world grown increasingly secularized, celebrity allows for worship. Even the most skeptical among us have been known to set the stars of our own worlds into the firmaments we gaze on, in which we hope to shine.

# Notes ❧

## INTRODUCTION

1. Locke, *An Essay Concerning Human Understanding*, 67.
2. Locke, *Two Treatises of Government*, 351.

## 1. PATRONIZING, 1890–1901

1. A. G. Gardiner, "Pillars of Society" (1914); quoted in Cheshire, *Music Hall in Britain*, 53.
2. Trussler, *The Cambridge Illustrated History of Theatre*, 264.
3. *Stage*, January 17, 1890, 12.
4. Ibid.
5. Ibid.
6. *Era*, January 18, 1890, 16
7. *London Entre'Act*, March 8, 1890, 10.
8. *Stage*, March 7, 1890, 9.
9. Banta, *Imaging American Women*, 9.
10. *Era*, February 22, 1890, 15.
11. *Era*, November 28, 1885; quoted in Bailey, "Rational Recreation and the Entertainment Industry," 165.
12. *Era*, February 8, 1890, 17.
13. *New York Times*, December 30, 1890, 1.
14. *New York Times*, November 19, 1895, 2.
15. *Era*, November 23, 1895, 9.
16. *Stage*, November 28, 1895, 10.
17. *Era*, November 23, 1895, 9
18. Ibid.
19. Ibid.
20. Kotsilibas-Davis, *Great Times, Good Times*, 40–1.
21. Ibid., 55–60.
22. Howells, "Drama and Society," 86.

23. E. Barrymore, *Memories*, 17.
24. *New York Clipper*, April 3, 1897, 76.
25. *New York Dramatic Mirror*, April 10, 1897, 17.
26. *New York Clipper*, April 3, 1897, 76; turns drawn from a Keith's Union Square bill reproduced in Kotsilibas-Davis, *Great Times, Good Times*, facing 323.
27. Kotsilibas-Davis, *Great Times, Good Times*, 394.
28. Ibid., 434.
29. Ibid., 141.
30. Mayer, "Parlour and Platform Melodrama," 221.
31. *New York Dramatic Mirror*, September 22, 1900, 18.
32. *Boston Herald Post*, March 29, 1897; quoted in Kotsilibas-Davis, *Great Times, Good Times*, 394.
33. Kotsilibas-Davis, *Great Times, Good Times*, 26.
34. Ibid., 451.
35. Norden, *John Barrymore*, 31–2.
36. Kotsilibas-Davis, *Great Times, Good Times*, 444–5.
37. *New York Herald*, March 30, 1901; in Robinson Locke (RL), "Maurice Barrymore," vol. 39.
38. Kotsilibas-Davis, *Great Times, Good Times*, 469.
39. *New York Dramatic Mirror*, April 13, 1901, 7.
40. Kotsilibas-Davis, *Great Times, Good Times*, 421.
41. Ibid., 457–8.
42. Ibid., 455–6.
43. Said, *Culture and Imperialism*, 53.
44. Porter, "The Edwardians and Their Empire," 134.
45. Donaldson, *The Actor-Managers*, 147.
46. Bingham, *The Great Lover*, 106.
47. Kipling, *Rudyard Kipling's Verse*, 457.
48. Rose, *Red Plush and Greasepaint*, 111–2.
49. Palace Theatre Archive (London), programs for October 31, 1899 and November 6, 1899.
50. Rose, *Red Plush and Greasepaint*, 112.
51. Kachur, "Shakespeare Politicized" 27–8.
52. Ibid., 37–9.
53. *Pall Mall Gazette*, November 1, 1899, 2.
54. Ibid.
55. Palace Theatre Archive, program dated November 6, 1899.
56. *Era*, December 16, 1899, 21.
57. Ibid.
58. Kachur, "Shakespeare Politicized," 39.

59. Schneer, *London 1900: The Imperial Metropolis*, 95–6.

## 2. PRECIOUS BRITS, 1904–1912

1. Hapgood, "The Life of a Vaudeville Artiste," 393.
2. H.F. May, *The End of American Innocence*, 30.
3. Rowell, *William Terriss and Richard Prince*, 77.
4. Kasson, *Houdini, Tarzan, and the Perfect Man*, 108.
5. Millward, *Myself and Others*, 267–8.
6. Weyl, *The New Democracy*, 219.
7. Clipping dated June 19, 1904; in Robinson Locke (RL), "Millward."
8. Ibid.
9. "Drama and Abroad" *Theatre Magazine* 41 (July 1904).
10. Clipping dated June 19, 1904; in RL, "Millward."
11. An Interview with "Jessie Millward," *Theatre Magazine* 7:745 (April 1907), 107.
12. *New York Dramatic Mirror*, June 4, 1904, 16.
13. An Interview with "Jessie Millward," 106.
14. *Variety*, May 2, 1908, 17.
15. *Variety*, February 8, 1908, 1.
16. Rowell, *William Terriss and Richard Prince*, 89.
17. Millward, *Myself and Others*, 286–7.
18. Clipping dated May 27, 1912; in RL, "Millward," envelope 1478.
19. *Variety*, October 7, 1911; in RL, "Millward."
20. Millward, *Myself and Others*, 286.
21. Ibid., 291.
22. See chapter 4, this volume.
23. An Interview with "Jessie Millward," vii.
24. Quoted in Faulkner, *The Decline of Laissez Faire*, 80.
25. LaFeber, *The Cambridge History of American Foreign Relations*, 190.
26. Higham, *Strangers in the Land*, 149.
27. *New York Times*, May 13, 1904, 9.
28. *New York Dramatic Mirror*, May 28, 1904, 16.
29. Norris, *Advertising and the Transformation of American Society*, 86.
30. Hawtrey, *The Truth at Last*, 268.
31. Millward, *Myself and Others*, 271.
32. Hawtrey, *The Truth at Last*, 268.
33. *New York Dramatic Mirror*, May 28, 1904, 16.
34. Sutro, *Celebrities and Simple Souls*, 105.

35. *New York Dramatic Mirror*, May 28, 1904, 16.
36. Huizinga, *America*, 114.
37. *New York Clipper*, May 21, 1904, 302; *New York Dramatic Mirror*, May 28, 1904, 16.
38. Clipping dated September 10, 1904; in RL, "Hawtrey."
39. Weintraub, *Edward the Caresser*, 251–69.
40. Unidentified and undated clipping; in RL, "Langtry," vol. 309.
41. *Grand Rapids Herald*, May 31, 1906; in RL, "Langtry," vol. 309.
42. Gerson, *Because I Loved Him*, 89.
43. *New York Clipper*, October 6, 1906, 880.
44. *Variety*, September 26, 1906.
45. Clipping dated October 1, 1906; in RL, "Langtry," vol. 310.
46. Golden, "The Romance of the Jersey Lily," 70.
47. Langtry, *The Days I Knew*, 173.
48. *Variety*, October 20, 1906, 9.
49. *Variety*, October 6, 1906, 12.
50. *New York Times*, September 30, 1906, 9.
51. Green and Laurie, *Show Biz from Vaude to Video*, 29.
52. *New York World Review*, October 1, 1906; in RL, "Langtry," vol. 310; and Colonial program, Firestone Library, Princeton University.
53. Dudley, *The Gilded Lily*, 195.
54. Campbell, *My Life and Some Letters*, 309.
55. Ibid., 309–10.
56. Grau, *Forty Years of Observation of Music and the Drama*, 26.
57. Campbell, *My Life and Some Letters*, 309.
58. Ibid., 310.
59. *New York Clipper*, February 26, 1910, 53.
60. *New York Clipper*, February 19, 1910, 19.
61. *Variety*, February 19, 1910; in RL, "Campbell," vol. 98.
62. Campbell, *My Life and Some Letters*, 310.
63. Peters, *Mrs. Pat*, 298.
64. *Chicago Tribune*, May 23, 1910; in RL, "Campbell," vol. 98.
65. *New York Times*, January 16, 1910, pt. 3, 3.
66. Peters, *Mrs. Pat*, 297.
67. Clipping dated May 26, 1910; in RL, "Campbell," vol. 98.
68. Unidentified and undated clipping; in RL, "Campbell," vol. 99.
69. "Campbell," *New York Telegraph*, November 21, 1926.
70. H. G. Rhodes, "The American Invasion of the London Stage," in Wolter, ed., *The Dawning of American Drama*, 235.
71. *Era*, June 29, 1912, 15.

## 3. GROWING PAINS, 1910–1913

1. Denton, "The Technique of Vaudeville," 1074.
2. *Play Pictorial* (London), 10:58 (1907), iii.
3. Beerbohm, *Last Theatres*, 29; in a review dated February 27, 1904.
4. Hibbert, *Fifty Years of a Londoner's Life* , 77.
5. Ibid., 78.
6. Kift, *The Victorian Music Hall*, 23.
7. Barker, *The House That Stoll Built*, 19.
8. Newton, *Idols of the "Halls,"* 133.
9. See chapter 2, this volume.
10. *Era*, February 8, 1908, 22.
11. *Era*, August 27, 1910, 20.
12. Blow, *Through Stage Doors*, 20.
13. Graham, *An Old Stock-Actor's Memories*, 245–6.
14. Everding, "Shaw and the Palaces of Variety," 14.
15. See chapter 6, this volume.
16. *Era*, January 15, 1910, 19.
17. *British Theatre in the 1890s*, 145.
18. Croxton, *Crowded Nights—and Days*, 187.
19. *Daily Telegraph*, September 21, 1910; in Coliseum pamphlet (1954).
20. Stevenson, *British Society 1914–45*, 32.
21. *Stage*, September 22, 1910, 12.
22. Gold and Fizdale, *The Divine Sarah*, 295.
23. *Play Pictorial* (London) 16:98 (1910), iv.
24. *Era*, September 24, 1910, 25.
25. *Stage*, September 21, 1911, 13.
26. Aston, *Sarah Bernhardt*, 137.
27. Barker, *The House That Stoll Built*, 72–4.
28. *Era*, October 28, 1911, 23.
29. *Era*, October 14, 1911, 23.
30. Croxton, *Crowded Nights—and Days*, 96–7.
31. *Stage*, October 10, 1912, 13.
32. *Era*, October 12, 1912, 23.
33. Agate, *Madame Sarah*, 174.
34. *Era*, October 26, 1912, 23.
35. *Era*, September 10, 1913, 21.
36. Croxton, *Crowded Nights—and Days*, 219.
37. Ibid.
38. *Stage*, September 11, 1913, 14.

39. Croxton, *Crowded Nights—and Days*, 219.
40. *Era*, October 15, 1913, 27; *in* Croxton, *Crowded Nights—and Days*, 221.
41. See chapter 5, this volume.
42. See chapter 4, this volume.
43. *Era*, December 31, 1910, 25.
44. *"Stage" Year Book* 1912, 37–8.
45. *Era*, January 20, 1912, 16.
46. See chapter 1, this volume.
47. Foulkes, *Performing Shakespeare in the Age of Empire*, 131.
48. *Era*, October 15, 1910, 17.
49. Rutherford, " 'Harmless Nonsense,' " 143.
50. *Daily Graphic*, January 15, 1912.
51. *Era*, January 27, 1912, 23.
52. Ibid.
53. Ibid.
54. Ibid.
55. Titterton, *From Theatre to Music Hall*, 65–6.
56. H. Pearson, *Beerbohm Tree*, 160.
57. Truman, *Beerbohm Tree's Olivia*, 108.
58. H. Pearson, *Beerbohm Tree*, 160.
59. *Era*, September 28, 1912, 19.
60. Kennedy, "The New Drama and the New Audience," 146.
61. *Era*, January 13, 1912, 21.
62. *Stage*, July 8, 1915, 15.
63. *Era*, July 14, 1915, 10.
64. MacCarthy, "In the Stalls," 225.
65. Deane, "Imperialism/Nationalism," 359.
66. *Era*, February 1, 1913, 24.
67. Mason, *Sir George Alexander and the St. James's Theatre*, 206–7.
68. *Era*, February 8, 1913, 15.
69. *Era*, February 15, 1913, 22.
70. *"Stage" Year Book* 1913, 27.
71. *Era*, October 29, 1913, 22.
72. Hibbert, *Souvenir Comprising the Story of the Music Hall*, 29.
73. *Era*, February 1, 1913, 20.
74. Titterton, *From Theatre to Music Hall*, 115–6.
75. Abrahams, *The Lyrical Left*, 47, 49.
76. Le Bon, *The Crowd*, 17–8.
77. Banta, *Imaging American Women*, 94.
78. Higham, *Strangers in the Land*, 149.

79. Vrettos, *Somatic Fictions*, 81–5.
80. Ibid., 81.
81. Brownstein, *Tragic Muse*, 255.
82. *New York Times*, December 2, 1912, 11.
83. Bernhardt, *The Art of the Theatre*, 161.
84. *Los Angeles Examiner*, February 23, 1913; in Robinson Locke (RL), "Bernhardt," vol. 66.
85. Palace Theatre (NYC) program for Sarah Bernhardt, 1913; Rare Books and Special Collections, Hatcher Graduate Library, University of Michigan.
86. Unidentified and undated clipping; in RL, "Bernhardt," vol. 66.
87. *Variety*, December 20, 1912, 52.
88. Ibid.
89. *Variety*, March 28, 1913, 5.
90. *Variety*, May 9, 1913, 20, and May 23, 1913, 16.
91. *Variety*, May 23, 1913, 16.
92. Ibid.
93. *Variety*, August 8, 1913, 1.
94. Davison, "The Music-Hall Tradition," 44.
95. Hobsbawm, "Inventing Traditions," 4–5.

## 4. SUFFER THE WOMEN, 1910–1914

1. MacKaye, "Art and the Women's Movement," 680.
2. *New York Times*, December 2, 1912, 11.
3. Hirshfield, "The Actresses' Franchise League," 131.
4. Corbett, *Representing Femininity*, 131.
5. *Montreal Star*, January 23, 1911, 15.
6. Stevens, *Jailed for Freedom*, 27.
7. Ormond, *J. M. Barrie*, 114.
8. Kent, *Gender and Power in Britain*, 267.
9. Coliseum programs for March 1912, catalogued by the year and housed in the Theatre Museum Library, London.
10. I. Vanbrugh, *To Tell My Story*, 105.
11. *Stage*, November 2, 1911, 14.
12. *Sketch*, February 26, 1913, 256.
13. Barrie, *The Plays of J. M. Barrie*, 798.
14. *Macbeth*, Act 5, scene 1.
15. *Era*, March 15, 1913, 22.

16. I. Vanbrugh, *To Tell My Story*, 83.
17. Hirshfield, "The Actresses' Franchise League," 144.
18. Ibid., 143.
19. Ibid., 144.
20. I. Vanbrugh, *To Tell My Story*, 84.
21. Ashwell, *Myself a Player*, 129.
22. *Stage*, October 2, 1913, 16.
23. *Era*, October 29, 1913, 26.
24. Holledge, *Innocent Flowers*, 71.
25. I. Vanbrugh, *To Tell My Story*, 104.
26. Ibid., 104–5.
27. Corbett, *Representing Femininity*, 140.
28. Ashwell, *Myself a Player*, 157.
29. Ibid., 165.
30. Marcus, ed., *Suffrage and the Pankhursts*, 309.
31. Ashwell, *Myself a Player*, 165.
32. *Stage*, October 5, 1911, 13.
33. Ashwell, *Myself a Player*, 157.
34. *Era*, October 7, 1911, 24.
35. Ibid.
36. Palace Theatre program, dated October 18, 1911, at the Palace Theatre Archive, Palace Theatre, London.
37. *Era*, November 26, 1910, 21.
38. *Stage*, February 22, 1912, 15.
39. *Era*, February 24, 1912, 25.
40. *Stage*, March 7, 1912, 13.
41. *Era*, March 9, 1912, 22.
42. *Stage*, March 7, 1912, 13.
43. Ibid.
44. *Era*, October 20, 1915, 16.
45. *Era*, October 13, 1915, 10.
46. Ashwell, *Myself a Player*, 275–6.
47. Marcus, ed., *Suffrage and the Pankhursts*, 310.
48. Holledge, *Innocent Flowers*, 75.
49. McCarthy, *Myself and My Friends*, 149.
50. *Times* (London), February 7, 1911, 10e.
51. *Era*, February 18, 1911, 24.
52. *Era*, February 4, 1911, 22.
53. *Era*, December 17, 1910, 25.
54. *Stage*, December 15, 1910, 15.

55. *Era*, March 18, 1911, 21.
56. See chapter 2, this volume.
57. *Stage*, March 9, 1911, 13.
58. *Era*, February 10, 1912, 27.
59. Rosen, *Rise Up, Women!* , 157.
60. Hirshfield, "The Actresses' Franchise League," 140.
61. *Variety*, October 4, 1912, 16.
62. *Brooklyn Eagle*, October 15, 1912; in Robinson Locke (RL), "Lillie Langtry," vol. 310.
63. Unidentified and undated clipping; in RL, "Langtry," vol. 310.
64. *Era*, January 4, 1913, 20.
65. Unidentified and undated clipping; in RL, "Langtry," vol. 310.
66. Ibid.
67. Ibid.
68. Reilly, "A Forgotten 'Fallen Woman,' " 106.
69. *New York American*, October 7, 1913; in RL, "Olga Nethersole," vol. 364; *New York Clipper*, October 11, 1913, 9.
70. Millward, *Myself and Others*, 284.
71. *Era*, November 5, 1913, 22.
72. *New York Telegraph*, November 7, 1913; in RL, "Nethersole," vol. 364.
73. *New York Review*, November 8, 1913; in RL, "Nethersole," vol. 364.
74. *Boston Herald*, October 28, 1913; in RL, "Nethersole," vol. 364.
75. Kibler, *Rank Ladies*, 48.
76. *New York Times*, October 10, 1913, 7.
77. Ibid.
78. Lumsden, *Rampant Women*, 151.
79. Glenn, *Female Spectacle*, 31.
80. Finnegan, *Selling Suffrage*, 81.
81. Kaplan and Stowell, *Theatre and Fashion*, 80.
82. Finnegan, *Selling Suffrage*, 107.
83. Blatch, *Challenging Years*, 138.
84. See chapter 1, this volume.
85. *New York Evening World*, April 27, 1913; in RL, "Barrymore," vol. 37.
86. Unidentified and undated clipping; in the Chamberlain and Lyman Brown Collection (C&LBC), "Ethel Barrymore," vol. 4.
87. Barrymore, *Memories*, 176.
88. Ibid.
89. Ibid.
90. From an unidentified clipping dated March 12, 1911; in RL, "Ethel Barrymore," vol. 37, under Walter P. Eaton's byline.

91. *New York Mirror*, January 29, 1913; in RL, "Barrymore," vol. 37.
92. Clipping from a September issue of the *Chicago News*; in RL, "Ethel Barrymore," vol. 37.
93. Ibid.
94. *Variety*, September 13, 1912, 18.
95. *Toledo Blade*, January 9, 1913; in RL, "Ethel Barrymore," vol. 37.
96. Kibler, *Rank Ladies*, 219.
97. Unidentified and undated clipping; in RL, "Ethel Barrymore," vol. 37.
98. *New York Times*, May 30, 1912, 4.
99. *New York Dramatic Mirror*, April 30, 1913, 6.
100. *New York Telegraph*, April 29, 1913; in RL, "Ethel Barrymore," vol. 37.
101. *Variety*, May 2, 1913, 18.
102. *New York Telegraph*, April 29, 1913; in RL, "Ethel Barrymore," vol. 37.
103. *New York Dramatic Mirror*, December 16, 1914, 17.
104. *New York Evening Mail*, December 22, 1914; in RL, "Ethel Barrymore," vol. 38.
105. *Billboard*, July 17, 1923; in C&LBC, "Barrymore," vol. 4.
106. *Variety*, June 12, 1923, 32.
107. *Knickerbocker Press*, January 2, 1927; in C&LBC, "Barrymore," vol. 7.
108. *New York Telegraph*, September 8, 1923; in C&LBC, "Barrymore," vol. 5.
109. *New York Times*, April 30, 1923; in C&LBC, "Barrymore," vol. 5.
110. *New York Times*, September 21, 1924; in C&LBC, "Barrymore," vol. 6.
111. Barrymore, *Memories*, 174.
112. Everding, "Shaw and the Palaces of Variety," 18.
113. Holledge, *Innocent Flowers*, 98–9.
114. Ibid., 101.

## 5. WAR AND PEACE, 1914–1918

1. Quoted in Wolter, ed., *The Dawning of American Drama*, 233.
2. *Era*, March 10, 1915, 12.
3. *Era*, October 20, 1915, 10.
4. *Henry V*, Act 4, scene 3.
5. *Stage*, August 20, 1914, 11.
6. Quoted in Mullin, *Victorian Actors and Actresses in Review*, 490–2.
7. *Era*, August 26, 1914, 10.
8. *Era*, September 2, 1914, 10.
9. *Era*, December 2, 1914, 19.

10. *Stage*, November 5, 1914, 18.
11. *Era*, December 9, 1914, 14.
12. Irving, *The Amusement of the People*, 19.
13. *Era*, December 9, 1914, 14.
14. Kent, *Gender and Power in Britain*, 274–6.
15. Barker, *The House That Stoll Built*, 119.
16. Thompson, *Outsiders*, 171.
17. Barrie, *The Plays of J. M. Barrie*, 12.
18. Ibid., 39–40.
19. *Times* (London), December 22, 1914; viewed at Westminster City Archives, London.
20. Croxton, *Crowded Nights—and Days*, 235.
21. Coliseum programs for the weeks of December 21, 1914, and January 4, 1915; housed at the Theatre Museum Library, London.
22. Barker, *The House That Stoll Built*, 119–20.
23. MacKail, *The Story of J. M. B.[arrie]*, 478.
24. *"Stage" Year Book 1914*, 22.
25. Schneider, *American Women in the Progressive Era*, 169.
26. Ibid., 198.
27. Press release dated September 20, 1914; in Robinson Locke (RL), "Alla Nazimova," vol. 356.
28. Senelick, "The American Tour of Orlenev and Nazimova," 8.
29. *New York Dramatic Mirror*, February 3, 1915, 18.
30. *War Plays by Women*, ed. Tylee, 13.
31. Blair, *The Torchbearers*, 133.
32. Wynn, *From Progressivism to Prosperity*, 27.
33. *Variety*, January 16, 1915, 18.
34. Spears, *The Civil War on the Screen*, 125.
35. *New York Dramatic Mirror*, February 3, 1915, 18.
36. Middleton, *These Things Are Mine*, 265.
37. Peiss, *Cheap Amusements*, 152.
38. Banner, *American Beauty*, 196.
39. Glenn, *Female Spectacle*, 143.
40. Auster, *Actresses and Suffragists*, 86.
41. *New York Telegraph*, January 26, 1915; in RL, "Nazimova," vol. 357, under Nellie Revell's byline.
42. *Variety*, January 30, 1915, 18.
43. *New York Times*, January 26, 1915, 11.
44. *New York Dramatic Mirror*, February 3, 1915, 18.
45. *New York Times*, January 26, 1915, 11.

46. Undated interview with *American Magazine*; in the "Alla Nazimova" file at the Billy Rose Theatre Collection, Public Library of New York at Lincoln Center, catalogue number MWEZ + n.c. 13,512.

47. *Pittsburgh Leader*, May 11, 1915; in RL, "Nazimova," vol. 357.

48. *Los Angeles Examiner*, July 20, 1915; in RL, "Nazimova," vol. 357.

49. *Memphis Commercial Appeal*, November 2, 1915; in RL, "Nazimova," vol. 357.

50. *Pittsburgh Post*, December 14, 1915; in RL, "Nazimova," vol. 357.

51. Undated interview with *American Magazine*; in the "Alla Nazimova" file, Billy Rose Theatre Collection.

52. Wentworth, *War Brides*, 3.

53. Spears, *The Civil War on the Screen*, 127.

54. *War Plays by Women*, ed. Tylee, 13.

55. *Era*, March 3, 1915, 12.

56. Shaw, *The Drama Observed*, 368.

57. *Stage*, March 4, 1915, 15.

58. *Era*, April 21, 1915, 12.

59. *Era*, October 13, 1915, 10.

60. Holledge, *Innocent Flowers*, 98–9.

61. *Era*, June 21, 1916, 14.

62. Ibid.

63. Ibid.

64. *Stage*, October 12, 1916, 15; *Era*, October 11, 1916, 1.

65. *Era*, February 14, 1917, 14.

66. Barker, *The House That Stoll Built*, 119.

67. See chapter 2, this volume.

68. *Stage*, August 30, 1917, 8.

69. *Era*, August 16, 1916, 12.

70. Donaldson, *The Actor-Managers*, 122.

71. *Era*, August 16, 1916, 12.

72. *Stage*, February 1, 1917, 12.

73. Spoken by the character soon to be crowned Richard III in *3Henry VI*, Act 3, scene 2.

74. *Macbeth*, Act 2, scene 4.

75. *Era*, January 17, 1917, 14.

76. Weintraub, *Bernard Shaw 1914–1918*, 142.

77. *Era*, January 31, 1917, 16.

78. Trewin, *Benson and the Bensonians*, 220.

79. Lady [Mrs. Frank] Benson, *Mainly Players*, 301.

80. *Romeo and Juliet*, Act 2, scene 2.

81. Barker, *The House That Stoll Built*, 135.
82. *Stage*, February 1, 1917, 11.
83. Ibid.
84. Coliseum program for the week of January 29, 1917, at the Theatre Museum Library, London.
85. *Stage*, April 26, 1917, 10.
86. *Era*, November 7, 1917, 17; *Stage*, November 8, 1917, 8.
87. *The Merchant of Venice*, Act 4, scene 1.
88. *Stage*, July 20, 1916, 13.
89. *Era*, July 19, 1916, 23.
90. *Stage*, July 20, 1916, 13.
91. McCarthy, *Myself and My Friends*, 188.
92. Kent, *Gender and Power in Britain*, 279.
93. *Stage*, April 5, 1917, 9.
94. See chapter 2, this volume.
95. *Era*, April 4, 1917, 12.
96. Holroyd, *Bernard Shaw: The Pursuit of Power*, 379.
97. McCarthy, *Myself and My Friends*, 190.
98. Holroyd, *Bernard Shaw: The Lure of Fantasy*, 91.
99. McCarthy, *Myself and My Friends*, 190–2.
100. Ibid., 191.
101. *Era*, January 23, 1918, 1.
102. *Stage*, January 24, 1918, 10.
103. *Stage*, February 7, 1918, 10.
104. Langtry, *The Days I Knew*, 309.
105. Ibid., 306.
106. Barrie, *The Plays of J. M. Barrie*, 949.
107. *Era*, July 31, 1918, 11.
108. Bernhardt, *The Art of the Theatre*, 144.
109. Gold and Fizdale, *The Divine Sarah*, 316–7.
110. Ibid., 315.
111. Skinner, *Madame Sarah*, 322.
112. *Era*, January 5, 1916, 16.
113. *Stage*, January 6, 1916, 15.
114. *Stage*, January 20, 1916, 16.
115. *Era*, January 19, 1916, 18.
116. Barker, *The House That Stoll Built*, 121.
117. Jelavich, *Berlin Cabaret*, 119.
118. *Era*, April 12, 1916, 12.
119. See chapter 3, this volume.

120. Agate, *Madame Sarah*, 212.
121. Ibid., 213.
122. *Era*, April 12, 1916, 12.
123. Hathorn, *Our Lady of the Snows*, 216.
124. *Variety*, February 16, 1917, 8.
125. Green and Laurie, *Show Biz from Vaude to Video*, 147, 149.
126. *Variety*, December 7, 1917, 1; and *Variety*, October 19, 1918; in RL, "Bernhardt," vol. 68.
127. *Era*, October 20, 1915, 10.
128. Ibid.
129. Wynn, *From Progressivism to Prosperity*, 30.
130. *Variety*, December 7, 1917, 1.
131. *Variety*, December 21, 1917, 20.
132. *Variety*, January 11, 1918.
133. Unidentified and undated clipping; in RL, "Bernhardt," vol. 68.
134. Bernhardt file; an unidentified obituary.
135. Kasson, *Houdini, Tarzan, and the Perfect Man*, 222.
136. Green and Laurie, *Show Biz from Vaude to Video*, 126.
137. Flexner, *Century of Struggle*, 284–5.
138. Revell, "When Vaudeville Goes to War," 356.

## 6. PARTING, 1921–1934

1. Quoted in Leach, *Land of Desire*, 34.
2. Schickel, *Intimate Strangers*, 44.
3. Fowles, *Starstruck*, 226.
4. Manvell, *Ellen Terry*, 323.
5. Auerbach, *Ellen Terry*, 443.
6. *Era*, July 21, 1921, 13.
7. *The Merchant of Venice*, Act 4, scene 1.
8. *2Henry IV*, Act 3, scene 1.
9. Steen, *A Pride of Terrys*, 335–6.
10. Ibid., 336
11. *2Henry IV*, Act 3, scene 1.
12. *Manchester Guardian*, July 19, 1921, 14.
13. *Manchester Evening News*, July 19, 1921, 2.
14. *Manchester City News*, July 23, 1921, 2.
15. Auerbach, *Ellen Terry*, 444.
16. Ibid.

17. Steen, *A Pride of Terrys*, 336.
18. "Ellen Terry" file at the Theatre Museum Library, London, England.
19. Manvell, *Ellen Terry*, 324.
20. See chapter 5, this volume.
21. Spears, *The Civil War on Screen*, 150.
22. Middleton, *These Things Are Mine*, 267.
23. *Variety*, November 1, 1923, 33.
24. Middleton, *These Things Are Mine*, 267.
25. *New York Herald*, October 31, 1923; from the "Nazimova" file at the Billy Rose Theatre Collection, Public Library of New York at Lincoln Center, catalogue number MWEZ + n.c. 13,512.
26. *New York Times*, October 31, 1923; from the Nazimova file.
27. *Variety*, April 21, 1926, 14.
28. Lambert, *Nazimova*, 287.
29. *Variety*, February 2, 1927, 21.
30. *Era*, June 1, 1927, 12.
31. "Nazimova" file at the Theatre Library, London.
32. Lambert, *Nazimova*, 294.
33. Ibid., 293.
34. *Variety*, January 18, 1928, 38.
35. Lambert, *Nazimova*, 292–8.
36. *Variety*, January 18, 1928, 37.
37. Ibid.
38. Smith, *The Vaudevillians*, 16.
39. Negri, *Memoirs of a Star*, 346.
40. *Stage*, February 12, 1931, 3.
41. *Era*, February 4, 1931, 1.
42. Negri, *Memoirs of a Star*, 361.
43. Coliseum programs for June 1928; in the Theatre Museum Library, London.
44. *Stage*, July 7, 1927, 8.
45. *Stage*, June 21, 1928, 11.
46. *Era*, June 20, 1928, 13.
47. *London Evening News*, July 19, 1927; from the "Fannie Ward" file at the Mander and Mitchenson Collection, Kent, England.
48. *Variety*, July 25, 1933, 12.
49. "Ethel Barrymore" file, City Museum of New York.
50. *Stage*, February 8, 1934, 3.
51. *Era*, February 7, 1934, 1.
52. Peters, *The House of Barrymore*, 350.

53. Burian, "Aileen Stanley: Her Life and Times," 112.
54. E. Barrymore, *Memories*, 274.
55. Peters, *The House of Barrymore*, 606.
56. E. Barrymore, *Memories*, 177.
57. *Chicago Record Herald*, September 15, 1912; in RL, "Barrymore," vol. 37.
58. Undated clipping; in RL, "Bernhardt," vol. 68.
59. *Variety*, March 1920; in RL, "Bernhardt," vol. 68.
60. Hippodrome program, at the Firestone Library Theatre Collection, Princeton University, Princeton, New Jersey.
61. Gold and Fizdale, *The Divine Sarah*, 327.
62. Ibid., 329–30.
63. Middleton, *These Things Are Mine*, 258.

## AFTERTHOUGHTS

1. Rojek, *Celebrity*, 198.
2. Cooper, *Pivotal Decades*, 194.
3. Quinn, "Celebrity and the Semiotics of Acting," 154.
4. Bernhardt, *The Art of the Theatre*, 144.
5. Cowen, *What Price Fame?*, 68.
6. Stafford, *Good Looking*, 4.

# Bibliography ❧

For those who like to sift: nostalgic writing and memoirs treating vaudeville include Caffin (1914), Seldes (1924, rpt. 1957), Marks (1934), Gilbert (1940; rpt. 1963), Marston and Feller (1943), Green and Laurie (1951), Laurie alone (1953), Sobel (1961), Spitzer (1969), Zellers (1971), DiMeglio (1973), the Samuelses (1974), Smith (1976), Toll (1976), McNamara (1983), Stein (1984), the Fieldses (1993) and Trav S.C.' (2005)] For colorful writing, likewise, about music halls and variety, see Stuart and Park (1895), Titterton (1912), Hibbert (1916), Haddon (1922 and 1935), Calthrop (1925), Newton (1928; rpt. 1975), Alltree (1932), Croxton (c. 1934), Boardman (1935), Haddon (1935), Disher (1938), Newton (1940), Felstead (1946), Macqueen-Pope (1950 and 1951), Bevan (1952), Barker (1957), Rose (1964), Mander and Mitchenson (1965), the collected journalism of Max Beerbohm (1969 and 1970), Gammond (1971), Farson (1972), Honri (1973), Read (1985), and Wilmut (1985). The span of years across which the books above have appeared shows the ongoing appeal of variety entertainments, owing something, at least, to the older stuff's fostering or feeding mass media including, in the order of first impact, film, radio, and television.

In grouping books together, as I've done, I don't mean to equate them. The quality of the writing varies widely, as does the rigor applied to performances, performers, and other events. Writing in the spirit of nostalgia takes it for granted that vaudeville and variety were good things, and it recalls them in good spirit. And so, of course, do the biographies of performers, though one might be struck at how consistently variety entertainments are relegated to venues deemed more worthy by veterans of the stage until after World War II. To find further information about particular performers, one can take a look at the endnotes that document their doings or for their names in the index or bibliography.

British writers have had longer to mourn music halls, as began to happen even before 1900 with the gentrification that distinguished variety from the music halls. In Britain, even before World War I, nineteenth-century music halls were associated with working-class empowerment, or, failing that, solidarity, or, failing that, jollity in the brotherhood of drink. Champions of the music halls have tended to favor working-class heroes; and so do champions of vaudeville who favor a brand of egalitarianism not quite so class-coded as British models are. Michael Kammen, the contemporary American historian, explains the longer-standing writing about music halls: "There is a tendency to locate the genesis of commercialization in cities as a major impetus for popular culture much earlier in time than Americanists do for the United States" (1999, 47). British writers have been more disposed to criticize commercialism, and to do so systematically, than their American counterparts.

Several books can help organize the nostalgia and memorabilia, and other aggregates, too. Excellent guides to vaudeville and variety writing include, on vaudeville and music halls together, Wilmeth (1980 and 1982), and on music halls alone, Senelick et al. (1981), which lists bibliographies for individual performers. McNamara (1983) and Stein (1984) have collected original documents around vaudeville, as Cheshire (1974) has done for music halls. Slide (1994) has documented the encyclopedic qualities of vaudeville in his own encyclopedia, organized by name and topic. In broader scope, Bryan (1985) furnishes an index, by actors' names, to theatrical biographies in English, and he includes both British and American actors, though ones who flourished chiefly in entertainments considered them more respectable than variety entertainment was. Slide and Senelick are the best sources for catching up on the people, by name, who gave the turns.

Neither vaudeville nor variety received serious scholarly attention until the 1960s. This came with the advent of what came to be called the counterculture. As notions gained currency that literature and high culture, in their European derivatives, had become morally bankrupt, vaudeville and variety took their places among an assortment of entertainments devised, it was argued, for and by the people, whoever they might be. For approaches inflected by populist and countercultural values in the spirit of the 1960s, see McLean (1965) and DiMeglio (1973) on vaudeville. For counterparts in British scholarship on music halls, see Farson (1972) and Davison (1982). Taken together, this class of book shows vaudeville, and even more the British music halls, less institutionalized, more spontaneous, and more widely popular than the theatre and more literary entertainments ever were.

In the 1980s, Warren I. Susman headed a group of Americans who focused on the role of entertainments in shaping culture as well as reflecting it. Susman and his circle saw complex and fruitful relationships between popular entertainments and what had formerly been considered to be weightier issues. Social and cultural history is the mode adopted by Lynes (1985) in looking at performances and the visual arts in the United States. Bratton (1986) and Bailey (1986) broach a social history of music halls in the collections each author has edited.

Bailey (1978) was also a pioneer in applying Marxist critique to popular entertainments and, later (1998), in calling on "hegemonic" models that have values constantly pitted against one another and negotiated in the public space. Hegemony was an idea first advanced by the Italian cultural critic Antonio Gramsci in the 1930s. In the 1980s, then, one-half century after his death, Gramsci gained a wider following in socialist circles in across Europe and the Americas. Russell (1996) takes his cue from Gramsci and is rare among British scholars for treating variety to the near exclusion of music halls in his interest in variety producers' calculated, concerted efforts to draw clientele across the boundaries of class. McConachie (1992, twice) is foremost among American scholars to have applied hegemonic models to performances that achieved widest popularity.

Treatments of vaudeville as a platform for ideology emerge from Allen (1991), who also wrote a dissertation about the commerce in films featured in vaudeville (1977). He is more skeptical than Nasaw (1993), who praises vaudeville—as Russell does variety—for bringing social classes into contact, if not harmony.

For more considered assessments of vaudeville stressing the play of many voices against the riot of market-driven forces, or coercion, see Erenberg (1981), Snyder (1989 and 1991), and Jenkins (1992). In Britain, Summerfield (1986), Bratton (1986), Bailey (1978 and 1986), and Crowhurst (1992) join Russell (1996) in fine-tuning Gramsci's notions of hegemony and applying them to spheres that sound less formidable than "ideology" often does. Kift (1996) has undertaken the most massive statistical treatment of music halls by reconstructing audiences, using means in sociology and demography, to reinforce the notion of multivocality that accommodates dissent and resistance. Kift also offers a comprehensive survey of the range of scholarly writing around music halls. Hodin (1997) takes a similar statistical approach, in much smaller compass, in trying to uncover the kinds of audiences that visited vaudeville.

Tracy C. Davis (1991 and 1992) documents feminism by using statistical measures to track women's lot in the British theatres and in music halls. Feminism also animates the work of Maitland (1986) on music halls and of Staples (1984) on vaudeville. Kibler (1999) offers rich treatments of audiences as well as performers in vaudeville, and the ways that gender was defined and performed. Writing about working-class women in New York City, Peiss (1986) finds a pragmatic, economically driven proto-feminism, focused firmly in the material world, in a range of pastimes and entertainments.

Since the 1960s, British and European scholarship around music halls has sprung more steadily from the perspectives of sociology and economics. Scholarly writing around music halls has concentrated most heavily on the nineteenth century, while American scholarship about vaudeville has tended to dwell on events in the first two decades of the twentieth century. Nicoll (1973), Stedman Jones (1973–1974), Bailey (1982 and 1986), and Crowhurst (1997) all study the finances of music halls. Among these writers, Stedman Jones is heavily indebted to traditional Marxism in the manipulative functions he finds in music halls and their management. Strictly Marxist approaches have given way to others that favor the resistive capacity of popular entertainments, in line with Mikhail Bakhtin's seminal writings on carnival (see Davison 1982).

Hostility to popular entertainment has often sprung from notions, dating back at least as far as the nineteenth century: that crowds grow stupider and more dangerous the larger they get (Le Bon 1895; rpt. 1960). More recently, negative commentary has focused on the tendency of popular entertainments to trade in images rather than words, particularly as this is seen to influence repression as to gender, race, and class. Phelan (1993) and Dudden (1994) see sexism inherent in images hatched to appeal to mass audiences, whereas Cima (1993) and Kibler (1999) dispute the same assertions based on the discretion they see individual performers applying in their work and communicating to their viewers. Stafford (1996) sees more enlightened and benevolent, or at least multivalent, power in images. She can be read to imply that celebrity, dependent as it is on visual culture, is not necessarily unitary, degraded, or coercive therefore.

\*   \*   \*

Anyone who criticizes things that appeal to large numbers of people—often *because* the things appeal to large numbers—has been disposed to criticize celebrity or to hold it in low regard. As a result, with a few recent exceptions, the institution of celebrity hasn't found the same critical favor that single celebrated persons attract routinely. Much of the writing hostile to celebrity adds moral repugnance to a certain condescension.

Many scholars who hold Karl Marx and his interpreters dear have counted celebrity among the by-products of mass entertainment packaged using assembly-line models. Mass entertainment, the argument goes, is a commercialized substitute for religion, which Marx called an opiate for the masses. The Soviet critic Mikhail Bakhtin praised folk- and pre-commercial pastimes for giving voice to the disadvantaged. At the same time, he argued that popular fare had spoken for the lowly across history because—he implies rather than states it—the amusements hadn't been a mouthpiece for the mighty in the way he thought modern mass entertainments had become, subject to central control to serve oppressive agendas. Bakhtin, writing at the height of Soviet power and under its scrutiny, had to be careful as to what he said about totalitarian regimes.

The Frankfurt School was spawned and expelled by a rival totalitarianism. This cluster of cultural theorists came to life in Germany, but gained wider influence more quickly than Bakhtin did outside the Soviet Union. Members of the Frankfurt School fled Nazi Germany in the 1930s with their influence on the rise and their righteousness at high boil. Their arguments that mass entertainments served up ideology confirmed a benighted present that Bakhtin only hinted at. Members of the Frankfurt School who landed in the United States deplored what they were first and most famous for, coining the term "culture industry." The School was afraid that, sooner or later, culture industry would support the same anti-intellectualism, aggression, and genocide that fascist governments sponsored before and during World War II.

Theodor Adorno and Max Horkheimer, among the Frankfurt School transplanted to America, never implicated vaudeville. That may have been because it had become a shadow of itself by the time they arrived. Still, with radio and films featuring former vaudevillians such as Jack Benny, Milton Berle, Burns and Allen, and Bob Hope, the Frankfurt School nursed an ongoing skepticism, in fact hostility, to vaudeville's lineal descendants: films, radio, and, with the 1950s, commercial television. In 1944, Leo Lowenthal wrote his School-worthy derision of celebrity, specifically, for increasing the popularity of entertainers as leading subjects for American biographies.

The School's views stood largely unchallenged, in learned circles at least, though briefly, after the war. It was the sudden, spectacular rise of commercial television that brought widening debates about the advantages and liabilities of mass entertainments. The partisans of popular culture formed a growing unnamed school of their own to argue, in a populist way, that the broadest kinds of culture had been instrumental in winning the war and deserved some of the credit for doing so. The American sociologist David Reisman argued that consumption expresses free choice and is itself a kind of democratic exercise. His views implied that celebrity, too, was an exercise in consumption, with other moral and ethical considerations inherent but subordinate to the vastness of the American economy. Reisman's arguments challenged the liberal wing for calling popular culture pablum, and more conservative commentators for blaming pop culture for the slavishness and conformity they saw as endemic to American life. In the 1960s, radicals saw the kinds of popular culture they did not endorse as manipulated by a corrupt ruling class.

In the 1980s, the presidency of Ronald Reagan drew fresh attacks on the same entertainments that Reisman had championed in the 1950s and that the counterculture favored and exploited in the 1960s and early 1970s. Reagan's rise put celebrity under closer scrutiny and made it more distinct from popular entertainment. Reagan's critics—there were many—mocked celebrity as an institution that could be turned to nefarious ends and cited the political career of the fortieth president as living proof. Liberal pundits thought that Reagan's film stardom, derived from his playing good guys, was indistinguishable from his electoral success and complicit in what Reagan's adversaries considered, oddly, given celebrity's brief history, to be the president's retrograde effect on the political process.

Daniel Boorstin, in *The Image: A Guide to Pseudo-Events in America* (published originally in 1961; reprinted in 1972 and 1987), anticipated and, later, followed others who, when Reagan was President, saw his celebrity as a poor, latter-day, and distinctively *American* substitute for more traditional and legitimate qualifications for high office. Anticelebrity theorists denigrated Reagan so vehemently that they bred a counter-reaction that had American cultural historians such as Warren I. Susman (1984) and Michael Kammen (1991) treating celebrity, if only in passing, as a kind of referendum for large societies in need of finding, or failing that, manufacturing grounds for common values.

Recently, apologists for celebrity have marshaled arguments against those who say that all storytelling, called "narrative" these days in academic parlance, is devious in one way or another. Most of those who call themselves poststructuralists, and many who have called themselves postmodernists— the latter including social theorists as well as literary and cultural critics— have attacked narrative for being uncritical, antiquated, and fanciful entirely. This group holds that storytelling, and with it any performance that unfolds a story, is constructed not only to control others, but to mask what is controlling *it*.

Views such as these implicate the arts, together with the most vital commercial entertainments, in the workings of power seen to drive all other institutions and the construction of meaning itself. The implication is left to stand that any decisions individuals make are so compromised that they might as well have been made on their behalf by people in power and the institutions those people control.

The United States, where capitalism has enjoyed steadier favor than on any other continent, with the possible exception of Australia, might have been expected to generate greater sympathy for celebrity. But many Americans have believed, and do still, that popular entertainment, and the celebrity that beckons the masses, feed simplification, or worse, irrationality. In Britain, where the monarchy and aristocracy are still relatively lively, celebrity has imposed itself less, or to take another view, been adapted to the needs of the heirs of the same elites whose standing predated the commercializing of fame. The foothold that socialism has enjoyed in British politics has promoted views of celebrity as one of the noxious products of America's voracious economy and its invasive popular culture.

Over time, Marx's ideas of social class influenced cultural theory more than his economics did. Those who have found Marx most persuasive tend to attribute celebrity's appeal to the effects of alienation. Charles Rearick (1985), for one, has written that in metropolitan areas "the entertainment . . . was not to enjoy someone's act or works but just to see the celebrities themselves. In the modernized huge city of so many anonymous faces . . . to recognize some that many could recognize was somehow appealing" (173). Rearick's view, though common, to my mind overlooks celebrity's broader appeal—as to the privileged, for instance, or to those with strong traditional or ethnic ties, or the devoutly religious.

Much of the celebrity-writing that Americans have turned out, aside from journalism, has been hostile. Richard Gilman (1982) has written that "the social impulse to create celebrities clearly springs from an insufficiency of true heroes" (124). Richard Schickel (1985) has denounced celebrity for "corrupting us by corrupting language . . . to coercively diminish our capacity for making fine distinctions." "The defenders of our language," Schickel writes urgently, "need reinforcement" (298). Michael Quinn (1990) has noted, more equivocally, that "the absolute qualities of the celebrity threaten the evaluations of the critic" (157). Celebrated actors, as has been conceded, can bring works the few deem inferior to greater attention. Critics see the potential as subversive, and not only insofar as it stands to affect them.

In *The Frenzy of Renown: Fame and Its History* (1986), Leo Braudy has offered the first heavily historicized, if still largely skeptical, account of celebrity. Braudy's *The World in a Frame: What We See in Films* (1976) touches on matters of celebrity in the context of film criticism and reception. And so, in more popular veins, do Alexander Walker in *Stardom: The Hollywood Phenomenon* (1970), and George W. S. Trow in *Within the*

*Context of No Context* (1978). Richard Dyer has trained an acute eye on Marilyn Monroe, Judy Garland, and Paul Robeson, in *Heavenly Bodies* (1986; 2nd edition 2004).

Film critics and historians, as Quinn notes, have been largely inclined to consider how celebrity influences what we see and understand. Quinn cites Charles Affron's *Star Acting* (1977) as an example of more balanced and neutral treatment of celebrity. I would add Richard deCordova's *Picture Personalities: The Emergence of the Star System in America* (1990), published in the same year as Quinn's essay, and Richard Dyer's "*A Star Is Born* and the Construction of Authenticity" brought out the year following. Jib Fowles's *Starstruck* (1992) follows Walker's book in being focused on stardom made in Hollywood. Hollywood, indeed, has been as central to revisionist views as it has been to denigrators of celebrity. Writing as one of the revisionists, Quinn concedes that Boorstin's *The Image: A Guide to Pseudo-Events in America* (1961), "while ahead of its time, is typical in its emphasis on celebrity as a typically American problem coincident with capitalism and the arrival of cinema" (160).

Quinn takes his point of departure not only from a fellow American but also from the Prague structuralists. Quinn names Jiri Veltrusky's "Contribution to the Semiotics of Acting" (1976) for identifying the components of celebrity, including the effects on particular viewers. Keir Elam, in *The Semiotics of Theatre and Drama* (1980), writes briefly but clearly about celebrity, as does Marvin Carlson in *The Haunted Stage: The Theatre as Memory Machine* (2001) and Joseph Roach in "It" (2004).

P. David Rogers (1997), among recent theorists of celebrity, seems to integrate the functionalism of Reisman with the post-Marxist corrections of the Gramscians. His synopsis of the literature on celebrity, especially for including European writers, is the most comprehensive I've seen. David Giles (2000) has approached celebrity by way of the social sciences, as his subtitle, "A Psychology of Fame and Celebrity," indicates. His survey is thorough, and his taxonomy of the kinds of celebrity is provocative. Chris Rojek (2001) also gives a thorough account of contemporary celebrity, and he traces it farthest back in history. Joshua Gamson (1994) considers the effects Reagan had on celebrity writing in the United States. Reagan's celebrity will almost surely impinge on views of celebrity in years to come. His grinning through old movies gives him a mythic proportion not to be underestimated.

Charles Ponce de Leon (2002) gives a colorful, detailed account of journalism's part in shaping celebrity in the United States, and he documents the ways in which celebrities from different fields have been covered in different ways. John Seabrook's *Nobrow: The Marketing of Culture, The Culture of Marketing* (2000) offers an entertaining account of the breakdown of traditional boundaries between high and low culture. Tyler Cowen, in *Commercial Culture* (1998) and *What Price Fame?* (2000), examines market-driven forces in ways that mark him off from the many cultural historians who, he notes, "tend to look sympathetically on modern popular culture but . . . dislike capitalism and the forces of the market" (1998, 11).

Sympathetic as Cowen is to latest-stage capitalism, his approach recapitulates the appeal of economic determinism among celebrity's harsher critics, then and now. In my view, these groups have steadily underestimated the force of individual fantasy and cultural mythmaking. Like culture itself, celebrity's products are no more simple, or belonging to any single group, than the processes that produced them. The writing I admire most tends to credit more voices as opposed to fewer.

*   *   *

Abrahams, Edward. *The Lyrical Left: Randolph Bourne, Alfred Stieglitz and the Origins of Cultural Radicalism in America*. Charlottesville: University Press of Virginia, 1986.

Adams, William Scovell. *Edwardian Heritage: A Study in British History 1901–1906*. London: Frederick Muller, 1949.

Affron, Charles. *Star Acting*. New York: Dutton, 1977.

Agate, May. *Madame Sarah*. London: Home & Van Thal, 1945.

Allen, Robert C. *Horrible Prettiness: Burlesque and American Culture*. Chapel Hill: University of North Carolina Press, 1991.

———. "Vaudeville and Film 1895-1915: A Study in Media Interaction." Diss. University of Iowa, 1977.

Alltree, George W. *Footlight Memories: Recollections of Music Hall and Stage Life*. London: Sampson, How, Marston & Co., 1932.

Anderson, Amanda. *Tainted Souls and Painted Faces: The Rhetoric of Fallenness in Victorian Literature*. Ithaca: Cornell University Press, 1993.

Anderson, Olive. *Suicide in Victorian and Edwardian England*. Oxford: Clarendon Press, 1987.

Archer, Stephen M. "*E Pluribus Unum*: Bernhardt's 1905–1906 Farewell Tour." In *The American Stage: Social and Economic Issues from the Colonial Period to the Present*. Ed. Ron Engle and Tice L. Miller. Cambridge: Cambridge University Press, 1993. Pp. 159–74.

Armstrong, Carol. *Scenes in a Library: Reading the Photograph in the Book, 1843–1875*. Cambridge: MIT Press, 1998.

Ashwell, Lena. *Myself a Player*. London: Michael Joseph, 1936.

Aston, Elaine. *Sarah Bernhardt: A French Actress on the English Stage*. Oxford: Berg, 1989.

Auerbach, Nina. *Ellen Terry: Player in Her Time*. New York: W. W. Norton & Company, 1987.

Auster, Albert. *Actresses and Suffragists: Women in the American Theatre, 1890–1920*. New York: Praeger, 1984.

Bailey, Peter. "Custom, Capital and Culture in the Victorian Music Hall." In *Popular Culture and Custom in Nineteenth-century England*. Ed. Robert D. Storch. London: Croom Helm, 1982. Pp. 180–208.

———. *Leisure and Class in Victorian England: Rational Recreation and the Contest for Control, 1830–1885*. London: Routledge & Kegan Paul, 1978.

———, ed. *Music Hall: The Business of Pleasure*. Philadelphia: Open University Press, 1986.

———. *Popular Culture and Performance in the Victorian City*. Cambridge: Cambridge University Press, 1998.

———. "Rational Recreation and the Entertainment Industry: The Case of the Victorian Music Halls." In *Leisure and Class in Victorian England* (1978). Pp. 147–68.

Baker, Michael. *The Rise of the Victorian Actor*. London: Croom Helm, 1978.

Banner, Lois W. *American Beauty*. New York: Alfred A. Knopf, 1983.

Banta, Martha. *Imaging American Women: Idea and Ideals in Cultural History*. New York: Columbia University, 1987

Barker, Felix. *The House That Stoll Built: The Story of the London Coliseum*. London: Frederick Muller, 1957.

Barrie, James M. *The Plays of J. M. Barrie*. Ed. A. E. Wilson. London: Hodder and Stoughton, 1947.

Barrymore, Ethel. *Memories: An Autobiography*. London: Hulton Press, 1956.

"Barrymore, Ethel" file, MWEZ + n.c. 19,268; at the Billy Rose Theatre Collection, New York Public Library at Lincoln Center.

"Barrymore, Ethel." Unidentified clipping (headlined "Ethel Barrymore in Five-a-Day") at the City Museum of New York.

Baudrillard, Jean. *Simulations*. Trans. Paul Foss et al. New York: Semiotext(e), 1983.

Beerbohm, Max. *Herbert Beerbohm Tree: Some Memories of Him and of His Art Collected by Max Beerbohm*. London: Hutchinson & Co., c. 1920.

———. *Last Theatres 1904-1910*. London: Rupert Hart-Davis, 1970.

———. *More Theatres 1898-1903*. London: Rupert Hart-Davis, 1969.

Begbie, Harold. *The Handy Man and Other Verses*. London: Grant Richards, 1900.

Benson, Lady (Mrs. Frank). *Mainly Players: Bensonian Memories*. London: Thornton Butterworth, 1926.

Bernhardt file. Unidentified obituary from the Firestone Library, Princeton University, Princeton, New Jersey.

Bernhardt, Sarah. *The Art of the Theatre*. 1924; rpt. New York: Benjamin Blom, 1969.

Bevan, Ian. *Top of the Bill: The Story of the London Palladium*. London: Frederick Muller, 1952.

Bingham, Madeleine. *The Great Lover: The Life and Art of Herbert Beerbohm Tree*. London: Hamish Hamilton, 1978.

Binns, Archie. *Mrs. Fiske and the American Theatre*. New York: Crown Publishers, 1955.

Blair, Karen J. *The Torchbearers: Women and Their Amateur Arts Associations in America, 1890–1930*. Bloomington: Indiana University Press, 1994.

Blatch, Harriot Stanton. *Challenging Years: The Memoirs of Harriot Stanton Blatch*. New York: G.P. Putnam's Sons, 1940.

Blow, Sydney. *The Ghost Walks on Fridays: In and Out of the Stage Door*. London: Heath Cranton, 1935.

———. *Through Stage Doors; or Memories of Two in the Theatre*. Edinburgh: W. & R. Chambers, 1958.

Boardman, W. H. ("Billy"). *Vaudeville Days*. Ed. David Whitelaw. London: Jarrolds Publishers, 1935.

Booker, M. Keith. *Dystopian Literature: A Theory and Research Guide*. Westport, CT: Greenwood Press, 1994.

Boorstin, Daniel. *The Image: A Guide to Pseudo-Events in America*. New York: Atheneum, 1961; rpt. 1987.

Brandon, Ruth. *Being Divine: A Biography of Sarah Bernhardt*. London: Mandarin, 1992.

Bratton, J. S., ed. *Acts of Supremacy: The British Empire and the Stage, 1790–1930*. Manchester: Manchester University Press, 1991.

———. "English Ethiopians: British Audiences and Black Face Acts, 1835–1865." *Yearbook of English Studies* (1981), 127–42.

———, ed. *Music Hall: Performance and Style*. Philadelphia: Open University Press, 1986.

Braudy, Leo. *The Frenzy of Renown: Fame and Its History*. Oxford: Oxford University Press, 1986.

———. *The World in a Frame: What We See in Films*. Chicago: University of Chicago Press, 1976.

Braybon, Gail. "Women and the War." In *The First World War in British History*. Ed. Stephen Constantine, Maurice W. Kirby, and Mary B. Rose. London: Edward Arnold, 1995. Pp. 141–67.

Bridges-Adams. W. "Theatre." In *Edwardian England 1901-1914*. Ed. Simon Nowell-Smith. London: Oxford University Press, 1964. Pp. 367–409.

Briscoe, Johnson. *The Actors' Birthday Book*. 3rd series. New York: Moffat, Yard and Company, 1909.

*British Theatre in the 1890s: Essays on Drama and the Stage*. Ed. Richard Foulkes. Cambridge: Cambridge University Press, 1992.

Brown, Jared. *The Fabulous Lunts: A Biography of Alfred Lunt and Lynn Fontanne*. New York: Atheneum, 1986.

Brownstein, Rachel M. *Tragic Muse: Rachel of the Comédie-Française*. New York: Alfred A. Knopf, 1993.

Bryan, George B. *Stage Lives: A Bibliography and Index to Theatrical Biographies in English*. Westport, CT: Greenwood Press, 1985.

Bulliet, C. J. *Robert Mantell's Romance*. Boston: John W. Luce & Company, 1918.

Burian, Grayce Susan. "Aileen Stanley, Her Life and Times." In *Women in American Theatre*. Ed. Helen Krich Chinoy and Linda Walsh Jenkins. New York: Crown Publications, 1981.

Burrows, Edwin G. and Mike Wallace. *Gotham: A History of New York City*. New York: Oxford University Press, 1999.

Buruma, Ian. *Anglomania: A European Love Affair*. New York: Random House, 1998.

Butler, Lawrence and Harriet Jones, eds. *Britain in the Twentieth Century: A Documentary Reader*. London: Heinemann, 1994.

Butsch, Richard. *The Making of American Audiences: From Stage to Television, 1750–1990*. Cambridge: Cambridge University Press, 2000.

Caffin, Caroline. *Vaudeville*. New York: Mitchell Kennerley, 1914.

Calthrop, Dion Clayton. *Music Hall Nights*. London: John Lane, 1925.

"Campbell, Mrs. Patrick." Clippings file at the Theatre Collection, New York, Public Library at Lincoln Center, New York City. Catalogued as MWEZ + n.c. 6490.

Campbell, Mrs. Patrick (Beatrice Stella Cornwallis-West). *My Life and Some Letters*. New York: Dodd, Mead and Company, 1922.

Carlson, Marvin. *The Haunted Stage: The Theatre as Memory Machine*. Ann Arbor, MI: University of Michigan Press, 2001.

Carlson, Susan. "Conflicted Politics and Circumspect Comedy." In *Women and Playwriting in Nineteenth-Century Britain*. Ed. Tracy C. Davis and

Ellen Donkin. Cambridge: Cambridge University Press, 1999. Pp. 256–76.

Cary, Alice and Phoebe Cary. *The Poetical Works of Alice and Phoebe Cary*. Boston: Houghton, Mifflin & Co., 1881.

Chamberlain and Lyman Brown Collection (C&LBC), Billy Rose Theatre Collection, New York Public Library at Lincoln Center: "Ethel Barrymore," volumes 4, 5, and 7.

Cheshire, David F. *Music Hall in Britain*. Newton Abbot: David & Charles, 1974.

Cima, Gay Gibson. *Performing Women: Female Characters, Male Playwrights, and the Modern Stage*. Ithaca: Cornell University Press, 1993.

Clarke, Ian. *Edwardian Drama: A Critical Study*. London: Faber and Faber, 1989.

Coliseum pamphlet (1954). At the Theatre Museum Library, London.

Coliseum programs. At the Theatre Museum Library, London, and at the Raymond Mander and Joe Mitchenson Theatre Collection, Beckenham Place Park, Kent, England.

Collins, Philip, ed. *Charles Dickens: The Public Readings*. Oxford: Clarendon Press, 1975.

Cooper, John Milton, Jr. *Pivotal Decades: The United States 1900-1920*. New York: W. W. Norton & Company, 1990.

Corbett, Mary Jean. *Representing Femininity: Middle-Class Subjectivity in Victorian and Edwardian Women's Autobiographies*. Oxford: Oxford University Press, 1992.

Cornwallis-West, George. *Edwardian Days; or A Little About a Lot of Things*. London: Putnam, 1930.

Cott, Nancy F. *The Grounding of Modern Feminism*. New Haven: Yale University Press, 1987.

Cowen, Tyler. *Commercial Culture*. Cambridge: Harvard University Press, 1998.

———. *What Price Fame?* Cambridge: Harvard University Press, 2000.

Crow, Duncan. *The Edwardian Woman*. London: George Allen & Unwin, 1978.

Crowhurst, Andrew John. "Big Men and Big Business: The Transition from 'Caterers' to "'Magnates' in British Music-Hall Entrepreneurship, 1850–1914." *Nineteenth Century Studies* 25:1 (Summer 1997), 33–59.

———. "The Music Hall, 1885–1922: The Emergence of a National Entertainment Industry in Britain." Diss. Cambridge University, 1992.

Croxton, Arthur. *Crowded Nights—and Days: An Unconventional Pageant.* London: Sampson Low, Marston & Co., c. 1934.

*Daily Call* (London).

*Daily Graphic* (London).

*Daily Mail* (London).

Davies, Acton. "What I Don't Know About Vaudeville." *Variety*, December 16, 1905, 2.

Davis, Michael M. *The Exploitation of Pleasure: A Study of Commercial Recreations in New York City.* New York: Russell Sage Foundation, 1911.

Davis, Ronald J. *Augustus Thomas.* Boston: Twayne Publishers, 1984.

Davis, Tracy C. *Actresses as Working Women: Their Social Identity in Victorian Culture.* New York: Routledge, 1991.

———. "Indecency and Vigilance in the Music Halls." In *British Theatre in the 1890s: Essays on Drama and the Stage.* Ed. Richard Foulkes. Cambridge: Cambridge University Press, 1992. Pp. 111–31.

Davis, Tracy C. and Ellen Donkin, eds. *Women and Playwriting in Nineteenth-Century Britain.* Cambridge: Cambridge University Press, 1999.

Davison, Peter. "The Music-Hall Tradition." In *Contemporary Drama and the Popular Dramatic Tradition in England.* London: Macmillan, 1982, Pp. 13–66.

Deane, Seamus. "Imperialism/Nationalism." In *Critical Terms for Literary Study.* Ed. Frank Lentricchia and Thomas McLaughlin. 2nd edition. Chicago: University of Chicago Press, 1995. Pp. 354–68.

DeCordova, Richard. "The Emergence of the Star System in America." In *Stardom: Industry of Desire.* Ed. Christine Gledhill. London: Routledge, 1991. Pp. 17–29.

———. *Picture Personalities: The Emergence of the Star System in America.* Urbana: University of Illinois Press, 1990.

De Leon, Charles L. Ponce. *Self-Exposure: Human Interest Journalism and the Emergence of Celebrity in America, 1890-1940.* Chapel Hill: University of North Carolina Press, 2002.

Denton, Harvey. "The Technique of Vaudeville." *Green Book Album* 1:5 (May 1909), 1068–74.

DiMeglio, John E. *Vaudeville U.S.A.* Bowling Green, OH: Bowling Green University Press, 1973.

Disher, M. Willson. *Winkles and Champagne: Comedies and Tragedies of the Music Hall.* London: B. T. Batsford, 1938.

Donaldson, Frances. *The Actor-Managers.* London: Weidenfeld and Nicolson, 1970.

Dorfman, Ariel. *The Empire's Old Clothes: What the Lone Ranger, Babar, and Other Innocent Heroes Do to Our Minds.* New York: Pantheon Books, 1983.

Drinnon, Richard. *Rebel in Paradise: A Biography of Emma Goldman.* Chicago: University of Chicago Press, 1961.

Dudden, Faye E. *Women in the American Theatre: Actresses and Audiences.* New Haven: Yale University Press, 1994.

Dudley, Ernest. *The Gilded Lily: The Life and Loves of the Fabulous Lillie Langtry.* London: Oldhams Press, 1958.

Dyer, Richard. *Heavenly Bodies: Film Stars and Society.* 1986; 2nd edition. London: Routledge, 2004.

———. "*A Star Is Born* and the Construction of Authenticity." In *Stardom: Industry of Desire.* Ed. Christine Gledhill. London: Routledge, 1991. Pp. 132–40.

Elam, Keir. *The Semiotics of Theatre and Drama.* London: Methuen, 1980.

*Era* (London).

Erenberg, Lewis A. *Steppin' Out: New York Nightlife and the Transformation of American Culture, 1890–1930.* Westport, CT: Greenwood Press, 1981.

Everding, Robert G. "Shaw and the Palaces of Variety." In *Shaw: The Annual of Bernard Shaw Studies 10.* Ed. Stanley Weintraub and Fred D. Crawford (1990). Pp. 12–26.

Falk, Candace. *Love Anarchy, and Emma Goldman.* New York: Holt, Rinehart and Winston, 1984.

Farson, Daniel. *Marie Lloyd and Music Hall.* London: Tom Stacey, 1972.

Faulkner, Harold U. *The Decline of Laissez Faire, 1897–1917.* New York: Rinehart & Company, 1951.

Felstead, S. Theodore. *Stars Who Made the Halls: A Hundred Years of English Humour, Harmony and Hilarity.* London: T. Warner Laurie, 1946.

Fields, Armond and L. Marc Fields. *From the Bowery to Broadway: Lew Fields and the Roots of American Popular Theatre.* New York: Oxford University Press, 1993.

Finnegan, Margaret. *Selling Suffrage: Consumer Culture and Votes for Women.* New York: Columbia University Press, 1999.

Flexner, Eleanor. *Century of Struggle: The Woman's Rights Movement in the United States.* New York: Atheneum, 1974.

Fornäs, Johan. *Cultural Theory and Late Modernity.* London: Sage Publications, 1995.

Foulkes, Richard, ed. *British Theatre in the 1890s: Essays on Drama and the Stage.* Cambridge: Cambridge University Press, 1992.

————. *Church and Stage in Victorian England.* Cambridge: Cambridge University Press, 1997.

————. *Performing Shakespeare in the Age of Empire.* Cambridge: Cambridge University Press, 2002.

Fowles, Jib. *Starstruck: Celebrity Performers and the American Public.* Washington: Smithsonian Institution Press, 1992.

Gammond, Peter. *Your Own, Your Very Own!: A Music Hall Scrapbook Compiled by Peter Gammond.* London: Ian Allan, 1971.

Gamson, Joshua. *Claims to Fame: Celebrity in Contemporary America.* Berkeley: University of California Press, 1994.

Gerson, Noel B. *Because I Loved Him: The Life and Loves of Lillie Langtry.* New York: William Morrow & Company, Inc., 1971.

Ghent, W. J. *Our Benevolent Feudalism.* New York: The Macmillan Company, 1902.

Gilbert, Douglas. *American Vaudeville: Its Life and Times.* 1940; rpt. New York: Dover Publications, 1963.

Giles, David. *Illusions of Immortality: A Psychology of Fame and Celebrity.* London: Macmillan Press, 2000.

Gillette, William. *The Illusion of the First Time in Acting.* New York: Columbia University Press, 1915.

Gilman, Richard. "The Actor as Celebrity." *Humanities in Review.* Ed. David Reiff. Cambridge: Cambridge University Press, 1982. Pp. 106–24.

Glenn, Susan A. *Female Spectacle: The Theatrical Roots of Modern Feminism.* Cambridge: Harvard University Press, 2000.

Gold, Arthur and Robert Fizdale. *The Divine Sarah: A Life of Sarah Bernhardt.* New York: Alfred A. Knopf, 1991.

Golden, Sylvia B. "The Romance of the Jersey Lily." *Theatre Magazine* (December 1930), 39–40, 69–70.

Goldman, Emma. *Living My Life.* 1931; rpt. Garden City, NY: Garden City Publishing Company, 1934.

Graham, Joe. *An Old Stock-Actor's Memories.* London: John Murray, 1930.

Gramsci, Antonio. *Selections from the Prison Notebooks of Antonio Gramsci.* Ed. and trans. Quintin Hoare and Geoffrey Nowell-Smith. London: Lawrence & Wishart, 1971.

Grau, Robert. *The Business Man in the Amusement World.* New York: Broadway Publishing Company, 1910.

————. *Forty Years of Observation of Music and the Drama.* New York: Broadway Publishing Company, 1909.

————. "The Growth of Vaudeville." *Overland Monthly* 54 (October 1914), 392–6.

————. *The Stage in the Twentieth Century.* 1912; rpt. New York: Benjamin Blom, 1969.

Green, Abel and Joe Laurie, Jr. *Show Biz from Vaude to Video.* New York: Henry Holt and Company, 1951.

Haddon, Archibald. *Green Room Gossip.* London: Stanley Paul, 1922.

————. *The Story of the Music Hall: From Cave of Harmony to Cabaret.* London: Fleetway Press, 1935.

Hamilton, Cicely. *Life Errant.* London: J. M. Dent & Sons, 1935.

Hapgood, Norman. "The Life of a Vaudeville Artiste." *Cosmopolitan* 39 (February 1901), 393–400.

Harper, Charles H. "Mrs. Leslie Carter: Her Life and Acting Career." Diss. University of Nebraska, 1978.

Hart, Jerome A. *Sardou and the Sardou Plays.* Philadelphia: Lippincott and Company, 1913.

Hartley, Marsden. *Adventures in the Arts: Informal Chapters on Painters, Vaudeville, and Poets.* 1921; rpt. New York: Hacker Arts Books, 1972.

Hathorn, Ramon. *Our Lady of the Snows: Sarah Bernhardt in Canada.* New York: Peter Lang, 1996.

Hawtrey, Charles. *The Truth at Last.* Boston: Little, Brown, and Company, 1924.

"Hawtrey, Charles" file. Theatre Museum Library, London.

Henderson, Mary C. *The City and the Theatre: New York Playhouses from Bowling Green to Times Square.* Clifton, NJ: James T. White & Company, 1973.

Henig, Ruth. "Foreign Policy." In *The First World War in British History.* Ed. Stephen Constantine, Maurice W. Kirby, and Mary B. Rose. London: Edward Arnold, 1995. Pp. 204–30.

Hibbert, H. G. *Fifty Years of a Londoner's Life.* London: Grant Richards, 1916.

————. *Souvenir Comprising The Story of the Music Hall.* London: Palace Theatre, 1912.

Higham, John. *Strangers in the Land: Patterns of American Nativism 1860-1925.* New Brunswick, NJ: Rutgers University Press, 1955.

Hilliard, Robert. "Memories." Unpublished manuscript in the Billy Rose Theatre Collection, New York Public Library at Lincoln Center.

Hippodrome (New York) program. Firestone Library Theatre Collection, Princeton University, Princeton, New Jersey.

Hirshfield, Claire. "The Actresses' Franchise League and the Campaign for Women's Suffrage 1908–1914." *Theatre Research International* 10:2 (Summer 1985), 129–53.

Hobsbawm, Eric. "Inventing Traditions." In *The Invention of Tradition.* ed. Hobsbawm and Terence Ranger. Cambridge: Cambridge University Press, 1983. Pp. 1–14.

Hodin, Mark. "Class, Consumption, and Ethnic Performance in Vaudeville." *Prospects: An Annual of American Cultural Studies* 22 (1997), 193–210.

Holledge, Julie. *Innocent Flowers: Women in the Edwardian Theatre.* London: Virago, 1981.

Holroyd, Michael. *Bernard Shaw: The Lure of Fantasy.* Volume 3: 1918-1950. London: Chatto & Windus, 1991.

———. *Bernard Shaw: The Pursuit of Power.* Volume 2: 1898-1918. London: Chatto & Windus, 1989.

Honri, Peter. *Working the Halls: The Honris in One Hundred Years of British Music Hall.* Farmborough, Hampshire: Saxon House, 1973.

Howells, William Dean. "Drama and Society." *Harper's Weekly* 41 (January 30, 1897). In *A Realist in the American Theatre: Selected Drama Criticism of William Dean Howells.* Ed. Brenda Murphy. Athens: Ohio University Press, 1992.

Huizinga, Johan. *America: A Dutch Historian's Vision, from Afar and Near.* Trans. Herbert H. Rowen. 3rd edition. 1928; rpt. New York: Harper & Row, 1972.

Irving, H. B. *The Amusement of the People.* London: Arthur L. Humphreys, 1916.

Jelavich, Peter. *Berlin Cabaret.* Cambridge: Harvard University Press, 1993.

Jenkins, Henry. *What Made Pistachio Nuts? Early Sound Comedy and the Vaudeville Esthetic.* New York: Columbia University Press, 1992.

Kachur, B. A. "Shakespeare Politicized: Beerbohm Tree's *King John* and the Boer War." *Theatre History Studies* 12 (1992), 25–44.

Kammen, Michael. *American Culture, American Tastes: Social Change and the 20th Century.* New York: Alfred A. Knopf, 1999.

———. *Mystic Chords of Memory: The Transformation of Tradition in American Culture.* New York: Alfred A. Knopf, 1991.

Kaplan, Joel H. and Sheila Stowell. *Theatre and Fashion: Oscar Wilde to the Suffragettes.* Cambridge: Cambridge University Press, 1994.

Kasson, John F. *Houdini, Tarzan, and the Perfect Man: The White Male Body and the Challenge of Modernity in America.* New York: Hill and Wang, 2001.

Kennedy, Dennis. "The New Drama and the New Audience." *In The Edwardian Theatre: Essays on Performance and the Stage.* Ed. Michael R. Booth and Joel H. Kaplan. Cambridge: Cambridge University Press, 1996. Pp. 130–47.

Kent, Susan Kingsley. *Gender and Power in Britain, 1640-1990.* London: Routledge, 1999.

Kibler, M. Alison. *Rank Ladies: Gender and Cultural Hierarchy in American Vaudeville.* Chapel Hill: University of North Carolina Press, 1999.

Kift, Dagmar. *The Victorian Music Hall: Culture, Class and Conflict.* Cambridge: Cambridge University Press, 1996.

Kipling, Rudyard. *Rudyard Kipling's Verse.* Definitive Edition. Garden City, N.Y.: Doubleday and Company, 1940.

Kirby, E. T. *Ur-Drama: The Origins of Theatre.* New York: New York University Press, 1975.

Kirkland, Alexander. "The Woman from Yalta." *Theatre Arts* 33:11 (October 1949), 28–9, 48, 94–5.

Konijn, Elly A. *Acting Emotions: Shaping Emotions on the Stage.* Trans. Barbara Leach with David Chambers. Amsterdam: Amsterdam University Press, 2000.

Kotsilibas-Davis, James. *Great Times, Good Times: The Odyssey of Maurice Barrymore.* Garden City, NY: Doubleday & Co., 1977.

LaFeber, Walter. *The Cambridge History of American Foreign Relations.* Volume 2: "The American Search for Opportunity, 1865-1913." Cambridge: Cambridge University Press, 1993.

Lambert, Gavin. *Nazimova: A Biography.* New York: Alfred A. Knopf, 1997.

Langtry, Lillie (Lady de Bathe). *The Days I Knew.* 2nd edition. London: Hutchinson & Co., 1925.

Laurie, Joe Jr. *Vaudeville: From the Honky-Tonks to the Palace.* New York: Henry Holt and Company, 1953.

Leach, William. *Land of Desire: Merchants, Power, and the Rise of a New American Culture.* New York: Pantheon Books, 1993.

Le Bon, Gustave. *The Crowd: A Study of the Popular Mind.* Intro. Robert K. Merton. New York: Viking Press, 1960.

Lentricchia, Frank and Thomas McLaughlin, eds. *Critical Terms for Literary Study.* 2nd edition. Chicago: University of Chicago Press, 1995.

Leuchtenburg, William E. *The Perils of Prosperity 1914-32.* Chicago: University of Chicago Press, 1958.

Levine, Lawrence W. *Highbrow/Lowbrow: The Emergence of Cultural Hierarchy in America.* Cambridge: Harvard University Press, 1988.

Locke, John. *An Essay Concerning Human Understanding (1690-95).* Ed. Peter H. Nidditch. Oxford: The Clarendon Press, 1975.

———. *Two Treatises of Government* (1690-98). Ed. Peter Laslett. 2nd edition. Cambridge: The University Press, 1967.

Lowenthal, Leo. "The Triumph of Mass Idols." In *Literature, Popular Culture, and Society.* 1944; rpt. Palo Alto, CA: Pacific Books, 1961. Pp. 109–36.

Lumsden, Linda J. *Rampant Women: Suffragists and the Right of Assembly.* Knoxville: University of Tennessee Press, 1997.

Lynes, Russell. *The Lively Audience: A Social History of the Visual and Peforming Arts in America, 1890-1950.* New York: Harper & Row, 1985.

MacCarthy, Desmond. "In the Stalls." *Herbert Beerbohm Tree: Some Memories of Him and of His Art Collected by Max Beerbohm.* London: Hutchinson & Co., c. 1920. Pp. 216–26.

MacKail, Dennis. *The Story of J. M. B.[arrie]: A Biography.* London: Peter Davies, 1941.

MacKaye, Percy. "Art and the Woman's Movement: A Comment on the National Suffrage Pageant." *Forum* 49 (1913), 680–4.

Macqueen-Pope, W. J. *Ghosts and Greasepaint: A Story of the Days that Were.* London: Robert Hale, 1951.

———. *The Melodies Linger On: The Story of Music Hall.* London: W. H. Allen, 1950.

Maitland, Sara. *Vesta Tilley.* London: Virago, 1986.

*Manchester City News.*

*Manchester Guardian.*

*Manchester Evening News.*

Mander, Raymond and Joe Mitchenson. *British Music Hall: A Story in Pictures.* London: Studio Vista, 1965.

———. *The Lost Theatres of London.* London: Rupert Hart-Davis, 1968.

Manvell, Roger. *Ellen Terry.* New York: G. P. Putnam's Sons, 1968.

Marcus, Jane, ed. *Suffrage and the Pankhursts.* London: Routledge & Kegan Paul, 1987.

Marks, Edward B. as told to Abbott J. Leibling. *They All Sang: From Tony Pastor to Rudy Vallee.* New York: Viking Press, 1934.

Marshall, Gail. *Actresses on the Victorian Stage: Feminine Performance and the Galatea Myth.* Cambridge: Cambridge University Press, 1998.

Marston, William Moulton and John Henry Feller. *F. F. Proctor, Vaudeville Pioneer.* New York: Richard R. Smith, 1943.

Mason, A. E. W. *Sir George Alexander and the St. James's Theatre.* London: Macmillan and Co., 1935.

Matthews, Brander. *On Acting.* New York: Charles Scribner's Sons, 1914.

May, Henry F. *The End of American Innocence: A Study of the First Years of Our Own Time 1912-1917.* New York: Alfred A. Knopf, 1959.

May, Lary. *Screening Out the Past: The Birth of Mass Culture and the Motion Picture Industry.* New York: Oxford University Press, 1980.

Mayer, David. "Parlour and Platform Melodrama." In *Melodrama.* Ed. Michael Hays and Anastasia Nikolopoulou. New York: St. Martin's Press, 1996. Pp. 211–34.

McArthur, Benjamin. *Actors and American Culture, 1880-1920.* Philadelphia: Temple University Press, 1984.

McCarthy, Lillah. *Myself and My Friends.* New York: E. P. Dutton, 1933.

McConachie, Bruce A. *Melodramatic Formations: American Theatre and Society, 1820-1870.* Iowa City: University of Iowa Press, 1992.

———. "Using the Concept of Cultural Hegemony to Write Theatre History." In *Interpreting the Theatrical Past: Essays in the Historiography of Performance.* Ed. Thomas Postlewait and McConachie. Iowa City: University of Iowa Press, 1992. Pp. 37–58.

McLean, Albert F. *American Vaudeville as Ritual.* Lexington: University of Kentucky Press, 1965.

McNamara, Brooks. *American Popular Entertainments: Jokes, Monologues, Bits, and Sketches.* New York: Performing Arts Journal Publications, 1983.

Middleton, George. *These Things Are Mine: The Autobiography of a Journeyman Playwright.* New York: Macmillan Company, 1947.

Millward, Jessie, with J.B. Booth. *Myself and Others.* 2nd edition. Boston: Small, Mayward & Company, 1924.

———. "An Interview with Jessie Millward." *Theatre Magazine* 7:74 (April 1907), 106–8, vii.

Montgomery, Maureen E. *Displaying Women: Spectacles of Leisure in Edith Wharton's New York.* New York: Routledge, 1998.

*Montreal Star.*

*Morning Post* (London).

Morse, Frank P. *Backstage with Henry Miller.* New York: E. P. Dutton & Co., Inc., 1938.

"Mrs. Fiske and Maurice Barrymore" [Anon]. *Munsey's Magazine* 22 (January 1900), 594, 596–8.

Mullin, Donald. *Victorian Actors and Actresses in Review: A Dictionary of Contemporary Views of Representative British and American Actors and Actresses.* Westport, CT: Greenwood Press, 1983.

Nasaw, David. *Going Out: The Rise and Rall of Public Amusements.* New York: Basic Books, 1993.

"Nazimova, Alla." File at the Billy Rose Theatre Collection, New York Public Library at Lincoln Center. Catalogue number MWEZ + n.c. 13,512.

"Nazimova, Alla." File at the Theatre Library, London.

Negri, Pola. *Memoirs of a Star.* Garden City, NY: Doubleday & Company, 1970.

Newton, H. Chance. *Cues and Curtain Calls: Being the Theatrical Reminiscences of H. Chance Newton.* London: John Lane, 1927.

———. *Idols of the "Halls," Being My Music Hall Memories.* 1928; rpt. New York: British Book Centre, 1975.

*New York Clipper.*

*New York Dramatic Mirror.*

*New York Times.*

Nicoll, Allardyce. "Commercialism, the Music-Hall Empire and Trade-Unionism." In *English Drama 1900–1930: The Beginnings of the Modern Period.* Cambridge: Cambridge University Press, 1973. Pp. 30–40.

Norden, Martin F. *John Barrymore: A Bio-Bibliography.* Westport, CT: Greenwood Press, 1995.

Norris, James D. *Advertising and the Transformation of American Society, 1865-1920.* Westport, CT: Greenwood Press, 1990.

*Notable Women in American Theatre.* Ed. Alice M. Robinson, Vera Mowry Roberts, and Millie S. Barranger. Westport, CT: Greenwood Press, 1989.

Odell, George C. D. *Annals of the New York Stage.* Volume 14, 1888–1891. New York: Columbia University Press, 1949.

Offen, Karen. *European Feminisms 1700–1950: A Political History.* Stanford: Stanford University Press, 2000.

Oldenburg, Veena Talwar. *The Making of Colonial Lucknow, 1856-1877.* Princeton: Princeton University Press, 1984.

Olson, Scott Robert. *Hollywood Planet: Global Media and the Competitive Advantage of Narrative Transparency.* Mahwah, NJ: Lawrence Erlbaum Associates, 1999.

Ormiston Chant, Mrs. (Laura). *Why We Attacked the Empire.* London: Horace Marshall & Son, 1895.

Ormond, Leonee. *J. M. Barrie.* Edinburgh: Scottish Academic Press, 1987.

Orpheum (Brooklyn) program, dated March 11, 1915; at the Museum of the City of New York.

Orville, Miles. *The Real Thing: Imitation and Authenticity in American Culture, 1880–1940.* Chapel Hill: University of North Carolina Press, 1989.

Osborn, John. "The Dramaturgy of the Tabloid: Climax and Novelty in a Theory of Condensed Forms." *Theatre Journal* 46 (December 1994), 507–22.

Osborne, John. *The Entertainer.* New York: Criterion Books, 1958.

Ormsbee, Helen. *Backstage with Actors: From the Time of Shakespeare to the Present Day.* 1938; rpt. New York: Benjamin Blom, 1969.

Palace Theatre Archive, Palace Theatre, London.

"Palace Theatre" (New York) file. Museum of the City of New York.

Palace Theatre (New York) program for Sarah Bernhardt, 1913. Rare Books and Special Collections, Hatcher Graduate Library, University of Michigan.

*Pall Mall Gazette* (London).

Pearson, Hesketh. *Beerbohm Tree: His Life and Laughter*. London: Methuen and Co., 1956.

———. *The Last Actor-Managers*. 1950; rpt. London: White Lion Publishers, 1974

Pearson, Roberta E. *Eloquent Gestures: The Transformation of Performance Style in the Griffith Biograph Films*. Berkeley: University of California Press, 1992.

Peiss, Kathy. *Cheap Amusements: Working Women and Leisure in Turn-of-the-Century New York*. Philadelphia: Temple University Press, 1986.

*Performer* (London).

Peters, Margot. *The House of Barrymore*. New York: Alfred A. Knopf, 1990.

———. *Mrs. Pat: The Life of Mrs. Patrick Campbell*. New York: Alfred A. Knopf, 1984.

Phelan, Peggy. "Crisscrossing Cultures." In *Crossing the Stage: Controversies on Cross-Dressing*. Ed. Leslie Ferris. London: Routledge, 1993. Pp. 155–70.

Phillips, Kevin. *The Cousins' Wars: Religion, Politics, and the Triumph of Anglo-America*. New York: Basic Books, 1999.

*Play Pictorial* (London).

Pollock, Channing. *The Footlights Fore and Aft*. Boston: Richard G. Bader, 1911.

Porter, Bernard. "The Edwardians and Their Empire." In *Edwardian England*. Ed. Donald Read. London: Croom Helm, 1982. Pp. 128–44.

Pound, Reginald and Geoffrey Harmsworth. *Northcliffe*. London: Cassell, 1959.

Purdom, C. B. *Harley Granville Barker: Man of the Theatre, Dramatist and Scholar*. London: Rockliff, 1955.

Quinn, Michael L. "Celebrity and the Semiotics of Acting." *New Theatre Quarterly* 6:22 (May 1990), 154–61.

Read, Jack. *Empires, Hippodromes and Palaces*. London: Alderman Press, 1985.

Rearick, Charles. *Pleasures of the Belle Epoque: Entertainment and Festivity in Turn-of-the-Century France*. New Haven: Yale University Press, 1985.

Reilly, Joy Harriman. "A Forgotten 'Fallen Woman': Olga Nethersole's *Sapho*." In *When They Weren't Doing Shakespeare: Essays on Nineteenth-Century British and American Theatre*. Ed. Judith L. Fisher and Stephen Watt. Athens: University of Georgia Press, 1989. Pp. 106–20.

Revell, Nellie. "When Vaudeville Goes to War." *Theatre* 25 (June 1917), 356.

Rhodes, James Ford. *The McKinley and Roosevelt Adminstrations, 1897–1909*. New York: Macmillan, 1922.

*The Riverside Shakespeare*. Ed. G. Blakemore Evans, assisted by J.J.M. Tobin. 2nd edition. Boston: Houghton Mifflin, 1997.

Roach, Joseph. *Cities of the Dead: Circum-Atlantic Performance*. New York: Columbia University Press, 1996.

———. "The Emergence of the American Actor." In *The Cambridge History of American Theatre*. Ed. Don B. Wilmeth and Christopher Bigsby. Volume 1. Cambridge: Cambridge University Press, 1998. Pp. 338–72.

———. "It," *Theatre Journal* 56:4 (2004), 555–68.

———. "Slave Spectacles and Tragic Octoroons: A Cultural Genealogy of Antebellum Performance," 1992; rpt. in *Exceptional Spaces: Essays in Performance and History*. Ed. Della Pollock. Chapel Hill: University of North Carolina Press, 1998. Pp. 49–76.

Robinson Locke Collection (RL), at the Billy Rose Theatre Collection, New York Public Library at Lincoln Center.

"Ethel Barrymore," volume 37;

"Maurice Barrymore," volume 39;

"Sarah Bernhardt," volumes 66 and 68;

"Mrs. Patrick Campbell," volumes 98 and 99;

"Charles Hawtrey," series 2, volume 238, envelope 655;

"Lillie Langtry," volumes 309 and 310;

"Jessie Millward," envelope 1478;

"Helena Modjeska," volume 350;

"Alla Nazimova," volumes 356 and 357;

"Olga Nethersole," volume 364;

"Nance O'Neil," volume 372;

"James O'Neill," volume 370.

Rogers, P. David. *Celebrity and Power: Fame in Contemporary Culture*. Minneapolis: University of Minnesota Press, 1997.

Rojek, Chris. *Celebrity*. London: Reaktion Books, 2001.

Rose, Clarkson. *Red Plush and Greasepaint: A Memory of the Music-Hall and Life and Times from the Nineties to the Sixties*. London: Museum Press, 1964.

Rosen, Andrew. *Rise Up, Women! The Militant Campaign of the Women's Social and Political Union 1903-1914*. London: Routledge & Kegan Paul, 1974.

Rossetti, Christina G. *Poems*. London: Macmillan, 1894.

Rowell, George. *William Terriss and Richard Prince: Two Characters in an Adelphi Melodrama*. London: Society for Theatre Research, 1987.

Rubin, Martin. *Showstoppers: Busby Berkeley and the Tradition of Spectacle*. New York: Columbia University Press, 1993.

Russell, Dave. "Varieties of Life: The Making of the Edwardian Music Hall." In *The Edwardian Theatre: Essays in Performance and the Stage*. Ed. Michael R. Booth and Joel H. Kaplan. Cambridge: Cambridge University Press, 1996. Pp. 61–85.

Rutherford, Lois. " 'Harmless Nonsense': The Comic Sketch and the Development of Music-Hall Entertainment." In *Music Hall: Performance and Style*. Ed. J. S. Bratton. Philadelphia: Open University Press, 1986. Pp. 131–51.

Said, Edward. *Culture and Imperialism*. New York: Alfred A. Knopf, 1993.

Samuels, Charles and Louise Samuels. *Once Upon a Stage: The Merry World of Vaudeville*. New York: Dodd, Mead & Company, 1974.

Sanderson, Michael. *From Irving to Olivier: A Social History of the Acting Profession in England, 1880-1983*. New York: St. Martin's Press, 1984.

Schanke, Robert A. "Alla Nazimova: 'The Witch of Makeup.' " In *Passing Performances: Queer Readings of Leading Players in American Theater History*. Ed. Schanke and Kim Marra. Ann Arbor, MI: University of Michigan Press, 1998. Pp. 129–50.

Schickel, Richard. *Intimate Strangers: The Culture of Celebrity*. Garden City, NY: Doubleday & Company, 1985.

Schneer, Jonathan. *London 1900: The Imperial Metropolis*. New Haven: Yale University Press, 1999.

Schneider, Dorothy and Carl J. Schneider. *American Women in the Progressive Era, 1900–1920*. New York: Facts on File, 1993.

Seabrook, John. *Nobrow: The Culture of Marketing, the Marketing of Culture*. New York: Alfred A. Knopf, 2000.

Seldes, Gilbert. *The Seven Lively Arts*. 1924; rpt. New York: Sagamore Press, 1957.

Senelick, Laurence. "The American Tour of Orlenev and Nazimova, 1905-1906." In *Wandering Stars: Russian Emigré Theatre, 1905-1940*. Ed. Senelick. Iowa City: University of Iowa Press, 1992. Pp. 1–15.

———. *The Changing Room: Sex, Drag and Theatre*. London: Routledge, 2000.

———. "Lady and the Tramp: Drag Differentials in the Progressive Era." In *Gender in Performance: The Presentation of Difference in the Performing*

*Arts*. Ed. Senelick. Hanover: University Press of New England, 1993. Pp. 26–45.

Senelick, Laurence, David Cheshire, and Ulrich Schneider. *British Music Hall 1840–1923: A Bibliography and Guide to Sources*. Hamden, CT: Archon Books, 1981.

Shaw, George Bernard. *Annajanska*. In *Heartbreak House, Great Catherine, and Playlets of the War*. London: Constable and Company, 1919.

———. *Collected Letters*. Volume 4. Ed. Dan H. Laurence. London: Max Reinhardt, 1988.

———. *The Drama Observed*. Volume 2. Ed. Bernard F. Dukore. University Park: Pennsylvania University Press, 1993.

Shepperson, George. "Kipling and the Boer War." In *Rudyard Kipling: The Man, His Work and His World*. Ed. John Gross. London: Weidenfeld & Nicolson, 1972. Pp. 81–8.

Sims, George R. *Prepare to Shed Them Now: Ballads of George R. Sims*. London: Hutchinson, 1968.

*Sketch* (London).

Skinner, Cornelia Otis. *Madame Sarah*. Boston: Houghton Mifflin, 1967.

Slide, Anthony. *The Encyclopedia of Vaudeville*. Westport, CT: Greenwood Press, 1994.

Smith, Bill. *The Vaudevillians*. New York: Macmillan, 1976.

Snyder, Robert W. "Vaudeville and the Transformation of Popular Culture." In *Inventing Times Square: Commerce and Culture at the Crossroads of the World*. Ed. William R. Taylor. New York: Russell Sage Foundation, 1991. Pp. 133–46.

———. *The Voice of the City: Vaudeville and Popular Culture in New York*. New York: Oxford University Press, 1989.

Sobel, Bernard. *A Pictorial History of Vaudeville*. New York: Bonanza Books, 1961.

Spears, Jack. *The Civil War on the Screen and Other Essays*. New York: A. S. Barnes and Company, 1977.

Spitzer, Marian. *The Palace*. New York: Atheneum, 1969.

Stafford, Barbara Maria. *Good Looking: Essays on the Virtue of Visual Images*. Cambridge: Massachusetts Institute of Technology Press, 1996.

*Stage* (London).

*"The Stage" Year Book 1911*. Ed. L. Carson. London: St. Clements Press, 1911.

*"The Stage" Year Book 1912*. Ed. L. Carson. London: *The Stage* Offices, 1912.

*"The Stage" Year Book 1913*. Ed. L. Carson. London: *The Stage* Offices, 1913.

*"The Stage" Year Book 1914.* Ed. L. Carson. London: *The Stage* Offices, 1914.

Stanislavsky, Constantine. *An Actor Prepares.* Trans. Elizabeth Reynolds Hapgood. 1936; rpt. New York: Routledge, 1988.

Staples, Shirley. *Male-Female Comedy Teams in American Vaudeville, 1865–1932.* Ann Arbor, MI: UMI Research Press, 1984.

Stedman Jones, Gareth. "Working-Class Culture and Working-Class Politics in London, 1870–1990: Notes on the Remaking of a Working Class." *Journal of Social History* 7 (1973–1974), 460–508.

Steen, Marguerite. *A Pride of Terrys: Family Saga.* London: Longmans, 1962.

Stein, Charles W., ed. *American Vaudeville as Seen by its Contemporaries.* New York: Alfred A. Knopf, 1984.

Stetz, Margaret D. "The Laugh of the New Woman." In *The Victorian Comic Spirit.* Ed. Jennifer A. Wagner-Lawlor. Aldershot, England: Ashgate, 2000. Pp. 219–41.

Stevens, Doris. *Jailed for Freedom: American Women Won the Vote.* Ed. Carol O'Hare. 1920; rpt. Troutsdale, OR: New Sage Press, 1996.

Stevenson, John. *British Society 1914-45.* London: Penguin Books, 1984.

Strachey, Ray. *The Cause: A Short History of the Women's Movement in Great Britain.* 1928; rpt. Bath: Cedric Chivers, 1974.

Stuart, Charles Douglas and A. J. Park. *The Variety Stage: A History of the Music Hall from the Earliest Period to the Present Times.* London: T. Fisher Unwin, 1895.

*Suffrage and the Pankhursts.* Ed. Jane Marcus. London: Routledge & Kegan Paul, 1987.

Summerfield, Penny. "Patriotism and Empire: Music-Hall Entertainment, 1870-1914." In *Imperialism and Popular Culture.* Ed. John M. Mackenzie. Manchester: Manchester University Press, 1986. Pp. 17–48.

Susman, Warren I. *Culture as History: The Transformation of American Society in the Twentieth Century.* New York: Pantheon Books, 1984.

Sutro, Alfred. *Celebrities and Simple Souls.* London: Duckworth, 1933.

Taranow, Gerda. *Sarah Bernhardt: The Art Within the Legand.* Princeton: Princeton University Press, 1972.

"Terry, Ellen." File at the Theatre Museum Library, London, England.

*Theatre* (London).

*Theatre Magazine* (New York).

Thelan, David. "Of Audiences, Borderland, and Comparisons: Toward the Internationalization of American History." *Journal of American History* 79:2 (September 1992), 432–62.

Thomas, Augustus. *A Man of the World*. Unpaginated manuscript copy at the Museum of the City of New York.

Thompson, Dorothy. *Outsiders: Class, Gender and Nation*. London: Verso, 1993.

Tickner, Lisa. *The Spectacle of Women: Imagery of the Suffrage Campaign 1907–14*. London: Chatto & Windus, 1987.

Titterton, W. R. *From Theatre to Music Hall*. London: Stephen Swift and Co., 1912.

Toll, Robert C. *On With the Show: The First Century of Show Business in America*. New York: Oxford University Press, 1976.

"Trav S. C." (Travis Stewart), *No Applause—Just Throw Money; or The Book That Made Vaudeville Famous*. New York: Faber and Faber, 2005.

Trewin, J. C. *Benson and the Bensonians*. London: Barrie and Rockliff, 1960.

Trow, George W. S. *Within the Context of No Context*. Boston: Little, Brown and Company, 1978.

Truman, Olivia. *Beerbohm Tree's Olivia*. Ed. Isolde Wigram. London: André Deutsch, 1984.

Trussler, Simon. *The Cambridge Illustrated History of British Theatre*. Cambridge: Cambridge University Press, 1994.

Tunstall, Jeremy. *The Media Are American: Anglo-American Media in the World*. London: Constable, 1977.

Vanbrugh, Irene. *To Tell My Story*. London: Hutchinson & Co., 1949.

Vanbrugh, Violet. *Dare to Be Wise*. London: Hodder and Stoughton, n.d.

*Vanity Fair* (London); consulted at the Palace Theatre, Palace Theatre Archive, London.

*Variety* (New York).

Veltrusky, Jiri. "Contribution to the Semiotics of Acting." *Sign, System and Meaning: A Quinquagenary of the Prague Linguistic Circle*. Ed. Ladoslav Matejka. Ann Arbor, MI: Michigan Slavic Studies, 1976. Pp. 553–606.

Vermorel, Fred and Judy Vermorel. *Starlust: The Secret Life of Fans*. London: Comet, 1985.

Verneuil, Louis. *The Fabulous Life of Sarah Bernhardt*. Trans. Ernest Boyd. New York: Harper & Brothers Publishers, 1942.

Vrettos, Athena. *Somatic Fictions: Imagining Illness in Victorian Culture*. Stanford: Stanford University Press, 1995.

Walen, Denise A. "Sappho in the Closet." In *Women and Playwriting in Nineteenth-Century Britain*. Ed. Tracy C. Davis and Ellen Donkin. Cambridge: Cambridge University Press, 1999. Pp. 233–55.

Walker, Alexander. *Stardom: The Hollywood Phenomenon*. New York: Stein and Day, 1970.

"Ward, Fannie." File at the Mander and Mitchenson Collection, Kent, England."

*War Plays by Women.* Ed. Claire M. Tylee with Elaine Turner and Agnès Cardinal. London: Routledge, 1999.

Weintraub, Stanley. *Bernard Shaw 1914-1918: Journey to Heartbreak.* London: Routledge & Kegan Paul, 1973.

———. *Edward the Caresser: The Playboy Prince Who Became Edward VII.* New York: The Free Press, 2001.

Wentworth, Marion Craig. *War Brides.* New York: The Century Company, 1915.

———. *War Brides.* In *War Plays by Women.* Ed. Claire M. Tylee with Elaine Turner and Agnès Cardinal. London: Routledge, 1999. Pp. 16–26.

Wertheim, Arthur Frank. *Vaudeville Wars: How Keith-Albee and Orpheum Circuits Controlled Big-Time and Its Performers.* New York: Palgrave Macmillan, 2006.

Weyl, Walter E. *The New Democracy: An Essay on Certain Political and Economic Tendencies in the United States.* New York: Macmillan, 1912.

*Who Was Who in The Theatre, 1912-1976: A Biographical Dictionary of Actors, Actresses, Directors, Playwrights, and Producers of the English-Speaking Theatre.* Volume 2. Detroit: Gale Research Company, 1978.

Whitefield, Eileen. *Pickford: The Woman Who Made Hollywood.* Lexington: University Press of Kentucky, 1997.

Williams, Gary Jay. *Our Moonlight Revels: A Midsummer Night's Dream in the Theatre.* Iowa City: University of Iowa Press, 1997.

Wilmeth, Don B. *American and English Popular Entertainment.* Detroit: Gale Research Press, 1980.

———. *Variety Entertainment and Outdoor Amusements: A Reference Guide.* Westport, CT: Greenwood Press, 1982.

Wilmut, Roger. *Kindly Leave the Stage: The Story of Variety 1919-1960.* London: Methuen, 1985.

Winter, William. *Other Days, Being Chronicles and Memories of the Stage.* New York: Moffat, Yard and Company, 1908.

Wolter, Jurgen C., ed. *The Dawning of American Drama: American Dramatic Criticism 1746–1915.* Westport, CT: Greenwood Press, 1993.

Woods, Leigh "Actors' Biography and Mythmaking: The Example of Edmund Kean." In *Interpreting the Theatrical Past: Essays in the Historiography of Performance.* Ed. Thomas Postlewait and Bruce A. McConachie. Iowa City: University of Iowa Press, 1989. Pp. 230–47.

———. "American Vaudeville, American Empire." In *Performing America: Cultural Nationalism in American Theater*. Ed. Jeffrey D. Mason and J. Ellen Gainor. Ann Arbor, MI: University of Michigan Press, 1999. Pp. 73–90.

———. "Ethel Barrymore and the Wages of Vaudeville." *New England Theatre Journal* 4 (1993), 79–95.

———. " 'The Golden Calf': Noted English Actresses in American Vaudeville, 1904–1916." *Journal of American Culture* (Fall 1992), 61–71.

———. "Sarah Bernhardt and the Refining of American Vaudeville." *Theatre Research International* (Spring 1993), 16–24.

———. "Two-a-Day Redemptions and Truncated Camilles: The Vaudeville Repertoire of Sarah Bernhardt." In *Twentieth-Century Literary Criticism*. Ed. Jennifer Gariepy. Detroit: Gale Research Press, 1998. Pp. 62–9. Rpt. from New Theatre Quarterly (February 1994), 11–23.

———. " 'The Wooden Heads of the People': Arnold Daly and Bernard Shaw," *New Theatre Quarterly* 22:1 (February 2006), 54–69.

Woods, Leigh and Ágústa Gunnarsdóttir. *Public Selves, Political Stages: Interviews with Icelandic Women in Government and Theatre*. London: Harwood Academic Publishers, 1997.

Wynn, Neil A. *From Progressivism to Prosperity: World War I and American Society*. New York: Holmes & Meier, 1986.

Zangwill, Israel. "The Future of Vaudeville in America." *Cosmopolitan* 38:6 (April 1905), 639–46.

Zellers, Parker. *Tony Pastor: Dean of the Vaudeville Stage*. Ypsilanti: Eastern Michigan University Press, 1971.

# Index 〜

You'll notice many *see also*s. Professional and institutional interconnectedness was a fact of life among those who performed for their livings. For readers now, a sense of interconnectedness will convey some feeling of the lives stage professionals lived back in the day, and of the sometimes curious alliances that were struck in and through vaudeville and variety.

The word "performer" or "actor" appearing after a name distinguishes a person who gave turns primarily from who appeared chiefly in the theatre or in films. Play titles appear under the names of the actors who performed them, and in a handful of cases, under the names of playwrights whose names will be most familiar. When a performer or an actor was relatively obscure, and is mentioned only in passing in the book, the name may not appear in the Index.

Be reminded that actors, and by no means the women only, have often fudged their birthdates forward. Illustrations are indicated in **boldface**.

## DATE DUE